THE IRISH CONSTRUCTION CYCLE
1970–2023

THE IRISH CONSTRUCTION CYCLE 1970–2023: POLICIES AND ESCAPE ROUTES

Nicholas Mansergh

EASTWOOD BOOKS

First published in 2024
Eastwood Books
A member of the Wordwell Group
Unit 9, 78 Furze Road,
Sandyford Industrial Estate,
Dublin 18
www.wordwellbooks.com

ISBN: 978-1-913934-31-6 (paperback)
ISBN: 978-1-916742-54-3 (ebook)

British Library Cataloguing-in-Publication Data.
A catalogue record for this book is available from the British Library.

Typeset in Ireland by Wordwell Ltd
Copy-editor: Heidi Houlihan
Cover design and artwork: Wordwell Ltd
Printed by: SprintPrint, Dublin

CONTENTS

LIST OF FIGURES

LIST OF TABLES

LIST OF BOXES

The boxes in chapters 3–6 put forward suggestions on how the cyclicality of the Irish construction industry might be managed more successfully, in each stage of the development process.

ACKNOWLEDGEMENTS

The origins of this book lie in my 2001 Ph.D. thesis 'Spatial Planning and the Construction Policy Sector', and much of the material relating to the 1970–2000 period in Chapters 3–6 is derived from that thesis. I am grateful to UCC for the fellowship which facilitated this research, and more particularly to Professor William Smyth and my supervisor Dr Barry Brunt of the Department of Geography, for their support and encouragement. I am also grateful to the late Noel Dillon, Cork County Manager, and Brendan Kelleher, Chief Planning Officer, for allowing me the necessary leave of absence.

As the final sections of the thesis were written at the height of the boom, they focused more on construction cyclicality than I had originally intended, and subsequent events reinforced my view that this was a key issue, which needed to be addressed directly. After my retirement from Cork County Council in 2015, I had more time to research and develop my ideas on how this might be done. My sincere thanks to Ronan Colgan of Eastwood Books, for agreeing to publish the somewhat unorthodox book that resulted, to Heidi Houlihan, for editing its somewhat unorthodox prose, and to Nick Maxwell, for finalising its design, and for giving it the vital last push, to get it on its way to the printers.

CHAPTER 1

AN UNUSUALLY
UNSTABLE SECTOR

Summary: The construction industry is more cyclical in Ireland than in most other developed economies. This leads to alternating shortfalls and surpluses in output, with a destabilising effect on property prices, housing affordability, and businesses and workers in the sector. Typically, Irish public policy reacts to the problems generated by this instability in successive phases of the construction cycle, but these reactive measures are often belated and ineffective, as they do not allow for lead times. As the cycle cannot be forecast reliably, semi-automatic measures – put in place in advance – are suggested. This study examines the scope for them in the various stages in the construction process: development land, planning and infrastructure, and construction/property markets.

The Irish construction industry is unusually unstable, and not just in the 'Celtic tiger' period which began in the late 1990s, and in the crash which followed this, from 2008 onwards. It has been much less stable than the economy as a whole, from the late 1970s. It has grown faster than the rest of the economy during cyclical upturns, and fallen further during downturns. The construction sector's share of total employment is an easily quantified symptom of this, and one that lends itself to international comparisons. As Figure 1.1 shows, its share in Ireland rose to around 9% in the late 1970s, fell to slightly over 6% by the late 1980s, climbed steeply in the late 1990s, and continued this climb after a brief pause in 2000–2, to a peak of 13% in 2007.

1

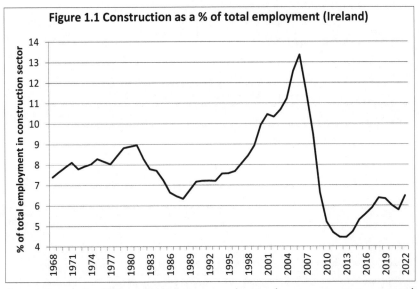

Sources: International Labour Organisation – employment by economic activity statistical series. Irish Labour Force Survey figures used for 1975–9 period for Ireland, as ILO figures for Irish construction employment appear to be incorrect for that period.

This is the norm for Ireland, not just for construction employment, but also for output volumes, property prices, development land and above all housing, which has been 'perpetually in crisis' – a crisis 'which predated the crash of 2007/8, building up for at least 20 years' (Kitchin et al., 2015, pp. 2–3). There has only been one worthwhile period of relative stability in the Irish construction sector since the late 1970s, between 1989 and 1995. That period was one of gradual recovery, in contrast to the steep decline which preceded it, and the steeper increase which followed it. Another recovery began in 2014, but it started from a very low base, as a result of the decimation of the industry after 2008, and this has led to the housing crisis continuing in another form.

Those of an age to remember the unstable sequence of events from the 1970s onwards may see them as the consequences of errors of economic and regulatory policy, particularly in the late 1970s and between 2003 and 2007, plus the very persistent after effects of those errors.

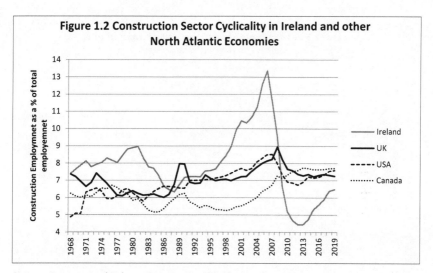

Figure 1.2 Construction Sector Cyclicality in Ireland and other North Atlantic Economies

Sources: International Labour Organisation (ILO) – employment by economic activity series, Irish Labour Force Survey (LFS) Series.

While there are reasons why construction industries tend to be more unstable and more cyclical than the economies of which they form part, the Irish one is more cyclical than most – more error and accident prone than most, if one chooses to see its instability in that light. In other English-speaking countries, employment in construction is not significantly more cyclical than in the economy as a whole, and departures from this are short-lived and relatively modest. Not so in Ireland. As Figure 1.2 shows, its contraction in the 1980s (-2.7%) was double the fall associated with negative housing equity in the early 1990s in Britain (-1.3%, 1989–93), and also greater than that associated with sub-prime housing loans in the United States (-1.8%, 2007–12).

As Figure 1.3 shows, the Irish construction sector had more similarities with those in central and northern European economies in the 1970s and 1980s. As in Ireland, the proportion of total employment in their construction sectors in the early 1970s was higher than in Britain or North America, but then fell, fairly persistently. By the end of the 1980s, construction in these different areas had converged at 6–8% of total employment.

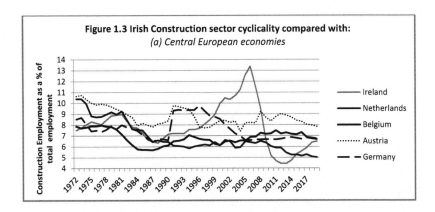

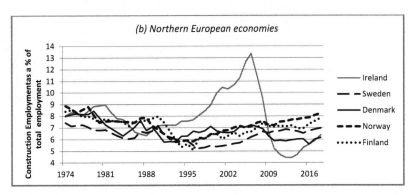

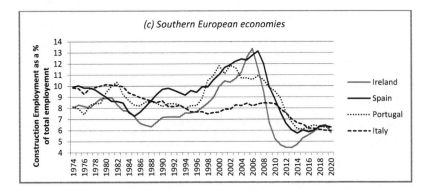

Sources: ILO employment by economic activity series, Irish LFS Series.

Geopolitics intervened at the beginning of the 1990s, as German reunification[1] prompted a steep but temporary rise in German construction employment, and Finnish construction employment fell sharply as a consequence of the collapse of the Soviet Union. These shifts were on a similar scale to the decline in Irish construction in the 1980s – around 3% in each case. There were also banking crises in the Scandinavian countries in the late 1980s and early 1990s, accompanied by falls in the percentage employed in construction of around 2%, and falls in house prices of over 30% in Sweden and over 40% in Norway (Reinhart and Rogoff, 2009, pp. 160, 360–76).

Since then, in sharp contrast to Ireland, the construction sector's share of total employment in central and northern Europe has remained fairly stable, with the curves for most countries being remarkably smooth, implying construction sectors in which cyclicality has not been a major issue, at any rate in output volume terms.

As Figure 1.3(c) shows, Ireland has an Iberian economy, at least for construction cyclicality purposes. The similarities with the construction cycle in Spain and Portugal are particularly striking from the mid-1990s onwards, but differences of c. 3% between peak and trough are evident before then in all three countries. They share a well-defined cyclical rise and fall in the construction share of total employment, and do not include long periods during which the construction share remains more or less constant. Italy, while included in Figure 1.3(c) as a southern European economy, conforms more to the central/northern European pattern.

While there may be a number of reasons for the similarities between cyclical patterns in the Irish and Iberian construction industries, one obvious common factor is that overall employment growth rates in those countries are also unusually variable, as Table 1.1 shows. The second column in that table shows the average annual rate of employment gain in national economies as a whole for the period between 1975 and 2019. This indicates that Ireland has an exceptionally high long-run average employment growth rate, reflecting its success in attracting foreign direct investment (FDI), and despite its highly cyclical construction sector.

5

TABLE 1.1   VARIABILITY IN OVERALL ANNUAL EMPLOYMENT CHANGE, 1975–2019

	Average employ-ment gain per annum (%)	No. of years in which gain is within 1% of this average	Standard deviation from this average gain (%)
Italy	0.52	32	1.46
USA	1.38	30	1.40
UK	0.69	30	1.55
Belgium	0.55	29	1.47
Austria	1.15	28	2.08
Sweden	0.53	27	1.56
Germany*	0.56	27	1.63
Canada	1.74	26	1.58
Denmark	0.44	24	1.68
Norway	1.13	24	1.49
Finland	0.34	23	2.29
Netherlands	1.51	20	1.84
Portugal	0.61	18	2.36
IRELAND	1.75	13	2.75
Spain	1.00	3	3.15

*West Germany from 1975–90, Germany from 1991–2019
Sources: International Labour Organisation (ILO) – employment by economic activity series, Irish Labour Force Survey (LFS) Series.

The third column shows the number of years in that period in which employment change has been less than 1% above or below that rate (e.g. the first line shows the average annual gain for Italy to be 0.52%, and that in 32 out of the 45 years in that period, employment change from the previous year was between +1.51% and -0.47%). This gives a crude measure of how much of the time employment growth in each country stays close to the long-run average. The table is arranged with the countries with the most years in which employment change was close to their long-run average gain at the top, and those with the fewest at the bottom. Spain, Portugal, and Ireland are in the latter category.

The right-hand column of Table 1.1 shows the standard deviation from the long-run average growth rate for each country in the 1975–2015 period. This is a measure of how far (on average) employment change in individual years varies upwards or downwards from a country's long-run rate of growth. Again, Spain and Ireland show the greatest variation, with average departures of around 3% from their respective long-run growth rates.

Construction industries have two main functions: to replace, rehabilitate or repair obsolescent existing structures, and to add to the stock of buildings and infrastructure to cater for increases in employment, population, and movement. The latter function is likely to be relatively stable in an economy which grows at a fairly constant rate, and unstable in one that grows erratically.

In principle, the need for extra capacity should reflect the rate of economic growth. This implies that when the economy is static or contracting, there will be little need for the construction industry to provide extra buildings, and in periods when it is growing at, say, twice its average rate, the output of extra buildings may need to double as well. Obviously, it is not quite that simple, but the underlying point – that an increase or decrease of 2% or 3% in the annual growth rate can trigger far larger percentage changes in construction output – is correct.

This is the main reason why economies with erratic growth rates can be expected to have highly cyclical construction sectors. However, the causal connection may work in reverse, in periods where growth in construction starts to drive national economic growth instead of being driven by it, due to a property bubble. In these circumstances, the sector is likely to be even more cyclical, as it was in the 2003–7 period in Ireland.

CYCLICALITY AND TIMING

A stable construction sector has considerable advantages. The volume of development is reasonably predictable, the capacity of the infrastructure needed to serve it can be planned and provided in an orderly way, and the lessons being learnt from current experience are likely to remain relevant for some time. By contrast, uneven growth seriously complicates management of the sector. Substantial increases or reductions in construction demand will occur quite frequently, and their timing will often be difficult to predict, leading to a surplus or shortfall in output, with a destabilising effect on prices, the construction sector, and the wider economy. Greater upward price variations lead to periodic housing affordability crises, and promote land speculation and property bubbles. Greater downward ones can put construction firms out of business and construction employees out of work, perhaps for long enough and on a large enough scale to do long-term damage to the capacity of the sector, as in the decade after the 2008 crash. Implementation of relevant longer-term public policies is likely to be disrupted.

Periodic exposure of the Irish construction industry to new and unexpected levels of demand triggers constructive responses, but these typically involve substantial lead times. The most obvious Irish examples of the lead-time problem involve surges in housing demand, a delay in matching them with an increase in output, and rapidly rising prices. In due course, market forces and the reactions of public authorities may produce a supply response to demand surges, but this takes time. Rising house prices raise development land prices, making landowners more inclined to sell their land to developers, but the decision to sell, the sale process, designing a development and securing planning permission all take time. Developers respond to increased profit margins by applying for more planning permissions and implementing them more quickly, but actually building, selling and occupying the housing will still take a further year or two.

Government-funded responses to surges in demand also involve significant lead times, after a shortfall in supply has been identified, but before the actions prompted by it become effective. There is a natural tendency to wait for a definite problem or opportunity to emerge before taking action. This is usually too late. From time to time, Irish governments have responded to cyclical crises in construction with measures which might have been highly effective, if taken three or four years earlier.

Since they were not, there is a painful interval in which acute problems persist, before the policy response can take effect.

In the most recent cycle, the incoming 2011–16 Fine Gael-Labour coalition looked back on the record of its predecessors, and commented (DoE, 2011) 'the previous policy response was to chase a fast moving target'. The comment was fair, and the implied inference that the state should adopt a less active role understandable, given its financial circumstances then. A more accurate inference would have been that the state had a few years to do what it could to prepare for the next phase in the cycle, if it was not to find itself chasing a fast-moving target once more.

The awkward implication is that some processes have to get underway earlier in the cycle than they actually do, to allow for lead times. There is no mystery as to why this does not, in fact, happen. Some builders and developers will anticipate trends in advance of a recovery and can raise the necessary finance, but more will wait for stronger evidence from the market, and may also find it pays to wait while prices rise. Public finances are under maximum pressure in a recession. Since no-one knows when a recovery will happen or on what scale it will be when it does, giving priority to preparing for a hypothetical future surge in demand over a host of more urgent and immediate needs is difficult to justify. Public interventions in a recession are more likely to try to make sure a recovery in construction output actually occurs than to take precautions to cope with an unexpectedly rapid one.

Construction is more exposed to the lead time problem than most other industries. Most products can be imported if domestic output is inadequate, but this is not normally possible with buildings. Output of goods from a production line can usually be increased at quite short notice by working extra shifts, but in the construction industry this approach is complicated by the need for each item produced to have its own plot of land. Where production takes place is normally a minor concern for buyers of products, but this is a key issue for purchasers of buildings.

Obviously, the problems associated with a volatile construction sector could be avoided, if the rate of growth in the Irish economy became more stable, as a result of more cautious Irish macro-economic policies, of changes in international conditions, or in how Ireland relates to them. While these possibilities cannot be excluded, they appear optimistic, and cannot be depended on.

Such problems could also be avoided with more accurate forecasts, and a greater willingness to act on them, but, in practice, this is difficult to achieve. The direction of change can be foreseen much, though not all, of the time, but forecasting its timing and extent reliably is much more difficult. Even when an accurate forecast is available, decision makers are naturally cautious in terms of how far they change policy or commit resources, in response to projections which differ widely from the current situation, and which may or may not turn out to be correct.

INSURANCE POLICIES AND CONTINGENCY PLANS

If it is accepted that overall economic growth in Ireland will probably remain erratic and difficult to forecast reliably, and that this will create continuing problems for the construction sector, some form of 'Plan B' is needed. This may need to involve alternative ways of coping with uncertainty about the future, which operate in a semi-automatic manner.

One routine way of dealing with uncertainty about the future is through insurance. Households have continuous insurance cover, because they cannot know in advance if or when a burglary or house fire will occur. This principle could, for instance, be applied to the infrastructure lead time problem. Governments could set infrastructure 'floors' – minimum levels of investment per annum in local infrastructure directly serving zoned housing areas in the larger urban areas[2] – which would apply throughout the cycle. This would result in spare capacity at the bottom of the cycle, and increase the supply of buildings and moderate price increases as the subsequent recovery accelerated – the point in the cycle when the problems caused by lead times are typically most acute. As with conventional insurance policies, this would not be costless, but the lower cost of providing infrastructure at the bottom of the cycle would help compensate for greater funding difficulties then.

The insurance principle could be combined with a form of contingency planning. This could involve publishing – in advance – information on how the government would respond to possible changes in market conditions. If, for instance, house prices were to rise, the government could indicate that it would gradually increase certain incentives or tax concessions for smaller, lower-cost dwellings in parallel, and what the main conditions would be. Builders could then consider whether they wished their developments to be eligible for such support under those circumstances, and design them to be capable of complying with the proposed conditions if they did. If and when prices rose, they could then respond, with minimal lead times.

If, for instance, they knew that any help to buy, tax rebate or grant scheme to help first-time buyers was and would remain limited to new houses selling at 80% of the average new house price in the relevant county or less, they would be more likely to make sure their planned developments included or could easily be adapted to include a worthwhile number of such houses. Any such scheme could be balanced by applying a higher rate of, say, stamp duty to large, expensive houses, so that in combination they would redirect supply rather than inflate demand.

This approach could replace recurrent, reactive initiatives on affordability for first-time buyers. Such schemes are typically introduced on an ad hoc basis, when a recovery in the housing market is already well underway. At that stage, the mix of dwelling types which developers are building or have planning permission for may be skewed towards the middle and upper parts of the market (e.g. semis and large detached houses), as margins on such developments may be higher than for starter homes. As a result, those designing such schemes are under pressure to take the mix of house types in the pipeline more or less as given, and to define eligibility to include averagely- or above-averagely-priced houses, so as not to apply an apparently arbitrary cut-off point to houses already under construction, and create an unexpected marketing disadvantage for those which fall just above it. This approach increases the risk of inflating house prices generally, to the benefit of builders more than purchasers.

Possible opportunities to use these and other principles have to be related to the way the processes to which they would be applied work at present, to existing policies affecting those processes, and (since they are not necessarily immutable) to possible alternatives to those policies.

It is accepted that there is a distinction between reactive, short-term government policies prompted by cyclically generated problems and longer-term, proactive policies designed to achieve positive changes in property markets, construction output and its spatial distribution. However, this distinction can break down in practice. While longer-term policies may be formulated initially in ways that pay little regard to the economic cycle, their implementation is often disrupted by it.

Also, some longer-term issues owe their prominence to the acute form they take in particular phases of the cycle. In the early 1990s – the last period in which 'normal' housing market conditions prevailed in Ireland – average new house prices (adjusted for construction cost inflation[3] and expressed in 2019 values) oscillated between €145,000 and €150,000 (€155,000 to €185,000 in Dublin), the land cost component of these prices was stable at 10–11%, and housing output, if adjusted for the difference in population, was around 32,000 per annum.[4] If the early 1990s had been normal in the other sense – i.e. representative of market conditions which prevail most of the time – issues such as the affordability and supply of new housing might now have a much lower profile.

The highly cyclical housing market conditions which have actually prevailed have led to a preoccupation with the quantitative side of new housing provision (number of units completed, price and rent levels, capital appreciation), arguably at the expense of more qualitative aspects, which are more important in the longer term.[5] While this book also focuses on these quantitative aspects, this is partly because reducing housing market cyclicality may be a precondition for qualitative issues getting more priority.

STRUCTURE OF THIS STUDY

The development process is often compared to a pipeline,[6] as projects have to move through three successive stages before they result in buildings ready for use. The central chapters in this book (Chapters 3–5) are organised around these three stages in the pipeline:

- Supply of land for development (Chapter 3)
- Provision of infrastructure to service that land (Chapter 4)
- The actual process of construction, together with its financing and transfer to final owners and users (Chapter 5)

The pipeline analogy is useful in drawing attention to the time it takes for a project to pass through these stages, and the need for flows through them to match demand and need in stages downstream, in terms of volume, cost, type, and location. This means that the current supply of development land and infrastructure needs to match demand a number of years into the future.

This may happen more or less automatically in a stable construction sector, in which pipeline flows and final demand do not vary much over time. In a highly cyclical one, current flows through upstream stages will often be out of line with the final output of completed projects that will be required half a decade or so later. Measures to improve the capacity of the Irish construction process to anticipate future needs have to be effective for each stage in the pipeline, not just the one that is giving most trouble at the moment.

Chapters 3–5 are primarily 'policy histories'. They each describe the evolution of government policies for the relevant stage in the development pipeline from around 1970 onwards. In many cases, these policies are prompted by specific phases in the cycle – particularly the late recovery or early boom phases, and depressed periods after a downturn. A historical review of policies prompted by different phases of the cycle takes more account of the variability of conditions in the construction sector than a narrower – though more natural – focus on the needs and problems which are uppermost in the current phase.

The policy histories include policies that were proposed but not adopted, or adopted mainly as aspirations, as well as those implemented effectively. This allows a range of possible policies to be assessed, wide enough to include ones too radical to have actually been implemented, but realistic enough to have been advanced in official reports. Limiting the range to policies which were put forward seriously at official level helps keep the policy options discussed within manageable proportions.

Each stage in the development process takes time. Ideally, increases in inputs at the upper end of the pipeline (e.g. development land) should precede cyclical increases in demand for completed projects at the lower end, but, in practice, they usually follow them, and time then has to elapse while the necessary increases in inputs pass down the pipeline. While the ideal is unachievable, rebalancing (e.g. of incentives, so as to encourage land sales earlier in the cycle, or funding patterns, so as to promote earlier provision of local infrastructure) is possible. Chapter 3 looks for practical ways to achieve such rebalancing in the supply of development land, and Chapter 4 considers the supply of local infrastructure. Chapter 4 also looks at how sub-regional or regional infrastructure projects can be planned realistically enough – having regard to the cycle – to prevent many of them spending long periods in funding queues, before they are actually constructed and used.

Coping with the construction cycle is not simply a matter of achieving a better match between the quantities of land and local infrastructure being provided now, and the quantity of completed buildings which will be needed in a few years time. Locational distribution of demand for buildings, and the mix of building types provided, also vary cyclically.

Chapter 5 therefore focuses on established public sector ways of influencing the mix and location of construction output, such as the physical planning and tax systems. At present, these are blunt instruments. Conventional land use planning tends to ignore the cycle, and rely on policy tools which give little control over the timing or rate of development (five-year permissions, zoning in plans revised on a six-year cycle), and often uses loosely worded zoning categories in the interests of flexibility. Tax codes, grants and public expenditure can be changed more quickly, but if changed in reaction to cyclical problems, there will still be a substantial time lag before projects can be created or adapted to match the change in development mix being promoted, and then be carried out, before they can be made available to users. Such measures need to encourage actors to anticipate what will be needed – for instance, by signalling in advance how they will be varied in response to different market conditions – so that these future responses can be factored into their expectations.

The main point of this book is to put forward a number of suggestions on how the cyclicality of the Irish construction industry could be managed more successfully, at each stage of the development process. These suggestions are put forward mostly in the form of digressions from the historical narratives in each chapter, inserted at the points when the relevant issues are at their most prominent. For ease of reference, they are summarised in a series of boxes. In some cases, these suggestions are alternatives to each other, but, in most, they are intended to be mutually complementary.

In order to create a clearer context for Chapters 3–5, they are preceded (in Chapter 2) by an overview of the Irish construction industry, its constituent sub-sectors, their characteristics and mutual interaction, and the way their output has varied over the last half century.

While this study treats cyclicality and the increased importance of lead times consequent on it as a pervasive factor, complicating the development process at every stage, there are alternative candidates for this role. One such candidate is unbalanced regional development. The concentration of growth in Dublin results in a development process and a property market in the Dublin area which are disproportionately difficult to manage, not least from a cyclical perspective, and this has spill-over effects on other parts of the country. Chapter 6 discusses the various regional policies which have been proposed or adopted, without obvious effect on the dominance of Dublin, and considers whether a more effective variant would reduce construction cyclicality.

As far as practicable, these largely historical chapters have been brought up to date. While they may seem unduly critical of current policies and proposals, this is not the intention. It is more that these policies often lack a clear cyclical perspective, and attempts to insert this almost inevitably lead to substantial modifications, or substitution of a different approach.

The final chapter (Chapter 7) recognises that the success or failure of the suggestions in the boxes in Chapters 3–5 may themselves depend on their introduction in a favourable phase of the economic cycle. In some cases, the optimum timing would be in a recession, or early in the recovery phase of the cycle. It is worth drawing attention to this, as public support for reforms relating to the construction sector typically peaks in a different part of the cycle, during a boom, late in a recovery or early in a downturn.

In order to get measures to reduce the cyclicality of the construction industry built into a reform package, a long-term view is needed. Unfortunately, short-term considerations loom larger in construction than in most other sectors, because firms need to know where the next project is coming from, and how the next budget will affect their profitability. Acute cyclicality typically reinforces this, by prompting a succession of hand-to-mouth measures. However, there is at present a stronger than usual sense that fundamental reforms are needed. It is also possible that some of the relevant agencies will see greater stability as being in their own longer-term institutional interests.

The unusual nature of this study reflects my fear that the Irish construction sector could continue to struggle with unresolved cyclical, and other problems for a long time to come, in the absence of a coordinated set of reforms. In an attempt to clarify what those reforms should consist in, it looks at the Irish construction process as a whole, and at its journey through time. This is partly in reaction to the tendency for existing publications to focus primarily on particular parts of the process (e.g. planning), particular outputs (e.g. housing), or particular phases of the economic cycle (e.g. booms). Media coverage is even more affected by a fragmented perception of the development process, and shines a cyclically prompted spotlight into one corner at a time, with governments under constant pressure to react to the issue of the moment.

This has to change. In 1971 (the starting date for this study), the Kenny report put the issue of development land on the public policy agenda. Since then, there have been sporadic initiatives on development land, at times when the housing market has been under maximum pressure. Most have been temporary, and exceptions such as Part V have been watered down. The underlying problem is far more acute than it was in 1971. Development land is only one of half a dozen major construction- or planning-related problems. If it takes half a century to not resolve one of them, the Irish construction process is going to remain dysfunctional indefinitely.

To some extent, the case for systematic reform of public policy on construction is separate from the specific suggestions on how this might be done. So, the book has two aims: firstly, to argue for the need for such reform – incorporating measures to control the sector's cyclicality – and secondly, to put forward ideas on how this might be achieved. Those who accept the former, but are sceptical about many of the latter, may be stimulated to come up with a more effective programme of their own.

CHAPTER 2

THE CONSTRUCTION CYCLE

Summary: This chapter provides an overview of the construction industry from the 1980s on, its sub-sectors, and their differing methods of operation. Different sub-sectors play slightly different roles in the overall cyclical pattern, for instance by leading or lagging it, and there is an element of repetition in the way variations in their outputs combine and interact to produce the overall construction cycle. Describing the sub-sectors and the phases of the cycle helps to set the context for the remainder of this book, and to define some of the terms used in it.

The Irish construction industry can be broken down into half a dozen broad sub-sectors. There are some important differences between them, not only in terms of what they produce, but also in how their output is organised and financed, and in how they are affected by the economic cycle.

The definition of sub-sectors is influenced by the availability of output data. A reasonably consistent output series, initiated by the Department of the Environment in 1980, allows housing, non-residential building and civil engineering to be distinguished from each other. For the period up to 2016, this series also allows construction and improvement of non-residential buildings to be subdivided between private building works, such as commercial and industrial development, and social infrastructure, such as schools and hospitals. New housing can be distinguished from the maintenance and improvement of existing houses, and (more approximately) new urban and suburban housing can be separated out from rural one-off housing.

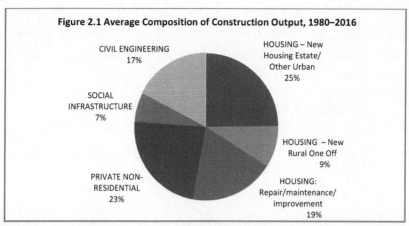

Figure 2.1 Average Composition of Construction Output, 1980–2016

Sources: Dept. of the Environment/DKM Construction Industry Review and Outlook series (1980–2009); RICS/DKM 'The Irish Construction Industry in 2012'; DKM 'Demand for Skills in Construction to 2020' (2016), CSO Census data on one-off houses and total dwellings constructed by inter-censal period. The allocation of new housing output between rural one-off and urban housing is approximate, and based on numbers of dwellings. One-off dwellings have greater average floorspace than urban ones, but lower costs per square metre.

While the proportion of overall output accounted for by each sub-sector is constantly varying, Figure 2.1 indicates the average share per sub-sector in terms of overall construction output, from 1980 to 2016. In order to include more recent data, albeit on a less detailed basis, Table 2.1 compares long-run shares of construction output with those in the 2014–19 recovery phase. Somewhat surprisingly, the share of housing is similar in both periods, but the recent civil engineering share was above the long-run average, and the non-residential development one below it.

TABLE 2.1   COMPARISON OF AVERAGE COMPOSITION OF OUTPUT,
1980–2016 & 2014–19

	Housing	Non-residential	Civil Engineering	Total
1980–2016	53	30	17	100
2014–2019	54	24	22	100

Sources: As for Figure 2.1, plus CSO Production in Building and Construction Index series

The 2014–19 recovery phase is put in historical context in Figure 2.2. Housing and non-residential output in 2019 were both similar to that in the mid-1990s in real terms, and civil engineering output was similar to that in 2000.

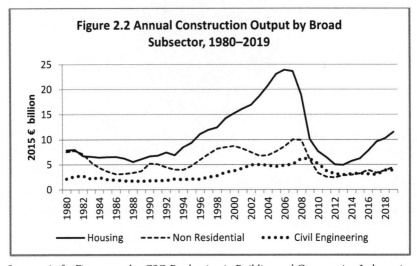

Sources: As for Figure 2.1, plus CSO Production in Building and Construction Index series

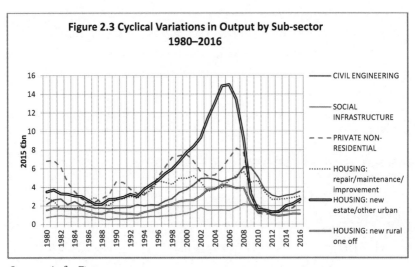

Sources: As for Figure 2.1

20

More detailed data on construction sub-sectors casts more light on how their relative positions have changed over time. New urban housing dominates public perceptions of the construction industry, and this reflected the actual situation in the 2000–8 period. As Figure 2.3 shows, private non-residential development (primarily commercial development) was of similar importance in other periods, and was the dominant sub-sector at the peak of the previous cycle, around 1980.

PRIVATE NON-RESIDENTIAL DEVELOPMENT

Differences in the way the various sub-sectors are affected by the economic cycle are also evident in Figure 2.3. For instance, the main periods of growth and contraction in housing output occur at the same time as rises and falls in private non-residential development, but the latter sub-sector also experiences intermediate rises and falls as well. There was a peak in 1990–1, and troughs in 1993–4 and 2002–3, which affected non-residential development but not housing.

Several reasons for these additional, intermediate periods of expansion and contraction in private non-residential development can be suggested. Firstly, this sub-sector includes commercial development, which is more prone to rapidly alternating periods of under- and over-supply, particularly in the Dublin office market. Undersupply lifts rents and capital values and encourages large amounts of new office floorspace, and this leads to oversupply, resulting in vacancy, falling rents and a lack of new development. In due course this triggers a fresh shortage.[1]

Secondly, private non-residential development seems more sensitive to fluctuations in the wider national and international economy, and their effects on business confidence and investment. For instance, the bursting of the dotcom bubble and the 9/11 attack on the World Trade Center had more effect on it than on housing output, and this also seems to be true of the 1993 currency crisis. This is not surprising. Economic shifts affecting the volume of employment are likely to influence demand for buildings used for employment purposes more directly and immediately than demand for housing.

Completed commercial developments are usually sold on to a financial institution, which becomes the landlord for the businesses occupying the completed floorspace. This pattern also applies to some industrial and tourism development (e.g. hotels), which also fall into the private non-residential category, but intending occupants may also develop or buy such buildings themselves. Prospects for the sale of buildings to financial institutions are obviously influenced by wider investment market conditions.

Figure 2.3 shows private non-residential development as the sub-sector most subject to large, steep rises and falls on a regular basis. The steepest and largest fall coincided with an even larger fall in new urban housing in 2008–10, and it was excessive lending and borrowing for site acquisition, construction, and property transactions in these two sub-sectors in the preceding boom which did most damage to the Irish banking system.

The other main form of damage liable to arise from excess private non-residential development is to town and city centre retailing. Local authority retail strategies typically overestimate growth in spending in shops. Local authorities favour new retail development because it increases rates income, and the consultants who draft retail strategies also do work for private developers, and have a motive for erring on the side of generosity. The government could encourage greater realism by asking the Central Statistics Office (CSO) to carry out a Census of Distribution, but no such census has been carried out since 1988. Extra retail floorspace is sometimes seen as increasing competitiveness and keeping prices down, but much of the extra space is taken up by the same small group of multiples, and consumers incur extra travel costs which are not reflected in prices. Typically, they travel further, and are more likely to use cars and increase traffic congestion.

PUBLIC SECTOR CONSTRUCTION

The public sector funds most investment in social infrastructure and civil engineering projects. Social infrastructure includes health and education, and other public and sports buildings. Civil engineering investment, in roads and other forms of transport, sanitary services, energy, and telecommunications, was almost all publicly funded in the 1980s and 1990s, but this has since been diluted by privatisation of energy generation and telecoms.

Investment in these sub-sectors is less volatile than urban housing or private non-residential development, but is still pro-cyclical rather than contra-cyclical. It expands when the construction sector as a whole is expanding, and contracts when it is contracting, but, in both cases, on a slightly delayed basis, with expansion and contraction phases typically starting a couple of years later than for the industry as a whole.

The probable reason for this is that the state only has the spare funds and confidence to substantially increase investment in physical and social infrastructure when the wider economy has been doing well for several years, and that competition between political parties puts it under pressure to invest heavily, once it is clear the resources are available. Similarly, after a downturn, the need to control public sector deficits in compliance with EU rules and to control borrowing costs may leave the state with little option but to reduce infrastructure investment drastically, particularly if the alternative is increased cuts to current expenditure. The need to complete large infrastructure projects which are already underway at the time of the downturn contributes to the time lag before its full effect is felt.

The tendency for investment in physical and social infrastructure to lag the cycle has awkward implications, particularly in the residential suburbs most affected by urban expansion. The lag makes it more difficult to put in place the physical and social infrastructure (e.g. local road improvements, footpaths, schools, public transport) to serve these areas in advance of the rapid development typical of booms, or even in parallel with it.

New public sector construction is overwhelmingly carried out by private sector contractors. There is a tendency for main contractors to become project coordinators and managers, and to employ sub-contractors to carry out much of the actual construction. Increasingly complex procurement processes favour larger firms with enough head office staff to cope with them.

NEW RURAL HOUSING AND HOUSE MAINTENANCE

A common feature affecting new rural housing and house maintenance is that both are normally carried out by small building contractors, for clients who already own the building or site, and will use the completed building. The practice of stage payments means contractors in these sub-sectors require little working capital and are at relatively low risk. Lead times are less of an issue for these two sub-sectors, because they do not normally need to wait for infrastructure to be put in place. One-off rural houses usually provide their own septic tanks or individual sewage treatment plants, and, if necessary, also private wells. Buildings undergoing repairs or improvement are usually already fully serviced.

Figure 2.3 also shows that new one-off rural housing fluctuates in tandem with new urban housing, but much less intensely. Higher development land values near the top of the cycle make building a house on family land more attractive, and the lengthening of average commuting journeys characteristic of such periods extends the rural area seen as being within commuting distance of the main cities. Existing or potential rural residents with construction experience can use their skills to save on labour costs, if they can acquire a site and build a one-off house for themselves.

However, housing repairs, maintenance and improvement do not necessarily conform to the pattern set by new housing. They dipped sharply in the 2000–4 period, more in line with private non-residential construction than new housing. This suggests that housing repairs and improvement are more affected by short-term fluctuations in business confidence.

The rise in housing repairs and improvement in the late 1980s was due to a government grant scheme for such works, introduced in 1985, partly as a way of stabilising construction employment, which was falling rapidly at the time. More generally, all construction sub-sectors are periodically affected by government decisions to take or withdraw funding or promotional measures for particular types of development, and variations in output are shaped by these decisions, as well as by changes in demand or underlying need.

NEW URBAN HOUSING

Figure 2.3 shows urban housebuilding can rise and decline even more steeply than private non-residential development, as in the 1996–2010 period, but it follows a less regular pattern. The 2008–10 downturn also showed housebuilders were more dependent on bank borrowing – and less reliant on reinvesting profits from previous schemes – than might have been expected. With hindsight, the expansion of urban house construction in the 2003–6 period may have been too rapid for even well-established housebuilders to maintain market share if they relied mainly on reinvested profits, and the banks were eager to lend. Unlike in Britain, few Irish housebuilders were public companies quoted on the stock exchange, with an ability to raise equity from shareholders.

Urban housebuilding is particularly vulnerable to steep rises and falls in output. In other sub-sectors, exposure is typically split between a developer who provides the site and arranges funding, and a contractor who carries out the actual construction. The contract usually makes provision for stage payments, which limits the main contractor's risk if the developer becomes insolvent, though sub-contractors may find it more difficult to protect themselves in this way. By contrast, new private housing in urban areas is usually provided by housebuilders, who combine the roles of developer and builder, and carry the risks associated with the project from site acquisition, through the construction stage, to sale of the completed dwellings. These risks are reduced if units can be sold off the plans, or if investment funds or local authorities agree in advance to purchase entire developments or apartment blocks, but not if units are built on a speculative basis for sale to individual purchasers on completion. The greater need for risk capital associated with the latter, and increased difficulty in obtaining it, has reduced the proportion of new housing units built on that basis. Banks are now only prepared to lend 50-60% of construction costs to housebuilders, as compared with 90% or more before 2008 (Reynolds, 2021, p. 66).

CONSTRUCTION INDUSTRY LOBBYING

The division of the industry into sub-sectors is reflected in the structure of its main representative organisation, the Construction Industry Federation (CIF). The CIF is a true federation, in the sense that it has around two dozen component associations. While most of these are for particular types of specialist sub-contractors, there are three major associations: the Irish Home Builders Association (IHBA), the Civil Engineering Contractors Association (CECA), and the Master Builders and Contractors Association (MBCA). The first two correspond to the two sub-sectors shown at the top of Figure 2.1, with the MBCA representing contractors in other sub-sectors, particularly private non-residential and social infrastructure. The CIF has regional branches, facilitating lobbying at local as well as national level.

The CIF magazine 'Construction' is a useful source on relations between the construction sector and government from the 1970s onwards, and on how these have been affected by successive phases of the construction cycle. It complements official sources, by making it clearer how far they coincide or conflict with construction industry views, and by using less guarded language.

The CIF and its component associations share permanent staff, who provide members with a variety of services, and coordinate lobbying of government and public bodies. However, the CIF is a trade association, not a trade union, and does not have a trade union's capacity to deliver the cooperation of its members, so government concessions to it are not necessarily reciprocated. Despite this, governments are anxious to gain the approval of the CIF, and benefit from any positive influence this may have on members' responses to government measures.

New, more broadly based lobby groups with membership extending well beyond the construction industry itself, such as Property Industry Ireland (PII), emerged during the cyclical low point in the cycle around 2012. These groups include property-related professionals, professional associations such as the Society of Chartered Surveyors (SCSI), property funds and companies, and banks and other financial institutions, as well as the CIF (Waldron, 2019, p. 692). Like the CIF, they have had very considerable success in influencing government policies. This can be interpreted as evidence of regulatory capture, or of government thinking which was so closely aligned with that of lobby groups that capture was unnecessary,[2] or of parallel responses by construction/property interests and governments to the same set of constraints.

DOWNTURNS

Construction firms usually try to maintain a core building team with the necessary range of skills and experience, and with the goodwill and reputational advantages resulting from satisfactory completion of previous projects, even under very unfavourable market conditions. Expanding this core team in a subsequent upturn is quicker and easier than trying to create one from scratch.

However, efforts to hold on to such teams may lead housebuilders to commit to new developments under obviously risky market conditions, and main contractors to bid below cost for contracts when work is scarce. For the latter, the choices can be stark: 'if you don't win work you go out of business, if you win work at a loss you also go out of business, but it takes longer' (Hillebrandt, 1995, p. 68). Housebuilders, while typically exposed to cyclical risk for longer periods, with less certainty on the price which will be paid for the finished product, have one compensating advantage. If their unit of output is small – individual detached houses or pairs of semis – this makes it easier for them to vary their rate of production in line with what the market can absorb.

Increased firm closures, bankruptcies and redundancies during downturns are a normal feature of economic life, and not peculiar to the construction industry. However, the unusually cyclical nature of the Irish construction sector periodically leads to disproportionate loss of firms, unusually severe job losses, and widespread damage to sub-contracting businesses, and so affects an abnormally large number of individuals and their families.

From the economic point of view, new firms can be created, and the construction workforce rebuilt from those of the unemployed, returning emigrants and migrant workers who have not been deterred by previous experience from re-joining it, but all this takes time, and may contribute to a slow response to a recovery in demand, and increase future cyclicality.

PHASES IN THE OVERALL CONSTRUCTION CYCLE

Figure 2.4 aggregates output in the construction sub-sectors from 1980 to 2016, to show how they combine to produce the overall construction cycle. Overall construction output figures are available from the early 1970s and these are shown in Figure 2.5.

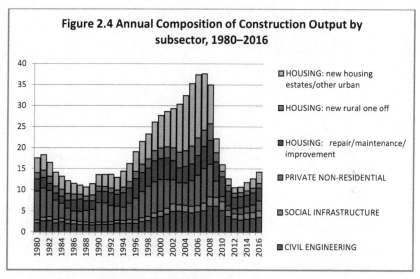

Figure 2.4 Annual Composition of Construction Output by subsector, 1980–2016

Sources: Department of the Environment/DKM Construction Industry Review and Outlook series (1980–2009); RICS/DKM 'The Irish Construction Industry in 2012'; DKM 'Demand for Skills in Construction to 2020' (2016).

There is a substantial literature on the construction cycle, which discusses various ways of classifying its phases (Ive and Gruneberg, 2000, pp. 227–31; Ball et al., 1998, pp. 169–74). Lewis (1965, pp. 13–14) defines cycles simply, through the identification of peak and trough values. While peaks and low points identify turning points in cycles, they also help identify phases, as they represent the end of boom and trough phases. If this principle is applied to the output data in Figure 2.4, the main peaks are in 1979 and 2007, and the main low points in 1988 and 2012.

These peaks and low points can be used to divide the period since the early 1970s into periods of expansion and contraction, with 1982–8 and 2008–12 falling unambiguously into the latter category. Similarly, 1977–9, 1989–90, 1994–2000 and 2003–6 are clearly periods of expansion.

However, there are also periods in which the direction of change was less clear, at least at the time: 1980–1, 1991–3 and 2000–2. In the last two cases, an 'intermediate' cyclical contraction in private non-residential

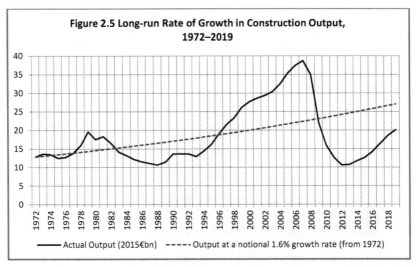

Figure 2.5 Long-run Rate of Growth in Construction Output, 1972–2019

Actual Output (2015€bn) — — — Output at a notional 1.6% growth rate (from 1972)

Sources: As for Figure 2.4, plus CSO Production in Building and Construction Index series

development, of the type noted above, offset continued growth in urban housing, resulting in a pause or slowdown within the longer-term period of aggregate construction industry growth from 1988 to 2007. These periods are classified as 'pauses'.

Some subdivision of periods of expansion and contraction is needed. It is natural to talk of 'recoveries' and 'booms', but opinions may differ on when exactly a period of expansion ceases to be recovery from a previous trough and becomes a boom. Two admittedly approximate ways of doing this can be suggested.

One possible way of defining the point at which a recovery becomes a boom, or a downturn becomes a trough, is to say that such transitions occur once the rate of expansion slows significantly after the year of fastest growth, after a trough, or the rate of contraction slows after the year of steepest decline, after a peak. As Ive and Gruneberg (2000, p. 231) note, 'business cycles usually begin with relatively rapid growth and decelerate towards the peak, after which decline is relatively rapid for a few quarters, thereafter slowing down until the trough is reached'.

For the Irish construction sector, 1983 and 2009 were the years of fastest decline, and arguably also points at which contraction in the sector ceased to be a possibly necessary or even desirable correction to a previously overheated market, and headed into a trough or slump or depression. Similarly, 1996 was the year of fastest growth (in percentage terms).

Another possible rule of thumb is to treat recoveries and downturns as periods in which construction output is converging on long-run average growth, and booms and troughs as periods in which it is diverging from it. Figure 2.5 shows that notional growth of 1.6% per annum from 1972 on intersects actual construction output in the years of fastest growth or decline noted above: 2009, 1996 and 1983. The two methods thus yield similar results.

Having regard to this, the years since 1974 have been classified as years of construction sector recovery, boom, downturn and trough in Table 2.2 below, plus 'pauses' (as defined above). The 2014–19 period has been treated as a recovery, as output remained well below the long-run 1.6% growth curve.

TABLE 2.2   CLASSIFICATION OF 1974–2019 PERIOD BY PHASE OF THE CONSTRUCTION CYCLE

Phase	Years	No. of Years
Trough*	1975–6, 1984–8, 2011–13	10
Recovery	1977, 1989–90, 1994–6, 2014–9	12
Boom	1978–9, 1997–9, 2003–6	9
Downturn*	1974, 1982–3, 2008–10	6
Pause	1980–1, 1991–3, 2000–2, 2007	9
TOTAL		46

*References to a (construction industry) recession mean downturn and trough phases combined.

Figure 2.5 and Table 2.2 are descriptive in purpose, and designed to make it clear what references to, say, 'periods of recovery' in the rest of this book mean. However, they also highlight boom and trough periods, in which actual output has been diverging from a possible definition of long-run average growth.[3] These account for 40% of the period since 1974. There is no realistic possibility of avoiding substantial future divergences from the long-run average, but their scale could be reduced, and ways of doing this are explored in the remainder of this book.

CHAPTER 3

THREE APPROACHES TO
DEVELOPMENT LAND

Summary: *There have been three main strands in official thinking on development land. Firstly, the (unimplemented) Kenny report proposed it be compulsorily acquired at existing use value +25%. Reviving this proposal could require a constitutional amendment to commit subsequent governments to it. The principle could be applied in a more limited way to new towns, and has been applied since 2000 to 10–20% of housing sites, via Part V. This would work better if it applied to any housing land, even if no planning application had been made.*

The second strand involves active management of the development land market. It is currently represented by the Land Development Agency, set up to manage public land. Privately owned land is managed effectively by public agencies in some continental countries, but they are in a stronger negotiating position, and the cycle disrupts their agreements less. Better communal services in new residential neighbourhoods will require increased land acquisition, but the principle that most on site infrastructure is provided by the developer should be retained, with equalisation mechanisms and compensation for works in excess of the needs of the development used where necessary.

The third strand involves the use of incentives and taxes to promote the supply of development land. Supply in the recovery phase of the cycle is often inadequate, leading to steep price rises, but might be improved if landowner expectations were influenced by announcing, in advance, an intention to raise tax rates on development gains and undeveloped sites on a step-by-step basis in a rising market, and reduce them in a declining one. This would be more likely to succeed if applied in conjunction with an increase in acquisition at existing use value.

Figure 3.1 represents the ways in which land is supplied for development, as a set of stocks and flows. The main sources of development land are farmland on the edges of towns and cities, vacant buildings and infill sites within them, and rural land. Land does not 'flow' automatically from these sources towards development, as 'except under conditions of compulsory purchase … all actors in the development process, including the owner, have to be in favour of the development of a particular site if development is to occur' (Goodchild and Munton, 1985, p. 177). If and when the relevant actors take the necessary decisions and actions to move a site towards development, these typically happen in a sequence, rather than all at the same time.

Figure 3.1 shows the most usual sequences, though a number of variations are possible. As there is often an interval between actions, stocks of land accumulate at intermediate stages in the development process.

FIGURE 3.1 THE SUPPLY OF DEVELOPMENT LAND

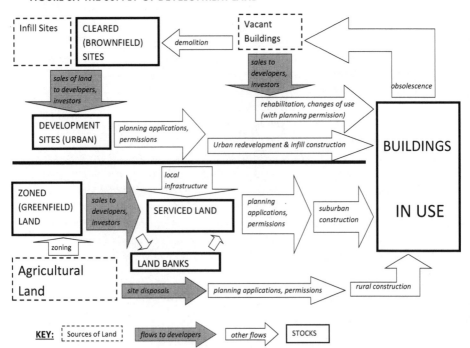

Most building land in Ireland is privately owned and developed, and flows from one stage to another mainly in response to incentives, in the form of increases in value.

On the face of it, these are ample. Table 3.1 compares the cost of development land to house-builders with its value as agricultural land, between 1990 and 2004. The ratio[1] was around 30:1 in the early 1990s, and around 60:1 under boom conditions a decade later.[2] While tax rates have varied quite a lot over the past four decades, most sellers of development land have only been required to pay a minority of their gains in taxes, and have kept the bulk of them.

The focus of this chapter is on the flow of sales[3] from landowners to developers, which are shown as shaded arrows in Figure 3.1. Obviously, those who develop land are sometimes also its original owners, especially where the development involves construction of a house or business premises for their own use. In most other cases they are not in a position to develop the land themselves, and sale to a professional developer is a necessary precondition for its development.

TABLE 3.1   RATIOS BETWEEN HOUSING LAND COSTS AND AGRICULTURAL LAND VALUES, 1990–2004

	1990	1993	1997	2001	2004
New house prices (€000s)	65.5	69.9	101.2	182.9	249.2
of which site cost (%)	11	10	18	23	23
(€000s)	7.2	7.0	18.2	42.1	57.3
Land cost per acre (assuming 10 units/acre)	72.1	69.9	182.1	420.6	573.1
Agricultural land value (€000 per acre)	2.5	2.3	4.0	7.9	9.1
Ratio – housing land cost: agricultural value	29:1	30:1	46:1	53:1	63:1

Sources: Department of the Environment/DKM Construction Industry in Ireland Review and Outlook series; Irish Statistical Bulletin, Agricultural Land Prices series for Mid-East region (a proxy for farmland close to urban areas).

While the high value of development land implies an expectation that this will be realised through its sale and development, its influence over the timing of a landowner's sales to developers is more uncertain. The main incentive influencing timing is not the difference between agricultural and development values, but the relation between currently available prices, and medium-term price expectations. Landowners are naturally reluctant to sell land, even at prices many times its agricultural value, if they expect its value to rise further. Such expectations are well founded at least some of the time. In the admittedly unusual period covered by Table 3.1, the cost[4] of development land more than doubled between 1993 and 1997, more than doubled again between 1997 and 2001, and had risen by a further 36% by 2004. Land costs were eight times 1993 levels by 2004, whereas house prices were less than four times 1993 levels.

The incentives affecting the timing of sales in the development land market may be perverse, from the point of view of moderating the cycle. Early in the upward half of the cycle, landowners have an incentive to delay sales, and investors have an incentive to buy for speculative reasons, even if they have no intention of developing themselves. Near the peak of the boom, the incentive to sell to a real developer is at its strongest, but a large volume of sales at that point may be too late to prevent prices reaching unsustainable levels, and may also facilitate oversupply.

There are some factors which limit the effects of these perverse incentives. Landowners sell for a variety of reasons, some of which encourage or force them to sell at times when prices are below values expected in the medium term. Also, since no-one knows for certain when the market will turn, some will prefer a satisfactory offer now to the prospect of a better one later, on the principle that a bird in the hand is worth two in the bush. On the other hand, the 1995–2012 period demonstrated how quickly and by how much values can vary, in both directions, and this has presumably increased awareness of the influence of timing on prices.

APPROACHES TO DEVELOPMENT LAND

While development land was a significant issue in Britain from the end of the nineteenth century, it only became so in Ireland in the 1960s, when the economy started to grow fast enough for its price to start spiralling upwards. Since then, housing problems in the boom phase of each construction cycle have prompted government initiatives and reports which deal with development land.

These interventions and proposals are mainly concerned with the availability of development land, its price and affordability, and the proportion of gains recovered by the public sector, with the relative prominence of these issues varying between and within cycles. They can be grouped into three main categories, on the basis of the main method of intervention envisaged, involving:

(1)   Nationalisation of development land, at or close to agricultural values
(2)   Active land management by public bodies, using public land and compulsory purchase
(3)   Fiscal interventions, involving new or modified taxes, levies or subsidies

While these three recurrent approaches have existed in parallel for almost half a century, they are described separately in the sections which follow, in the interests of clarity, and to avoid the constant switching between them necessary in a chronologically organised narrative account.

The widely held view that high housing land and house prices are the result of too much state intervention, and could be avoided by drastically reducing planning controls and taxes on development, has had some limited influence on reports and actions under (2) and (3), but no general case for this has been made at an official level in Ireland. A brief discussion of this approach is included at the end of this chapter, so as to cover that end of the policy spectrum.

The focus in this chapter is mainly on the practical effectiveness of these approaches. There are few success stories, but the reasons for limited success can usually be identified. Some relate to the economic cycle. Proposals and interventions are prompted by phases in the economic cycle, and not designed to cope with the cycle as a whole. The focus of policy is thus constantly changing, and interventions are rarely given a chance to bed down. Some proposals never get implemented at all, because the case for them builds in a particular phase of the cycle, but this only translates into political support when the cycle is about to move into the next phase.

There are other reasons. Any significant policy change will have gainers and losers, and may be opposed by the latter, and they may be more organised, motivated and politically influential than the gainers. Reform proposals may exacerbate this, by being unnecessarily diffuse, rather than targeted more precisely on actions with the most favourable balance between practical effects and likely opposition. One reason for this is the centralised nature of the Irish state, resulting in measures prompted by conditions in the larger cities being applied to the country as a whole.

This chapter follows the 'horses for courses' principle. In my view, each of the three generic approaches is the most appropriate one for dealing with certain aspects of development land supply. In the following sections – which deal with each of these three approaches in turn – the description of proposals, interventions and experience over the last half century suggests versions which might usefully be applied now. These possible reforms are outlined in Boxes 3.1–3.8. In cases where some of these reforms would be more effective if applied in combination, this is also noted.

A. NATIONALISATION OF DEVELOPMENT LAND AT EXISTING USE VALUE

Development land became a prominent issue in Ireland in the late 1960s, due to the difficulties the Dublin local authorities were experiencing in acquiring it. The then Dublin City and County Manager expressed concern at the effect of high land prices on small builders and local authority housing, and at the tendency for both to be outbid by larger builders and speculators. As an additional irritant, these competing bidders relied on local authorities to service this land and so underwrite their bids. He proposed that the Dublin authorities should buy land for resale to small builders, to help contain future land price rises. By 1972, some 350 acres had been sold to builders or as individual house sites. The Kenny report described this sympathetically (pp. 23–5) but felt the rate at which land was being supplied was probably too slow to have much effect.

(a) The Kenny Report

The Kenny Committee was appointed by Bobby Molloy, the Minister for Local Government. Its terms of reference focused on controlling the price of building land, and recovering 'betterment'[5] due to publicly-funded sanitary services. The report (completed in 1971, but not published until 1974) cited 16 recent cases where large profits had been made. In five, the local authority was the purchaser, and, in two, the landowner had reneged on a verbal commitment to sell to the local authority, following a better offer. In the Dublin area, average prices had risen from c. £1,000 per acre in 1961 to c. £7,000 in 1970, and c. 4,000 acres of unserviced land had been bought by large builders as land banks. The Committee saw rising development land values as an international trend, not peculiar to Ireland, which would continue. Scarcity of serviced land would accelerate price rises, but ample provision would not halt them. Price rises were largely due to rising demand, as population, incomes and urbanisation increased (Kenny, 1974, pp. 3–9, 10–13).

The Committee considered eleven proposals for controlling land prices and recovering gains/betterment for the community (Kenny, 1974, pp. 26–34). Most were rejected as not providing convincing answers to difficult questions. How was development land to be distinguished from other land? If a tax or levy was used, how did one define and measure the increase in value to be taxed? How did one stop landowners evading a tax, or passing it on to the house buyer (thus pushing up house prices further)? Would the legal and administrative costs of a solution complex enough to cope with these problems consume most of the betterment recovered?

The majority of the Committee recommended compulsory acquisition of land adjoining towns and cities, and likely to be developed within the next ten years. A high court judge, sitting with planning and valuation assessors, would designate such land. It would be acquired at existing use value plus 25%, where its value was probably increased by local authority works. Estimates of existing use value would be needed, but not development value. The 25% extra was to cover development value due to economic influences (e.g. rising demand), rather than works. Local authorities could recover betterment their works had created, and pass the benefit on to housing and schools by selling land for them at cost. Land for commercial and industrial purposes would be sold at full market value. Leasehold sales would allow local authorities to control what precisely land was used for, including the price bracket for private housing[6] (Kenny, 1974, pp. 35–41).

A minority of the Committee regarded any proposal to acquire land at less than full market value as unjust and probably unconstitutional. They also challenged the majority view that the system would produce price control over designated land not actually acquired. The majority felt that, as

> it is unlikely that anyone will pay more than the existing use value plus 25% ... for building land ... The local authority will be able to acquire the land at this price, and so no one will pay more than this for it (Kenny, 1974, p. 41).

The minority argued that it would lead to a dual land market instead, with one set of prices for compulsory transactions and another for open market ones, as had happened in Britain after the 1947 Town and Country Planning Act had introduced a somewhat similar system. It would also end local authority acquisition by agreement, which was more prevalent than compulsory purchase. Instead, acquisition would be fought tooth and nail, and new and drastic powers would be needed to cope with this. The scheme would also require large initial amounts of capital to fund acquisition, which central government might well have difficulty providing (Kenny, 1974, pp. 83–95). The minority report did not refer to the effects of the majority report on 'one-off' houses in rural areas close to towns, as this had not yet taken off at that time. However, the Kenny majority report probably would have stimulated dispersed development outside designated areas, as land within them became the subject of legal delays (Mansergh, 1983, p. 117).

The problem for the minority was to find any viable alternative to the majority report:

> *If ... open market value must continue to be the basic determinant of the price of land acquired for public purposes, it has to be considered whether any legislative action to deal with the land prices problem is feasible at all ...* (Kenny, 1974, p. 99)

However, the existing situation could not be allowed to continue: 'We do not accept that it is in the public interest that local authorities should be forced to compete with other parties in order to secure land needed for progressive and orderly development' (*Ibid.*).

Accordingly, they proposed that areas be designated as suggested by the majority report, but acquisition by compulsory purchase order (CPO) within them be at full market value. Local authorities would still benefit, as they would have a right of pre-emption, by which all vendors wishing to sell land in the designated areas would have to offer it to the local authority first. If the local authority did not wish to buy the land, it could issue a certificate to this effect, allowing sale to a private purchaser. All sales, to the local authority or a private purchaser, would be subject to a 30% levy, and there would be a similar levy on land developed by its original owner.

The majority on the Committee criticised this proposal, on the ground that the levy would be passed on to the house buyer or other final user, and that 'methods of avoiding payment would be discovered'. The minority conceded the levy might be passed on, but if open market value was to be retained, a levy was needed if the community were to get anything. Also, the right of pre-emption would allow a much more active local authority land policy (Kenny, 1974, pp. 35, 115–16).

While the stated role of the Kenny Committee was to examine the price of building land, its minimum aim – common to the majority and minority recommendations – was to improve access to land for local authorities. The minority report proposals might well have raised house prices, as the majority on the Committee argued, but its proposal for pre-emption would – like the majority report – have allowed local authorities to acquire enough land for their social housing programmes and to supply builders with land for lower-cost private housing.

(b) The Failure to Implement the Kenny Report

Neither version of the Kenny report was implemented. The most frequently cited obstacle was the protected status of property rights in the constitution. This difficulty could have been tested in the Supreme Court, and, if necessary, a referendum to amend the constitution could have been held. This would have been an unattractive option for the main political parties because it could split their supporters along urban/rural lines. The reaction attributed to the outgoing Minister for Local Government in the 1973–7 coalition after its defeat in 1977 suggests a simpler explanation:

> *Nobody claimed that his performance as a minister had affected the result. Had he not refrained from taking precipitate, or indeed any, action on the Kenny report of 1973 which sought to impose restrictions on speculation in building land, which would have threatened a powerful pressure group?* (Lee, 1989, p. 486)

Practical experience with similar measures in Britain was another deterrent. The 1975 Community Land Act in Britain had a lot in common with the majority report proposals,[7] and had not worked well. Local authorities there blamed the British government for under-funding their acquisition of land under that scheme, and, by the end of the second year, the Scheme was 'widely regarded as a failure, or at least as a non-event' (Barrett and Fudge, 1981, p. 71).

Funding difficulties in Britain would have struck a chord in Ireland in the mid-1970s, as both countries needed to reduce public expenditure. The Department of Finance would have been conscious of the initial outlay needed for land acquisition, even at existing use value. A dual land market, in which some transactions took place at existing use value + 25%, and others at much higher prices, leading to a strong sense of injustice among those required to sell at the lower price, would have been a certainty with an under-funded attempt to implement the Kenny report. Even with a well-funded attempt, a dual market would have been probable, as compulsory acquisition at existing use value + 25% would have ended urban expansion by consent, and legal and other delays where it was contested would have led to slow and uncertain land supply at that price.

These problems remain. Any future attempt to implement the Kenny report will be at least as vulnerable to the economic cycle and changes of government as it was in Britain, and more vigorously opposed, as Ireland has more dispersed land ownership, and stronger rural interest groups. At the same time, while no Irish government has even attempted to implement the Kenny report, it nevertheless had – and still has – a stronger hold on the minds of those dissatisfied with the current system of development land supply than any subsequent proposals.

This latent public support is for the majority report proposals – for compulsory acquisition at existing use value plus 25% – but limited awareness of the distinction between the CPO-based majority report and the levy-based minority one allows the mantle of Kenny to be draped over levies. For instance, Housing for All (2021, p. 75) introduces its Land Value Sharing (LVS) proposals as involving 'Updated, Kenny Report style, active land management powers with fairer sharing of the increase in land values resulting from zoning decisions'. The minority report accepted (p. 115) the levy it proposed could be passed on, and the majority (p. 35) thought that it would be, but their view on this point is not emphasised.

Given the latent public support for the majority report, careful timing and slightly more generous compensation might offer a reasonably determined government a way round some of these obstacles. In particular, could the phases of the cycle to be used to aid implementation? Box 3.1 explores this option:

Box 3.1 Cycle-friendly Implementation of the Kenny Report?

In the past, interest in the Kenny report has been greatest late in a boom (e.g. 1982, 2004), when land values are highest. This is understandable, but might be counterproductive if it resulted in legislation being introduced at that stage in the cycle. A downturn which restricted public funds for land purchases might well occur before it was fully operational.

A more cycle-friendly approach might involve giving advance notice of an intention to implement Kenny at or before the start of a recovery. This would discourage delaying sales, and buying land as an investment. Builders who could develop quickly would thus pay less for sites. However, it could also affect confidence and financing of the recovery.

Legislation (and any necessary constitutional change) could then be processed in the late recovery or boom phases, when there would be most political support. Slightly more generous compensation – e.g. double existing use value, or a lower multiple if this exceeded half open market value – could reduce opposition, and allow some urban expansion by consent to continue. The state would need to use increased construction-related tax revenue in these phases to build up a war chest for future compulsory purchases.

Compulsory purchases under the legislation could start gradually, but rise once a downturn was well underway. This would reduce the drop from development to existing use values, and resistance from landowners and developers. Also, there would be less time pressure in the downturn and trough phases, as demand for land would be quite low then. Initially, acquisition could be mostly in and near cities, where the market recovers first.

When the market recovered, local authorities would be well placed to resell compulsorily purchased land at a profit and on conditions, and to use the betterment recovered in this way to fund local infrastructure, and further purchases at existing use value. Once they had substantial land banks and a worthwhile flow of betterment income from them, the system might come to be seen as a success, and so be less vulnerable to shifting political conditions.

This approach would require long-term government commitment over a full economic cycle, normally equivalent to several electoral cycles. This is unlikely, unless a referendum on the legislation was necessary, and was passed with a reasonably convincing majority. In those circumstances, successive governments might consider themselves bound by the programme advanced at the time of the referendum. While the possible need for a referendum has, up until now, been seen as one of the main obstacles to the Kenny report, it might, in fact, be the only way of securing durable political commitment to it.

However, even if a referendum was passed, this approach would require a lot of patience, and depend on economic and other conditions developing more or less as anticipated. A more limited application of the Kenny approach might deliver quicker results more simply. Arguably, the original Kenny recommendations spread the net too wide, and would have cost more to implement and aroused more opposition than strictly necessary.

Land availability, excessive prices and development gains are much more of a problem in and close to large urban areas, and special measures are less necessary elsewhere. However, there are obvious difficulties in having radically different rights and obligations for landowners in different parts of the state. These difficulties could be circumvented by a variant on the Kenny majority report, narrowly focused on the creation of new or satellite towns, and largely consistent with existing provisions on compulsory purchase. This variant is outlined in Box 3.2.

Box 3.2 The Kenny Report and New Towns

While new towns are now seen from a planning perspective, with well understood pros and cons, they were originally proposed more as a way of overcoming the obstacle to better urban living conditions represented by high land values. Ebenezer Howard's 1898 classic *Garden Cities of Tomorrow* argued that economic growth in existing cities pushed up property prices, frustrating efforts to use it to improve housing conditions for many of those who contributed to it. To circumvent this, he proposed new towns at a distance from existing cities, on land acquired at agricultural values. Once the land was publicly owned, employment, population and services could be attracted, without pushing up land values.

Applying the Kenny proposals to acquire new town sites well outside cities would involve quite limited change. Rule 13(b) of the rules for assessment of compensation states that no account should be taken of 'the possibility or probability of the land … becoming subject to a scheme of development undertaken by a local authority'. If the 'scheme' was a complete new town, this should allow acquisition of its site at close to agricultural values, like land acquired for a rural motorway. As any such scheme would be preceded by public discussion and a planning process, legislation might be needed to explicitly confirm exclusion of compensation for any hope value which arose prior to its adoption, while a scheme was under consideration.

The Irish property market copes with rising house prices in cities partly through longer commuting journeys. Dependence on this is often undesirable, and needs to be reduced, but there is no realistic prospect of avoiding it completely. Creation of new towns on commuter rail corridors, where they would support more frequent services (e.g. as in the proposed new town of Monard in Co. Cork), would be a relatively sustainable version of this phenomenon.

The need among smaller builders for upfront finance could be reduced by agreements whereby the site remained publicly owned until houses were complete, and sale proceeds were then split on an agreed formula. Such agreements could also control timing and price. Release of land in the new towns would be publicly controlled, and varied in line with demand and need.

Infrastructure costs are usually higher in new towns, but this should be offset by the absence of development land value. The gap between affordable and open market values is generally less in commuter belts than in the cities themselves, so there would be less reliance on clawback clauses or other controls on the resale of affordable houses at market prices.

Unlike the Kenny proposals, this would not bring the bulk of development land under public control, but it would create a substantial alternative to the privately controlled housing market in the main cities, where price and availability problems are, typically, at their most intense.

(c) Part V (1999–2010)

While the boom of the late 1970s put the Kenny report[8] back on the political agenda, it did not the remain there long, partly because of criticisms of its approach in the 1985 report of the Joint Oireachtas Committee on Building Land (discussed below). Also, the boom was replaced by a deep recession, in which development land gains were too low for there to be much support for radical proposals to recover them. Land costs had been 14% of average new house prices in 1980–2, but had fallen to 9% by 1985, and were still only 10% in 1991–4.[9]

However, house and development land prices soared in the late 1990s. By early 1999, the government had become concerned not only by the rate at which house prices were rising, but also by the longer-term affordability problem for first-time buyers, even if prices stabilised.[10] Part V of the 1999 Planning and Development Bill included a requirement for developers to transfer up to 20% of private housing estate sites to the local authority for social and affordable housing, at existing use value.[11] Each local authority would produce a housing strategy, which would include an estimate of the percentage of new housing within its area which needed to be social or affordable, subject to the 20% upper limit. As most of the land would be provided at agricultural values, the price of this housing would be only marginally above construction cost. Social housing would be provided in the places where private housing was being built, so avoiding the previous tendency to ghettoisation.

Part V, like the Kenny report, involved public acquisition of land at existing use value, but only applied to 20% of zoned housing land, while Kenny envisaged it applying to most land, for any type of development. Part V also required transfer from developers as a condition of planning permission, giving them control over timing, whereas Kenny would have involved acquisition mostly from the original landowners, with CPO timing controlled by the local authority.

The construction industry was appalled. The cover story on the October 1999 edition of *Construction* was 'New Planning Bill – Recipe for Disaster'. The 1999 Bill included many changes to the planning system which the

Construction Industry Federation (CIF) had been pressing for, and the adverse overall reaction was due to Part V. The CIF argued it would do nothing to increase the supply of housing land, which was where the real problem lay. The only thing it would produce was uncertainty. It was an attempt to tackle the price of building land in the tradition of the Kenny and Joint Oireachtas reports, which, like them, would fail. Local authorities supported the Bill, but this was not surprising as they had 38,000 on their waiting lists, due to insufficient government funding for public housing (*Construction*, October 1999, pp. 5–7).

Continuing pressure from the construction industry did not prevent the legislation being enacted in 2000, or starting to be applied in the latter part of 2001, but it did lead to its drastic dilution after the 2002 general election. While s.96 of the 2000 Act required the transfer of up to 20% of the application site, in the form of land, or with houses or serviced sites on this land, an amending Act[12] allowed these to be provided on land other than the application site, or payment of a cash contribution instead. This resulted in developers offering Part V housing in areas which already had a lot of social housing, as their Part V contribution on developments in middle class areas, thus undermining the social mix intentions of the 2000 Act. However, transfer of land which was part of the application site remained the default option, and alternatives to this had to be agreed between the applicant and the local authority.

The practical effects of Part V as amended varied widely between local authorities. In some, a financial contribution became the norm. This had the merit of simplicity, and avoided service charges in apartment only inner–city developments, but reduced Part V to a new and complicated development levy.

Other local authorities wished to retain the social mix and access to land advantages of on-site property transfers, and these normally sought completed houses, and were reluctant to agree to a financial contribution. This led to considerable conflict. In defiance of planning conditions, many developers started building with no agreement in place, while delaying transfers through unrealistic negotiating positions, or declining to negotiate at all, forcing the local authority to take them to court. On the local authority side, the extent to which the planning, housing and estates functions were coordinated – giving developers a coherent inter-departmental team to negotiate with – also varied. Conveyancing of affordable housing was sometimes slow, and social housing transferred was not always allocated and occupied quickly.

The Department of the Environment reacted to these issues in several different ways. In 2005, 'following representations made by the Irish Home Builders Association' it decided[13] that the profit on the cost of constructing houses on land to be transferred to the local authority which developers were entitled to under Part V should allow for developer's profit of up to 15%, in addition to contractor's profit at 7½%.[14] Since such houses were being constructed on a contract basis, and did not involve the risks associated with speculative building which makes developer's profit necessary, this change made sense only as a way of making Part V more palatable to builders. It was not particularly successful in this, as there was continuing litigation,[15] and it also resulted in some local authorities agreeing to pay what became more than the open market value of Part V houses, once prices started to collapse in 2008.

In November 2006, a further circular[16] took a somewhat tougher line with house builders' delaying tactics, advising that planning applications which did not specify how a relevant development would comply with Part V should be treated as invalid. Where they did propose a particular method of compliance, and this was accepted by the local authority, the Part V condition attached to the permission should require the developer to comply in that specific way. Within local authorities, it recommended that where they were not already doing so, Part V proposals be circulated to the housing department, and their report incorporated in the planning assessment of an application, and also that they should arrange for direct sale of Part V houses to affordable purchasers, to avoid the delays involved in a double property transfer.

In the first decade of operation (2002–11), Part V resulted in the transfer of around 9,400 affordable and 5,700 social units, plus 68 hectares of housing land, 940 individual serviced house sites, and €150 million in financial contributions. Assuming the land, sites and contributions were fully used, the overall number of dwellings or equivalents transferred under Part V was 19,245, or 4.8% of total housing output in that period (Housing Agency, 2014, p. iii). This figure was low, partly because Part V did not apply to pre-2001 planning permissions, and only came fully into force when most of these had expired, by around 2006. Transfers peaked in 2008, at 12.6% of housing output, but this was at least partly because increasing selling difficulties rapidly overcame builders' reluctance to transfer them to local authorities.

(d) Review of Part V (2011–15)

The collapse in the housing market from 2009 on meant that open market new house prices were often at or below the price of houses transferred under Part V. In 2011, the Department of the Environment published a Housing Policy Statement, discontinuing the role of Part V in providing affordable housing as no longer necessary, and as reflecting the 'high and often disproportionate value' attached to owner occupation. Providing the state did not overstimulate the housing market, state interventions to make housing more affordable should not be necessary. However, there was still a strong need for social housing, so it favoured retention of this component of Part V as a way of providing this in a manner which promoted social mix. A Review of Part V was announced, to work out in more detail what revisions to it were necessary.

The Review was carried out by the Housing Agency and published in 2014. Its priority was speedy delivery of social housing, at a time when government expenditure was limited.[17] To promote this, it recommended that the Part V compliance options should be limited to providing housing on or off site, or land on site, with other options (e.g. financial contributions, land off site) being withdrawn. As it also felt provision of affordable housing via Part V was no longer needed, it suggested that the maximum transfer required should be reduced from 20% to 10%. The 2015 Urban Regeneration and Housing Act amended the Planning Acts in accordance with these recommendations. The National Economic and Social Council (NESC) (2020, p. 32) attributed this scaling back of Part V to concerns on its effects on viability.

The 2015 Act arguably made the same mistake as the 2000 one, in legislating for Part V in a form appropriate to housing market conditions and the phase of the cycle existing at the time of enactment, rather than for a more robust and flexible version, with the capacity to adjust to different phases of the cycle designed into it. Less than a year after the 2015 Act became law, the Society of Chartered Surveyors of Ireland (SCSI) produced detailed costings (summarised in Table 3.2) for a new three-bedroom semi-detached house in Dublin, which totalled €330,000[18] – about 10% above the maximum a couple who were both working and on the average industrial wage could afford, based on loans of 3.5 times income and in accordance with the Central Bank's loan limits. A 2020 SCSI report, updating the 2016 one, reached the same conclusion.

While a 114m² (1200 square foot) semi might be questioned as a test of affordability, further SCSI reports in 2017 and 2021 indicated that substituting 79m² apartments did not improve matters. The lowest cost version (low rise suburban apartments with surface parking) offered much less floorspace at a similar price, and other versions offered this at much higher ones.

If the affordable version of Part V had still been available in 2016, and the land costs were based on agricultural rather than development values, this would have reduced the overall price of semis and low-rise suburban apartments to be transferred[19] by more than enough to meet the SCSI's affordability criteria. Most local authorities would, in practice, have sought 1,000-square-foot terraced houses in preference to semis or low-rise apartments, reducing the cost further. The 2015 Act arguably discontinued affordable transfers under Part V at precisely the moment when they were once again becoming necessary, at least in Dublin.[20]

The 20% requirement was eventually restored by s.46 of the 2021 Affordable Housing Act, but this will not take effect on land bought between 2015 and 2021 until 2026.

TABLE 3.2 SCSI COST ESTIMATES FOR SEMI-DETACHED HOUSES AND APARTMENTS IN DUBLIN, 2016–21

Year	▢Dwelling type	▢Parking	m²**	Land	Construction, contingency	Finance, fees, sales	Levies, VAT	Profit	Total	Total cost per M²
					€ '000s					€
2016	**3 bed semi** (average cost)	surface	114	58	150	34	51	38	330	2895
2017	2 bed apartments (lower end of cost range;									
	low rise suburban	surface	79	33	166	40	56	38	333	4215
	medium rise suburban	undercroft	79	70	206	56	59	52	443	5608
	medium rise urban	basement	79	90	233	68	64	61	516	6532
2020	**3 bed semi** (average)	surface	114	61	179	31	58	43	371	3257
2021	2 bed apartments (lower end* of cost range;									
	low rise suburban	surface	79	29	186	40	63	41	359	4543
	medium rise:									
	–suburban	undercroft	79	46	201	47	70	47	411	5199
	–urban, 5–8 storeys	basement	79	65	230	58	83	57	493	6241
	–urban, 9–15 storeys	basement	79	65	245	60	85	59	514	6507

* Apartment costs at the upper end of the range in 2021 were 15-27% higher than those at the lower end, and mid-range ones were 8-13% higher.
** For apartments, net floorspace (i.e. excluding communal floorspace) is given in this column. Net floorspace of 79m2 was equated to 91m2 gross.
Sources: SCSI, 2016, 2017, 2020, 2021

The obvious argument against Part V transfers below market value are that they are a form of tax, levied in kind, and, like other taxes, reduce gains to landowners and/or builders, leading some of them to withhold land or houses they would otherwise have supplied. If demand remains constant, the reduction in supply will cause an increase in house prices, allowing some or all of the tax to be 'passed on' to open-market purchasers of other houses in the developments affected.[21]

Part V is vulnerable to 'withholding' because it takes effect near the end of the development pipeline, via conditions attached to planning permissions. A landowner normally has to sell the site to a developer, and the latter then has to secure and be about to implement a permission before any Part V transfer takes place. It is this control over timing and the rate at which land is released that can put both of them in a position to pass on some of the cost of compliance to house buyers. This is a weakness, relative to the Kenny proposals, which envisaged acquisition from the landowner rather than the developer, with the local authority controlling timing.

In a limited way, the differences between Part V and the Kenny approach could be reduced, by providing for advance acquisition of Part V land from the original landowner, prior to any planning application. This would remove control over the timing of the transfer of Part V land from landowners, and ensure compliance costs were specific to them, in line with the Kenny view that they were the ones benefitting from windfall gains. It would prevent this cost being passed on to households, who might sometimes be priced out of the market as a consequence, or to builders, whose developments it might sometimes make unviable.

In essence, the tendency to 'withhold' and 'pass on' would apply to less of the development pipeline if Part V transfers occurred further upstream. Once the Part V 20% had been transferred, it would become irrelevant to decisions on disposal of the remaining 80% downstream of that point. Box 3.3 outlines how this might be done:

Box 3.3 Advance Transfer of Part V Land

If local authorities had the power to acquire the Part V percentage of zoned blocks of housing land from landowners in advance of any planning application, the transfer would be involuntary, and at the landowner's expense. Transfer on Part V terms would be less cumbersome than through CPOs, and would be at existing use value. Landowners could then sell the remaining portion when they wished, free of Part V obligations for a specified period.

Crucially, advance acquisition would allow local authorities to develop Part V land when supply was tight and prices rising – circumstances in which it often suits landowners and developers to wait. The reinstatement of the 20% rate in the 2021 Affordable Housing Act will increase the size of sites transferred and make them easier to develop independently.

While provision of Part V housing by developers helps it blend in with that on the remainder of the site, transfers of land also have advantages, as they allow a more flexible response to market conditions. In secondary locations, and in small- or medium-sized towns, demand can vary greatly, growing rapidly in booms, and collapsing during recessions. A site transferred under Part V can be developed when needed, and held at low cost when it is not. Land transfer negotiations are simpler, quicker and less contentious than the transfer of houses, and subsequent construction of houses by a contractor would usually be cheaper.

Especially in Dublin, there are periodic reports of developers seeking very large amounts for the transfer of Part V units. Since the local authority has to pay the full construction cost of these units, plus a margin, developers have no incentive to keep their costs down. In some cases, it may be better to realise the cost savings achievable by acquisition of the relevant percentage of the site and its development by the local authority itself, with 'blending in' achieved by co-ordination of design rather than by construction of all units by the developer.

Housing for All emphasises (Sept. 2121, pp. 79–81) the difficulty local authorities have in recouping an adequate share of development gains through the (existing versions of) Part V and development contributions, as these 'take effect after the majority of the uplift in value has occurred, often to those other than the site developer'.

Once a developer has crystalised this uplift in a purchase price, subsequent efforts to recoup more of it may render development unviable. The proposed solution – 'Land Value Sharing' (LVS) – will be applied 'no later than a grant of permission for development' and is expected to 'act as a clear signal to landowners and purchasers of development land as to the obligations that will result from ... zoning of land for residential development'.

The same could be said of existing versions of Part V and development contributions, but it is doubtful whether they do much to dampen price expectations in practice, and the same problem may apply to LVS. Advance acquisition under Part V could do more to resolve this problem, as it would be more than just a signal, and could take direct effect soon after zoning.

B. ACTIVE LAND MANAGEMENT

In addition to their long-established non-market development roles (e.g. provision of social housing, roads etc), local authorities have also traditionally sold and rented out some property in the open market. These market transactions have mostly involved using surplus parts of land parcels acquired primarily for social housing or infrastructure, for purposes such as private sector housing, and industrial sites or estates. There have been periodic proposals to expand this market role, as a way of stimulating the development process, or resolving problems within it.

A legislative basis for local authority market transactions was provided by s.77 of the 1963 Local Government (Planning and Development) Act. This gave local authorities extensive powers to carry out a wide range of industrial, commercial and residential development and urban renewal themselves, to provide land and sites suitable for development, acquire land compulsorily, and enter into agreements with others for these and other purposes. These powers remain in force, with some minor amendments, as section 212 of the 2000 Planning and Development Act. Local authorities thus have the power both to actively manage development land, and to act as developers on a commercial basis. In principle, these positive powers complement the predominantly regulatory powers in the planning acts, which allow specific types of development through zoning and planning permissions, but cannot ensure that they actually happen.

The initial version of active land management encouraged local authority-led development. The 1971 White Paper on Local Government Reorganisation noted (pp. 14–15) that:

> *For many years local authorities … have been contributing to economic and social development, for example, by providing sites for industry and other developments in the course of their housing programmes. With the enactment of the 1963 Act, this developmental role has been statutorily recognised. Local authorities, therefore, must now regard themselves and be regarded as development corporations for their areas.*

It saw the 1963 Act as providing a mandate for development as well as for planning, and the 'development corporation' role of local authorities as including provision of sites for industrial, housing, and commercial development. It also noted that they had the power to carry out almost any type of development themselves.

These wider intentions may have been genuinely held, but were largely unrealised:

> *The 1963 Act was not called the Planning and Development Act by accident. The original objectives were twofold. One was to regulate the flow of private investment in land development … The other was for the local authorities to actively involve themselves in the creation of a better physical environment … by eliminating the legal obstacles to appropriate development or by engaging in joint venture projects for development themselves. The emphasis on the active was at least as strong as on the regulatory …*
>
> *The experience since then has been very disappointing. Firstly, no mention of finance was made in the 1963 or, indeed, in any other Act since then. Secondly, many local authorities struggled for up to 10 years to deal with their regulatory responsibilities. Thirdly … the dual hierarchy system actively hindered the undertaking of active initiatives. The experience has been that, even when they were mooted, the Planners were not practical enough, and the Managers abhorred the risk.* (Boland, 1986, p. 43)

THE JOINT OIREACHTAS COMMITTEE ON BUILDING LAND

In the 1980s, the Joint Oireachtas Committee[22] on Building Land argued for a different form of intervention, designed to rectify market failures in the development land market, through wider and more aggressive use of compulsory purchase. This seems to have been recommended as a less drastic and more market-friendly alternative to the Kenny report. Building land had come back onto the political agenda, due to another surge in house prices in the late 1970s, prompting what the CIF called a 'campaign' to implement the Kenny report (*Construction*, February 1982, p. 5). The incoming coalition government established a Joint Committee on the issue in 1983,[23] in response to this pressure, and probably also as a way of defusing the issue.

The Joint Committee's report, following the economic advice given to it, criticised the Kenny approach as being too concerned with the distributional issue – recovery of development gains for the community – and 'unduly concentrated on dealing with land prices, which are a symptom rather than a cause' (Joint Committee, 1985, p. 144).

The Joint Committee report considered land prices had an important function in ensuring land is used for the most appropriate purpose. Other things being equal, price is an indicator of the benefit available from alternative land uses. Replacing price signals by administered prices – as envisaged by Kenny – could lead to inappropriate and wasteful use of land. Artificially depressed land prices may encourage lower densities, undue reliance on new building on the periphery of urban areas, and insufficient renewal of existing housing areas. Management of the land market is an important task in its own right, not just a tool for achieving policy objectives in related areas, such as housing shortages, urbanisation patterns, or the level of construction activity.

Management was needed because open market land prices are not a completely reliable guide to what land should be used for. Markets are imperfect, and sometimes subject to market failure. They do not allow for externalities, and make insufficient provision for uses for which there is no effective market – public open space, for instance. However, the land market, in combination with planning policies which correct for these deficiencies, is the appropriate way of allocating development land between the various urban land uses (Joint Committee, 1985, pp. 4–10, 13–15).

The Committee subdivided management of the development land market into three main functions: supply, allocation and equity. It considered each of these in turn, to identify respects in which they were not operating satisfactorily, and propose measures to rectify these defects.[24]

(i) **Supply**: the task of policy was to identify and correct any tendency to price distortion and market failure. On a number of occasions, prices 'had been seriously distorted (i.e. prices did not reflect the development potential of the land)'. This was partly due to land being treated as an investment asset, rather than as an input to the development process:

> *The markets for urban land, in particular, and publicly serviced land to some degree are unduly affected by asset value to the point of contributing to market failure in the former case and short term price distortion in the latter.* (Joint Committee, 1985, p. 66)

There was a lot of vacant land in inner city areas at the time, but land availability was poor. The Committee quoted a NESC report suggesting this was due to unrealistic expectations: 'Low holding costs and anticipation of planning permission provide the incentive to hold land in anticipation of large capital gains' (Bannon *et al.*, 1981, p. 195; cited by Joint Committee, 1985, p. 65). This prompted the Committee's main recommendation, namely wider and more aggressive use of (a speeded-up form of) compulsory purchase, at prices which reflected current supply and demand, and excluded unrealistic long-term hope value.[25] This was supplemented by proposals to improve market research and information, so builders had a better understanding of the balance between supply and demand for particular types of development. It was recommended that it should also be made easier to identify landowners (Joint Committee, 1985, pp. 64, 70, 79, 90–3, 97).

The Joint Committee dealt with access to development land under 'supply', with the unstated implication that land is either available in adequate quantities or it is not, and, if it is, it is available to all on an equal basis. It did not share the Kenny report's concern that local authorities and small builders were, in practice, at a disadvantage.[26]

The proposal to use compulsory purchase more widely and aggressively was not acted on. Local authorities continued to acquire land for construction projects of their own, and occasionally also to remedy some high-profile problem, such as a prominent site which had been derelict for a long time. They were no more inclined to intervene systematically to make the market work more smoothly after the Committee's report than before. The solution to overvalued inner-city land which was actually adopted was to raise its value, by making designated urban renewal areas eligible for generous tax reliefs. This initiative came into force from 1986 onwards.

(ii) **Allocation:** pressures on the planning system caused it to allocate land inappropriately:

> *Zoning ... is a distributive influence which benefits certain property owners and not others. As a result, planning authorities may come under severe pressure from property owners who are attempting to acquire the windfall gains accruing to development land. This can lead to excessive or premature zoning of land, disruption of resources available for servicing and to the adoption of undesirable development patterns.* (Joint Committee, 1985, p. 7)

However, specific proposals were only advanced in relation to pressures exerted via the right to claim compensation for refusal of planning permission. The report suggested excluding the portion of development gains attributable to state subsidies and unrealistic hope value from the amount claimable, and restricting the right of connection to public sewers, which had been used to support a compensation claim in the Short case[27] (Joint Committee, 1985, pp. 77–9, 84). No proposals were advanced on pressures exerted through other channels, such as lobbying of elected members of local authorities. This is a logical weakness, since the Committee outlined the general pressures windfall gains create for planning in their analysis, but confined themselves to one symptom – compensation for refusal of planning permission – in their proposals.

While the government eventually acted on this latter issue, they took a more robust line than the Joint Committee. The 1990 Local

Government (Planning and Development) Act made zoning a non-compensatable reason for refusal of permission.[28] This was an important change. So long as refusal for zoning reasons was compensatable, local authorities were under pressure to grant permission, to avoid large claims, undermining their power to not zone land. The Joint Committee's recommendations on deducting value attributable to public subsidies, and disallowing claims based on an automatic right to connect to sewers, were included in the Act,[29] but as minor clauses.

(iii) **Equity**: the Committee (1985, p. 96) outlined three further 'equity' principles. Firstly, the community had a right to recover its own contribution to development values. Secondly, there was a need 'to eliminate distortions and pressures, arising from windfall gain, which are contrary to optimum development'. Thirdly, public acceptance that the distribution of gains was fair and reasonable was needed.

These principles were not accompanied by definite proposals on how they should be applied, and some of the Committee's comments imply that they thought the existing distribution acceptable. For instance, they considered (1985, p. 97) estimates of tax collected 'would stand comparison with' estimates of the gains made, but data on both were weak and needed verification. Also, their recommendations under the allocation and supply heads would 'substantially counteract' (*Ibid.*) adverse effects from windfall gain on the planning system and the market. If the proportion of gains recovered through the tax system needed to be raised, it should be done through a tax rather than via fixed levies, in view of the variability of windfall gain.

The report was unconvincing on its aim of eliminating 'distortions and pressures, arising from windfall gain, which are contrary to optimum development'. Reliance on the economists' distinction between efficiency and equity led to treatment of the distribution of development gains as a largely separate issue from supply and allocation, and discouraged recognition of the way distributional outcomes cause allocational problems. The Joint Committee at no point stated the obvious: that supply of development land had depended since the 1960s on landowners being allowed to keep the bulk of development gains, and that pressures on the planning system arose directly from this practice.

The main aim of the Joint Committee and its economist advisers may have been more theoretical than practical – to reassert the value of market processes in relation to development land. If so, it did succeed in exorcising the ghost of the Kenny report, at least until the end of the 1990s. The expansion in the use of existing compulsory purchase powers it recommended did not occur, and these powers remained a minor form of development land supply.

NESC AND DEVELOPMENT LAND

The lengthy 1997–2006 boom revived interest in the use of compulsory purchase, public land, and public-private partnerships as ways of improving the volume, affordability and quality of housing output. This interest increased once the market started to recover from 2014 on. The theoretical case for this was developed in a series of reports on housing and development land produced by the NESC, in which more active land management has been one main strand. These reports are conveniently book-ended by *Housing in Ireland: Performance and Policy (2004)* and *Urban Development Land, Housing and Infrastructure: Fixing Ireland's Broken System* (2018).

The 2004 report suggested (pp. 194–5) government policy was already moving towards more active land management, citing special development agencies in Dublin's Docklands and the Temple Bar area, the 1997 Serviced Land Initiative (SLI),[30] the 1999 Affordable Housing Scheme, the 2003 Affordable Housing Initiative,[31] and 2002 legislation facilitating public-private partnerships.[32] Like the Joint Oireachtas Committee, it suggested a stronger, reformed and streamlined form of compulsory purchase (of greenfield as well as derelict urban land). NESC also saw a strong case for compulsory purchase in advance of residential zoning, with the land so acquired normally being developed in partnership with the private sector.

However, the 2004 NESC report's motives differed from those of the Joint Oireachtas report. NESC was critical (2004, pp. 124–6) of the prevailing pattern of suburban housing development in Ireland, whereby individual housing estates were single use, and laid out on the 'pod' or cul-de-sac principle, separate from public services, employment and each other. NESC favoured a shift towards mixed-use neighbourhoods, which had well-defined centres, and grid or web-type road systems which put those centres within easy walking distance of housing within the neighbourhood, resulting in higher quality, more sustainable housing.

Developing complete neighbourhoods, rather than on a field-by-field basis, would require more coordination between adjacent land holdings. NESC cited (2004, p. 24) Evans (2004, p. 181) on owners of adjacent blocks of development land in the UK often having different motives for holding land and different perceptions of how values may change in the future, leading them to put their land on the market at very different times. This was not a serious problem for traditional housing estate development on the cul-de-sac model: it was car dependent anyway, and the sequence in which zoned land at various points on the perimeter of the existing built-up area was developed was rarely critical. It was a problem for neighbourhood-based development, not just for timing reasons, but also because the mix of uses would include a neighbourhood centre, a primary school, sports facilities and so on. This would result in different values per acre for different landowners, and in ones required to provide land for less remunerative uses having a sense of grievance and being less inclined to make their land available.

By 2018, NESC had developed its own ideas on how active land management could be used to promote coordinated developments of neighbourhoods, relying partly on established practice in Germany and the Netherlands. While a variety of approaches used in those countries are cited (NESC 2018, pp. 23–8), most feature:

- Negotiations between landowners and the relevant public authority
- Pooling and re-division of land, with some of it retained for public purposes
- Ensuring the cooperation of landowners through a credible (but rarely used) threat of compulsory acquisition below market value

To apply such approaches in Ireland would require highly skilled and respected, well-staffed and well-led urban development agencies that have 'the professional competence to draw up master plans and engage in complex arrangements for implementation with the private sector and community groups' (*Ibid.*, p. x). It would also require:

> ... *real engagement between the public and private actors, which depends on framework conditions, in particular the status of the public bodies, their planning powers and a credible system of compulsory purchase at below full development value, to be used as a last resort and under judicial supervision* (*Ibid.*, p. 51).

The new agencies would work with private landowners, making use of public land, joint ventures, and land readjustment, and have stronger compulsory purchase powers, as existing CPO powers in Ireland are considered cumbersome and costly (*Ibid.*, p. 52).

The government launched a new national Land Development Agency (LDA) in September 2018, intended to have many of these characteristics. Its immediate function was to manage the development of publicly owned land for housing, and it had an 'initial pipeline' of sites with capacity for 10,000 homes, of which 3,000 would be on land which was already serviced. On public land disposed of to private developers, 40% of the houses would have to be provided at below market rates – 10% social, and 30% affordable.

This immediate role makes sense. An agency specifically charged with reuse of publicly owned land may carry out this function more effectively than national/regional/local government agencies and departments which currently own such land, as the latter understandably tend to see their landholdings from the point of view of their own specialised responsibilities. The delays involved in transferring land from another state agency to the LDA and then to a developer could be minimised, if the LDA acted on behalf of that agency rather than as an intermediate owner.[33] Where another agency was already advancing delivery of land, the LDA would not complicate matters by becoming involved as well.[34]

The government had more ambitious long-term intentions for the LDA. Capital funding of €1.25 billion was earmarked for the agency, to support the provision of 150,000 new homes[35] over a 20-year period, on the basis that the LDA, working with developers, would 'assemble strategic landbanks from a mix of public and private lands, making them available for housing in a controlled manner which brings essential long term stability to the housing market' (DHPLG statement, 13/9/18).

As in the 2018 NESC report, this involved applying European models in Ireland:

> *The LDA is modelled on best European practice as already demonstrated in Germany and the Netherlands. By assembling land packages ahead of the planning and infrastructure stages, the Agency can lower development land costs and tackle upward pressure on house prices. (Ibid.)*

The Housing for All programme, launched in September 2021, indicated (p. 98) that the LDA's capital of €1.25 billion would be matched by another €1.25 billion of borrowing capacity, which was likely to be increased by a further €1 billion in 2024.

LIMITS TO ACTIVE LAND MANAGEMENT IN IRELAND

The forms of active land management proposed by NESC, and to some extent endorsed by government, address real problems, but go against the grain in Ireland in several respects:

(1) As Chapter 1 indicated, the construction industry in Ireland is unusually cyclical. If housing development relies too much on agreements with developers, on publicly owned land or in UDZs, these will be open to disruption by the cycle. After 2008, some agreements simply collapsed, but they would be vulnerable to less extreme market shifts, in so far as they price land and/or specify how neighbourhood services, infrastructure and social and affordable housing are provided and paid for. These provisions ultimately depend on housing values. If developers do not allow for unpredictable changes in values, deals may fall through; if they do (e.g. through generous margins), this results in poor value for the public sector. The LDA and Housing for All aim for 'long term stability to the housing market' but agreement-based active land management cannot deliver this. Broader efforts to increase the market's ability to adjust to successive cyclical phases are needed.

(2) In most new development areas in Ireland, land is held by farmers and investors as well as developers, and some of the developers will drastically revise their proposals, or sell on to other developers who have different proposals. At the local plan stage, only a minority of the land may be held by a developer. Where land is held by others, negotiations will centre on their efforts to maximise the value of their holding, but they are not in a position to deliver agreed development in return. Developers who buy land from them will normally try to renegotiate the deal, to make it more economic from their point of view, and, in the process, some of the public benefits of agreements reached previously will be lost.

(3) Considerable pressure may be needed to get agreement on coordinating the timing of development in neighbourhoods, where the land involved is in multiple ownership. Developers prefer not to have competitors building in the same area at the same time, and the variety of

motives which influence landowners' decisions makes it less likely they will want to release land in line with some planned programme.

(4)   These difficulties may increase reliance on compulsion. NESC cites ways of enforcing coordination, including threatened or actual CPOs below open market value, and pooling and re-division of landholdings in a planned neighbourhood (though it is unclear how far they are endorsed by Housing for All). The question is how much would get 'lost in translation' if we apply Dutch or German models in an Irish context. Recourse to litigation is more common in some countries than in others, and Ireland is not amongst the others. In the 2001–7 period, many housebuilders did not cooperate or used lengthy delaying tactics in relation to below market value transfers under Part V, despite explicit provisions on how it should be used in the legislation, and confirmation of its constitutionality by the Supreme Court. Active land management would be more discretionary. If public agencies can choose which landowners and developers are treated as uncooperative, or how blocks containing farmyards and one-off housing are re-divided, the scope for case-by-case litigation would be much greater than for Part V.[36]

Given these potential difficulties, negotiation-based active land management should be a supplement to more arms-length measures, to be used in appropriate circumstances, rather than as a substitute for them. The proposals for Urban Development Zones (UDZs) and Land Value Sharing (LVS) put forward in Housing for All, and outlined in more detail in 2021 and 2022 General Schemes of future legislation, seem reasonably compatible with an arms-length approach. On the other hand, Housing for All expects UDZ schemes and associated LVS provisions to provide 'market signalling to encourage negotiation between landowners', with the development agency playing a 'key role'.

URBAN DEVELOPMENT ZONES

UDZs are a variant on the Strategic Development Zones (SDZs) intro-duced in the 2000 Act, with a new preliminary appraisal stage added to the process prior to designation, and with the Planning Scheme redefined as a 'Planning and Delivery' Scheme. One aim of UDZ schemes will be to

> *address situations where speculation by early mover landowners … leads to increased price expectations on the part of the neighbouring landowners. This makes the assembly and provision of necessary community infrastructure diffi-cult and expensive. A combination of elevated land prices and infrastructural hurdles can ultimately render development unviable* (Housing for All, p. 82).

The proposed solution to the problem involves defining 'critical' land which is needed for community infrastructure in the UDZ scheme, and allowing local authorities to acquire such land as soon as it becomes the subject of a planning application. The cost to the local authority is its market value, less an LVS levy of 30% on the difference between that value and its existing use value immediately prior to designation. Non-critical land which forms part of the same application will also be subject to the levy, and this obligation can be set against the purchase price of the critical land. Depending on the balance between them, the landowner may end up entitled to a 'land credit' or owing a land equalisation amount.[37] The 30% levy would also apply to land purchased to land pur-chased compulsorily.

The proposal could be useful in the initial stages of development in a UDZ, as a way of facilitating the transfer of land needed for infrastructure which has to be in place before any buildings can be provided. Such infra-structure may include a sewage treatment plant or pumping station, or an initial section of new road needed to open up some adjacent land for development and avoid its timing being unduly under the control of a particular landowner. The approach would also be useful in public acquisition of sites for new schools.

However, the outline legislation does not explicitly relate 'critical land' to the main existing method of provision of communal infrastructure on developers' sites. The most obvious example is public open space, which is normally included in planning applications and/or required by conditions to them. This is provided by developers at their own expense, dedicated to public use, and in due course taken in charge by the local authority. The same applies to on-site physical infrastructure necessary for the development of a site, such as roads, footpaths, sewers, water pipes, and surface water drainage.

There is a risk that planning authorities will come under pressure to redefine some of the infrastructure currently provided on site by developers as being on critical land, which they will then have to acquire and construct the relevant infrastructure on themselves. This type of risk could arise in cases where site conditions make provision of open space in relatively large blocks appropriate, or where roads or other linear infrastructure serve both the site they are located on, and other developments beyond its boundaries.

For these purposes, it is usually preferable to leave provision to developers, because it avoids the acquisition and transaction costs involved in transfer of the land to the local authority, public procurement of the necessary works on it, and the delays involved in each of these stages. Also, the role of the LVS system in recovering betterment or 'uplift'[38] will be compromised, if much of the revenue has to be spent on public provision of on-site infrastructure currently provided by developers.

Box 3.4 outlines possible ways of avoiding these types of unintended consequence.

Box 3.4 Developer Provision of Shared Infrastructure in UDZs

Unnecessary transfers of land to local authorities, and the need for them to carry out works on them, could be minimised in several ways:

(a)   Where open spaces are an unusually large proportion of a development site, the excess over normal provision could be treated as eligible for 'land credits' under the proposed equalisation process, even if they have not been classified as critical land or acquired by the local authority. Alternatively, equalisation could be built into Development Contribution Schemes for new neighbourhoods or SDZs under existing legislation, by making provision for rebates on contributions.

(b)   UDZs institutionalise the shift from cul-de-sac type layouts to planned neighbourhoods sought by NESC and successive governments, but risk transferring some of the cost of on-site civil engineering infras-tructure from developers to local authorities. In cul-de-sac estates, roads and other on-site infrastructure normally only serve the housing within the particular estate in which they are provided, so there are no grounds for expecting anyone other than the developer to fund them. This relationship is weakened in planned neighbour-hoods, where on-site infrastructure is typically provided as part of networks which serve a number of developments. To avoid unin-tended transfer of costs, the legislation may need to indicate explicitly that network infrastructure which serves both a site for which planning permission is sought and other adjacent areas, should not be regarded as a creating a case for treating the land it is on as critical land. Also, it should only be regarded as justifying payment for works 'in excess of the immediate needs of the development' under s.34.4.(m) of the 2000 Act, where it is clear the external benefits of on-site works on the application site substantially exceed the benefits such works on other sites have conferred or will confer on the application site.

(c)   Public provision of short sections of local distributor roads, and the sewers and waterpipes often laid under or alongside them, can prevent individual landowners having undue control over the timing of development on adjoining landholdings. This is an argument for treating the relevant sections of such corridors as critical land, and acquiring it during the planning process, or compulsorily. However, public provision of longer sections of such road may be unnecessary, if the UDZ is planned so that there are a number of corridors along which develop-ment can proceed, creating alternative development sequences. This reduces the need for public acquisition and works, and also the need for intervention to force reluctant landowners and developers to develop at a particular time. The local authority can more easily afford to be patient, if progress in one corridor compensates for lack of it in another.

It is not easy to work out how acquisition- and negotiation-intensive land management will be in UDZs, and how far it will continue to rely in practice on arms-length regulation. S.34.4(m), which provides for the compensation of developers to the extent that the works they carry out are in excess of the immediate needs of their developments,[39] is perhaps underused at present, but the emphasis on public acquisition in the proposed legislation suggests this underuse may continue.

To summarise, while there has been an element of active land management in Ireland since at least the 1950s, expanding it to the point where a high proportion of development land passes through public ownership, and/or is the subject of public-private property agreements, is likely to lead to difficulties under Irish conditions. The need for this can be reduced, by making fuller use of existing planning and infrastructure powers, perhaps in ways outlined in Box 3.4. However, a strong active land management approach offers greater control over the timing of development, in cases where there is a genuine need to coordinate this on adjacent landholdings.

As a way of controlling the timing of development, active land management is an alternative to reliance on fiscal incentives and disincentives. In recent years, the government seems to be relying to some extent on both, as a vacant sites levy was legislated for in 2015, and Housing for All indicated (p. 92) this will be replaced by a new and more effective version. Limited control over the timing of development via active land management would be less of a problem if there was confidence in the effectiveness of fiscal measures. The fiscal tradition on development land – and the question of whether it offers an effective substitute for the more ambitious versions of active land management – is reviewed below.

C. TAXES, LEVIES, INCENTIVES

The third tradition has involved taxation measures, designed to increase the proportion of development gains recovered by the community, or the amount of land made available for development, or some mixture of the two.

(a) Capital Gains Tax on Development Land

In the 1970s and 1980s, the first of these aims dominated. Capital Gains Tax (CGT) was introduced in 1974, and applied to development land and other capital assets at a flat rate of 26%. In 1979, a distinction between development land and other capital assets was made, with the former being subject to a 30% rate, and being ineligible for lower rates which became applicable to other assets held for longer periods. In 1982, CGT rates in general were drastically increased, with a 60% rate for assets held for less than a year, and a 50% rate for ones held for one to three years. The distinction between development land and other capital assets was retained, with the former being subject to a minimum rate of 50%, and the latter to a 40% one.

These measures need to be seen in a cyclical context. In the early 1980s, development land issues loomed large, with a peak in real house prices around 1980, and land costs in 1980–2 were some 14% of these unusually high prices. Neither level was reached again until 1996. The boom had had obvious side effects, particularly in inner city areas. The *Irish Times* had published a scorching series of full-page articles on 'Derelict Dublin' by Frank McDonald (11–14 January 1982). In the first of these, he mapped the large amount of derelict land in central Dublin, and attributed much of it to speculative assembly of office sites, uncontrolled by government:

> *... between 1975 and 1980, planning permissions for 5½ million sq. ft. of offices were granted, but a staggering 65% of it was never built ... successive govern-ments have failed to act against speculators hoarding or dealing in development*

*land … despite oft repeated demands that penal rating … should be imposed
to discourage dereliction.*

Developers are least popular late in a boom. At that stage, their association in the public mind with the adverse side effects of construction
projects, high or unaffordable house prices, and disproportionate gains
to themselves, landowners, and speculators, is at its strongest. The rise in
CGT rates in 1982 reflected this cyclically prompted unpopularity.
Politicians could increase rates safely, as demand for property was falling,
vacancy was rising, and there was no longer any obvious need to stimulate
the supply of development land. The downturn was also putting public
finances under additional pressure, making it difficult not to seek additional revenue from this unpopular and apparently wealthy source.

One curious consequence of this was to establish the no doubt unintended pattern shown in Figure 3.2, whereby CGT rates are inversely
related to the health of the property market. For the rest of the 1980s, at
a time when a deep recession minimised gains on development land, a
CGT rate of 50–60% applied to such gains as were available. As the property market recovered, CGT on development land was gradually reduced,
to a flat rate of 50% in 1990, and to 40% in 1992.

CGT applies to individual taxpayers. However, Corporation Tax –
which applies to company profits, including those arising from gains on
development land – has followed a somewhat similar pattern, though for
different reasons. The general rate was 45% in the late 1970s, 50% for most
of the 1980s, and then fell in steps from 40% in the early 1990s to 12½%
in 2003. This reduction was a result of convergence between the general
rate and the special manufacturing rate, as required by the EU. A higher
rate of 20% or 25% applied where development land was being sold on
without having been developed. In so far as profits were distributed to
Irish taxpayers, they would have been subject to the (reduced) income tax
rates applicable to dividends as well.

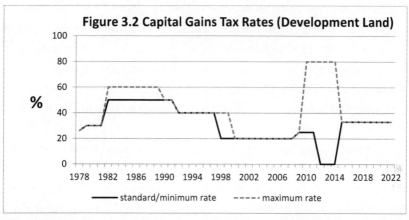

Source: Finance Acts

(b) The Bacon Reports (1998–2000) and Capital Gains Tax

In the late 1990s, the government lost control of the housing market, with annual house price increases in Dublin accelerating from 6% in 1995 to 12% in 1996, 26% in 1997 and 32% in 1998. In response, it commissioned the Bacon reports on house prices. The first of these – published in April 1998 – contained a wide range of recommendations, which will be discussed more fully in the next two chapters. They included a proposal to cut the CGT rate on serviced land zoned for housing from 40% to 20%, and this was implemented immediately.

The change increased the availability of development land, but suffered from obvious problems of timing. The second Bacon report, published a year after the first, quoted (1999, p. 52) an (unnamed) estate agent as estimating development land sales in the Greater Dublin area at 2,300 acres in 1997, 3,500 in 1998, and an expected 4,200 in 1999. However, this had not led to 'any significant slowdown in prices being paid for development land', perhaps partly due to a requirement that land benefiting from the 20% rate had to have outline planning permission for housing. The Irish House Builders Association (IHBA) was also quoted

(Bacon, 1999, pp. 4, 53) as saying that land supply in Dublin remained inadequate, having regard to the need for choice, and the lead time 'of three or more years' needed 'by developers planning future develop-ments'. The implication of such lead times is that the appropriate time for measures designed to moderate house price increases through greater availability of land is well before house prices start increasing at 26% per annum, not afterwards.

The first Bacon report (p. 89) had recommended that the reduction in CGT to 20% on housing land be compensated for by an increase back to 60% after four years (i.e. in 2002). The stated motive for this sting in the tail was to make the 20% rate self-financing in the longer term, but it did not happen. Instead, all development land became subject to a 20% rate from 2000 onwards.

This was perhaps unfortunate. As noted earlier, the incentive to sell to a real developer is at its strongest near the peak of the boom, but a large volume of sales at that point may be too late to prevent prices reaching unsustainable levels, and may also facilitate oversupply. Housebuilders were able to lay their hands on enough land to build around 80,000 houses each year from 2004 to 2007, but the effects included putting most of their recent customers into negative equity, raising the vacancy rate from a long-run average of around 11% to 15% by 2006, and making the Irish banking system and state much more insolvent than they other-wise would have been.

(c) Capital Gains Tax after 2008

CGT rates continued to be inversely related to the cycle after the housing market collapsed in 2008. The 20% rate for development land was left in place throughout the boom, but was raised to 25% in 2009, 30% in 2012, and 33% in 2013. An 80% rate, which applied to land zoned for the first time from 2010 to 2013, was the most extreme manifestation of this ten-dency. This was presented as a way of implementing the recommendations of the Kenny report,[40] though, in reality, it is unlikely to have had any practical effect, as no-one who had any choice in the matter would sell land at the bottom of the market with gains taxed at 80%. As soon as there was any indication of a renewed need for extra zoned land, the 80% rate was (predictably) dropped.

Development land bought between December 2011 and December 2014, and retained for seven years or more, was exempted from CGT. This might be seen as an exception to the tendency for CGT rates to be inversely related to the cycle. In reality, it is one that proves the rule, as its function was to help rescue excessive loans taken out on development land and commercial property during the previous boom, so as to reduce state and bank debt. This posthumous subsidy contributed to the housing shortage which was about to emerge, by encouraging investors to buy and retain development land.

The 2004 NESC Report on Housing provides a rationale of sorts for the inverse relationship between CGT rates and the health of the property market. It attributed (p. 191) the application of CGT to development land in 1974 and its increase in 1982 to 'government's awareness of high levels of betterment', and reductions in CGT in 1990, 1992 and 1998 to government's anxiety about its 'possible negative effect on land supply'. In other words, governments lower CGT rates (raising the after-tax prices paid to the landowners) at times when the construction industry is expanding and they risk running short of land, and raise CGT rates (lowering after tax prices) when the market has already peaked, and there is a surplus.

In practice, this supply and demand response has been left too late either to capture much of a share of 'high levels of betterment' before the downturn caused a collapse in gains and transactions (in 1974, 1982 or 2009) or to avoid a 'negative effect on land supply' before it has contributed to spiralling prices (in 1998).

As a result, anyone who considers the historical pattern will be aware that the potential for change in CGT rates on development land in a rising market is in a downward direction. This means that the CGT system is, at best, a neutral influence on whether land is brought forward then, and, at worst, encourages a wait and see approach.

(d) Vacant Land Levies

A levy on vacant development land is a possible alternative to CGT, and one which avoids tension between recovery of betterment and adverse effects on land supply. In a rising market, raising the rate levies are charged at should both capture more betterment and boost supply.

The possibility of some form of holding tax on development land, designed to put landowners under pressure to sell, increase supply, and help keep prices down has been suggested on a number of occasions. The Kenny report considered (pp. 32–3) an annual tax on site value, and a variant under which the rate of tax rose the longer the site remained undeveloped, but saw a number of practical difficulties in these proposals:

i. They would be expensive to administer
ii. Assessing the value of the land would be costly, and the subject of litigation
iii. Owners would pay the tax and retain the land
iv. They could not apply to land which did not have services in place
v. Owners would reduce exposure by seeking zoning or permission shortly before building
vi. They would apply to a small amount of land at any particular time, and have a small yield

These practical difficulties have not prevented subsequent, more specialised annual levies being enacted or proposed, even though at least some of them also apply to these levies as well.

The 1990 Derelict Sites Act provided for a 3% levy on urban land classified as derelict, with the possibility of a higher rate, subject to a maximum of 10%. While derelict sites were normally also vacant, vacant sites were not necessarily derelict, as derelict sites were defined in the Act as containing ruinous, derelict or dangerous structures, or being in a neglected, unsightly condition, or having litter, rubbish or debris on them. In principle, local authorities were obliged to register urban sites which, in their opinion, were derelict, and to apply the levy to them, but as classification was based on their opinion, in practice, they had discretion. Where they did use this power, it was quite easy for the owners to escape from 'derelict' status by cosmetic tidying up of the site. The levy did not put them under serious pressure to redevelop or reuse derelict land, and had no effect on land which was vacant but not derelict.

The derelict sites levy does not seem to have been widely used by local authorities. This may be partly because it was, in practice, discretionary, and partly because it was easy to escape from and not very effective as a way a getting land redeveloped. The process of registering land as derelict was also quite cumbersome, with each site needing to be valued individually, and revalued at least every five years, with these values being subject to appeal. In practice, this was not much of a problem, but only because the power to classify land as derelict was not much used.

The third Bacon report proposed (2000, pp. 4, 9, 78, 86) that the Strategic Development Zone (SDZ) process which had been proposed to speed up the development of industrial sites in the 1999 Planning and Development Bill also apply to significant housing sites in the Dublin area as well, and that an annual tax of £3000 per house site apply to land within an SDZ on which planning permission had not been sought within 12 weeks of approval of an SDZ Planning Scheme, or development commenced within 26 weeks of planning permission being granted. However, the latter recommendation was not acted upon, possibly because the 2000–2 'pause' in the boom made it (and other measures recommended by the Bacon reports) seem less necessary.

Nevertheless, this proposal had some features worth noting. It would have had a tight focus, as SDZs are geographically compact. Information on the appropriate number of houses in each block, and on when and where the various services were or would become available, would have already been collected during preparation of the Planning Scheme. The SDZ would have a team responsible for implementing the Scheme, which could also calculate liabilities under the levy. The standard levy of

£3000 per house site would have avoided the need to value or revalue sites.

The 2015 **Urban Regeneration and Housing Act** provided for a levy on vacant sites, at 3%, from 2019 onwards, and Budget 2018 indicated this would rise to 7% in 2020. The definition of vacancy in the Act was an elaborate one, and only covered land which was both vacant, and also:

(a) Zoned residential, physically suitable for housing, with all the necessary infrastructure and in an area in which there was a need for housing, to be judged on the basis of the Development Plan core strategy, the Housing Strategy, house prices and rents, the number of households qualifying for social housing supports, and whether the proportion of houses for sale or rent was less than 5%, or

(b) Having an adverse effect on the amenities or character of an area – identified in the Development Plan or Local Plan as being in need of urban renewal – by contributing to the prevalence of ruinous or neglected property, anti-social behaviour, declining housing stock, and falling population.

Local authorities had to be of the opinion that each block or site was actually vacant in accordance with these criteria, which were complicated enough for the matter to be largely at their discretion. Owners of sites classified as vacant could appeal to An Bord Pleanála on any of these criteria. Section 16(2) of the Act provided for a reduced or nil levy, to reflect the proportion any loan taken out to purchase the site bore to its overall value. It would not have been difficult to arrange such a loan if the levy was large enough to justify the effort. NESC (2020, p. 25) commented that:

there are indications that it is not as effective as hoped. Issues with the levy appear to include exemptions from its application, delay with local area plans, administrative difficulties, inability to demonstrate viability of construction or housing need in the area and problems with interpreting the legislation.

The **2022 Residential Zoned Land Tax (RZLT)** was announced in Budget 2022, as one of three taxes affecting development land and vacant property being developed in 2021–2. The RZLT is a replacement for the 2015 vacant sites levy, and involves a 3% rate which would apply after a two-to-three year lead in period. It would be simpler than its predecessor, in that value would be self-assessed and it would be collected by the Revenue Commissioners, instead of the planning authority being responsible for valuation and collection, as provided for under s. 12 and 15 of the 2015 Act.

The necessary provisions were inserted into the 2021 Finance Act (s.80). They omitted the various housing market and socio-economic criteria listed in the 2015 Act, but retained the requirement that liable land had to have all necessary infrastructure.[41] Local authorities spent much of 2022 drawing up draft maps of land which is zoned residential and has these infrastructural services, checked on an item-by-item basis. The Act made provision for submissions on the draft maps, amendments to them on supplemental maps, and appeals to An Bord Pleanála by dissatisfied landowners.[42]

The Minister for Finance said in his Budget statement that the interval before it came into effect would 'give scope to review the workings of the tax, to listen to stakeholders, and to ensure it is both acceptable and equitable'. However, the main categories of stakeholder have different characteristics, and a uniform 3% levy will have different impacts on them. Table 3.3 shows the effect of the levy on developers and farmers in two development scenarios.

There is a distinction between applying modest pressure to act, and more or less forcing a landowner to do so immediately. Farmers and developers may pay the same annual levy, but it would be a small fraction of developer's profit, and a large multiple of farm income. Developers would retain flexibility, as leaving their site undeveloped for a few years extra would make limited difference to their bottom line. Farmers would lose it, as continuing to farm for even a short period would be a fairly futile exercise, involving large annual losses and a need to take out large loans. Admittedly, some farmers might be willing to risk doing this, in the expectation that they could pay off the loans if the land was sold later, and land prices might rise in the meantime.

The levy introduced by the 2015 Act ran into immediate difficulties on the issue of agricultural land. The Act itself was not very clear on whether land in agricultural use counted as 'vacant' for levy purposes, but a subsequent departmental circular indicated (P7/2016, p. 16) that the levy could be applied to such land 'as the site is not being used for the purpose for which it was zoned'. When farm organisations reacted angrily to this, the Act was amended in 2018, so that the levy only applied to land purchased after it had been zoned residential.[43] The 2021 Act does not include this qualification and reverts to the previous position, but the special procedure through which landowners can seek to have their zoning changed immediately may have been included as a way of defusing the situation, by directing them towards an escape route.

These solutions have limited merit. While the 2016 one was harsh and politically unrealistic, exempting pre-existing owners completely under the 2018 one meant the levy could have no effect at all on a large proportion of residentially zoned land. The 2021 escape clause under-lines the dangerously strong incentive to seek dezoning of serviced residential land – which is counterproductive if the zoning was justified in the first place – or its rezoning for commercial or industrial purposes. This may lead to over-zoning of land for these uses, reducing the ability of the planning system to channel commercial uses into the most appropriate locations, with town and city centres most at risk from this. The risk of distortion also applies to brownfield and infill sites, where it could make the aim of consolidating residential development within existing built-up areas more difficult to achieve.

The interaction of the cycle with 'accidental' ownership of land by those who own it for reasons unrelated to its development potential may throw up hard cases which destabilise the system. Family circumstances may make quick disposal difficult, and time to adjust may be needed

TABLE 3.3 EFFECT OF THE RZLT AT 3% ON FARMERS AND DEVELOPERS

	LOWER VALUES SCENARIO				MEDIUM VALUES SCENARIO			
	per acre	per ha.	per unit	%	per acre	per ha.	per unit	%
Average sale price per unit (€)			250000				350000	
Density	10	25			14	35		
Sales income (€m)	2.5	6.25			4.9	12.25		
Land as % of sales income				10				15
Land value (€)	250000	625000			735000	1837500		
3% annual levy on land value (€)	7500	18750			22050	55125		
Net farm income per annum (€)	200	500			600	1500		
Developer's profit as % of sales				10				15
Developer's profit (€)	250000	625000			735000	1837500		

where farms are held more for emotional reasons than economic ones. Outside booms and strong recoveries, buyers are not always easy to find for land seen as being in secondary locations, or only developable in unusually favourable circumstances, or as suitable for specialised uses for which demand is sparse and sporadic, and this applies to urban sites as well as farms. Landowners could be forced to sell on very unfavourable terms, or get deep into debt. A levy at a rate which forces the pace for this type of landowner – but not for developers – could become difficult to sustain politically.

A version of RZLT responsive to different types of landownership?

These problems may seem to be generic ones, not easily avoided with this type of levy, but it may be worth considering what a levy specifically designed to avoid them might look like. To avoid the distorting effects of some types of development land being liable and others not, almost all serviced development land might be made liable for the levy. The diverse circumstances of its owners could be reflected in varying rates, with the advantage that any arguments would be mostly simple, easily resolved ones on whether the appropriate rate had been applied. Those benefitting most from these concessions might not pay very much, but would always pay something, so holding serviced development land would never be costless, and there would always be some pressure to look for ways in which the land might be developed. The likelihood of rates varying upwards and downwards in different phases of the cycle could be explicitly acknowledged from the start, so that the system would remain in place during downturns, rather than be faced with pressure for its drastic amendment or abolition then, and a need to reinvent it in the next cycle.

Box 3.5 outlines one way in which these aims might be realised.

Box 3.5 A Variable Annual Tax on Development Land

The rate structure of an annual tax on development land could differentiate between

(a)   Builders/developers and speculators/investors: These groups cannot easily be distinguished in advance, as some move back and forth between the two roles, but can on the basis of subsequent actions. A rebate on past levy payments could be allowed once newly con-structed new buildings were completed and ready for occupation, perhaps equal to payments for the four years prior to that date (but subsequent to the developer's acquisition of the site). Levy payments by the actual developer would thus be refundable, with the proportion refunded decreasing with the length of time between purchase and development. There is a somewhat similar provision in relation to the levy in the 2021 Finance Act (s.653AH.1 and 7(a)), which involves deferring payment once development has commenced, and then waiving it if development is completed within the lifetime of the planning permission.

(b)   'Accidental' and 'intentional' owners of land: A lower rate could apply to those who already owned development land when legislation was published, or inherited it from a deceased relative, than to those who bought it knowing a levy would apply. Amongst other things, this would make the two- to three-year delay in applying the new version of the levy in the 2021 Finance Act less necessary.

(c)   Land in agricultural use and other development land: A further reduction could apply to (a) and (b) if it was actively farmed agricultural land.

These features could be incorporated into a robust, administratively feasible levy by:

•   Ensuring, as envisaged in Budget 2022, that valuation and collection are modelled on the existing Residential Property Tax (RPT) system, with the owner submitting a value, and the Revenue Commissioners collecting the levy. To ensure that values were kept up to date, a 'default' value revised in line with estimated annual changes in the average value of development land could be calculated automatically for subsequent years, with the owners having the right to put forward their own estimate instead (e.g. if they felt the value of their site had increased by less than average).

•   Registering all vacant (in the normal sense of the word) urban land, and all zoned, serviced greenfield land. Sites exempted as unsuitable for development should be included in the register, with reasons for their exemption stated.

•   Limiting registration and application of the levy to the main cities and surrounding metropolitan areas, and towns on rail corridors converging on them.

In addition to revising values annually, to reflect changes to average development land values, the percentage rate at which land in each of the categories referred to in (a)–(c) above was charged could vary cyclically, e.g. in the manner shown in Table 3.3. This would be simpler than it sounds, as the amount levied for all the sites in each category would be increased or reduced by the same percentage.

The solution outlined in Box 3.5 involves changing the basis of the levy, so that it becomes a tax on unused infrastructural capacity. A good case can be made for this. The availability of infrastructure is what makes land developable, and growing urban areas need to keep adding to it. It is not unreasonable to expect owners of development land to start paying for public infrastructure once the cost of providing it has been incurred and it becomes available to them, rather than waiting until it has been developed and occupied before it becomes subject to rates or RPT. Nor is it unreasonable to expect owners of unused inner-city land served by infrastructure provided in the nineteenth century to pay such a levy, since the more serviced land lying unused, the greater the need to service further greenfield land.

A lot of work has already been carried out on the RZLT, but this would not necessarily be wasted if a different approach was adopted. The mapping carried out by local authorities in 2022 would remain relevant, with modest adjustments, so that it included serviced land zoned for non-residential purposes. However, a revised version of s.80 of the 2021 Finance Act would need to be inserted into a future one.

An inherent weakness of both the RZLT and the variant on it just outlined is that neither would do much to discourage the holding of development land as an investment. Figure 3.3 shows that a 3% levy would have had little effect on the gains available in the 1995–2007 period, and that setting it at a higher rate would not solve the problem. Even in less extreme periods, development land values respond disproportionately to rises and falls in the price of houses and other buildings. At any particular rate, an annual levy would capture too low a proportion of developer gains in years when they are high, and all of them (or more) when they are low. Even the average gain over a number of years is difficult to estimate in advance, because gains can be higher or lower than could reasonably be predicted, for quite long periods.

RZLT runs into this problem because it is an annual tax, which cannot realistically vary its rates widely enough to reflect variations in

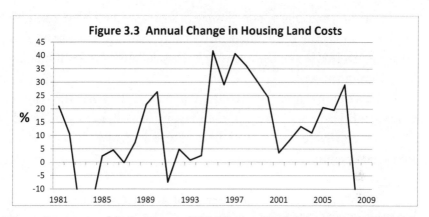

Source: Department of the Environment/DKM Construction Industry Review and Outlook
Series

development gains. Periodically levied taxes may be better placed to avoid
this problem. CGT, for instance, avoids it by taxing the difference
between the value of the land at the time of acquisition and its value at
the time of disposal, and ignoring any intermediate fluctuations.

COORDINATED USE OF TAXES ON UNDEVELOPED LAND AND DEVELOPMENT GAINS?

A non-penal annual levy on undeveloped land could nevertheless help
bring forward land for development, if – instead of being applied as a
stand-alone measure – it was combined with a CGT-type tax on development gains, designed to have the same effect. This would be possible if it
were known in advance that both taxes would be low at the start of a
recovery, and would rise in modest but cumulatively significant steps if the
recovery gathered strength and became a boom. This should encourage
landowners to bring land forward for development earlier in the cycle.[44]

The two taxes would be complementary, and compensate for each
other's weaknesses. A CGT type tax could recover a large enough proportion of gains to influence behaviour and expectations, but its weakness is

that it can be avoided by not developing or selling land. The levy on hold-ing land could not be avoided in this way, and the modest annual amounts involved would cumulatively become a deterrent to withholding land from the market long term.

Box 3.6 outlines how the two taxes could be applied in combination, as a way of rebalancing incentives in favour of earlier release of land. Figure 3.4 and Table 3.4 illustrate the possible effects of such taxes, in the 1988–2009 period.

Box 3.6 Capital Gains and Vacant Site Tax Rates which Anticipate the Cycle

As we have seen, CGT rate rises have roughly coincided with market down-turns (e.g. 1982, 2009), and reductions with recoveries and booms (e.g. 1992, 1998). This is a natural market response: the community needs more develop-ment land during upturns and so increases the after-tax price to the vendor, and vice versa in downturns. If landowners knew in advance that CGT rates on development land sales would be low early in a recovery and would then rise steadily while output continued to increase, this would reduce the incentive to retain land. In the previous cycle, the loss of control over house prices in 1997 would have been less if land supply in the early-mid 1990s had been greater. Higher CGT rates later in the boom would lead to less oversupply of land and housing, and fewer bad loans to fund site purchases.

For this approach to work, landowners would have to be sure CGT rates would rise as a recovery gathered strength. A series of modest rate increases could be used to reinforce this expectation. The Bacon proposal for a 20% CGT rate for four years, followed by an increase to 60%, was perhaps too drastic to be credible, and – as we have seen – did not in fact happen.

By themselves, CGT increases designed to tax away most of the gains in a rising market would have been too steep to be credible in the last boom. As noted at the start of this chapter, the cost of development land more than doubled between 1993 and 1997, and more than doubled again between 1997 and 2001. For CGT to tax away a doubling of values, the 40% rate which applied in 1993 would need to have risen to 70% in by 1997, and to 85% by 2001.

However, more moderate CGT increases could be effective if applied in tandem with a parallel policy of charging a simplified vacant sites levy at a low rate at the start of a recovery, with similarly moderate, pre-announced rate increases so long as output was expanding. This would require the levy to be more robust and comprehensive than the version introduced by the 2015 Act. Possible principles for this more robust version have been outlined in Box 3.5.

To illustrate the potential of this combination, Figure 3.4 shows the effect of the notional stepped, incremental changes to both set out in Table 3.3, on average house site prices during the last cycle. As CGT liabilities depend on when land is acquired, Figure 3.4(a) shows before- and after-tax prices on land acquired before 1987 at agricultural values (with the effects of actual historical CGT rates and a constant one at the current 33% rate shown for comparison). After tax prices would still have risen, but as time passed, cumulative levy payments plus the risk that they would be dead money in the event of downturn would encourage sales. As the last cycle was an extreme one, Figure 3.4(c) applies the same assumptions to a more moderate set of price changes – half the actual ones for 1988–2009 – with similar results.

Figure 3.4(b) shows the effect on average after-tax price of land bought in 1997 for investment purposes. It suggests combined use of CGT and an annual levy could reduce rises in after-tax prices to the point where they barely justified the risks involved in holding land, making it a much less attractive investment and minimising upward pressure on land prices from investor demand.

Figure 3.4 looks at recovering gains and reducing cyclicality in a historical context, testing variants on established methods of recovery against past price movements. The practical question for the future is whether some version of these ideas could be applied, and if so, how?

The taxation of development land is quite a crowded field in Ireland. Existing taxes like CGT, Corporation Tax and Stamp Duty are general taxes which raise revenue from a variety of other sources apart from land, but typically have special clauses or provisions which modify the way they are applied to development land. As we have seen, new taxes specific to residentially zoned land – RZLT and LVS – are in the process of being added to this list. LVS is partly designed to fund publicly provided infrastructure which will serve new housing development, and overlaps with existing local authority Development Contributions Schemes in this role.

In these circumstances, there is unlikely to be much enthusiasm for another new tax, so scope for applying the ideas outlined above may be limited to the possibility of influencing taxes which already exist, or are

TABLE 3.4 NOTIONAL 'CYCLICALLY PLANNED' CGT AND VACANT SITES LEVY PERCENTAGE RATES IN FIGURE 3.4

	1988–89	90–91	92–4	95	96	97	98	99	00	01	02	03	04	05	06	07	08	2009
Phase*	T, P	R	P	R	R	R	B	B	B	P	P	P	B	B	B	B	P	D
CGT	10	15	15	20	25	30	35	40	45	45	45	45	50	55	60	60	60	50
Levy (min)	0.1	0.2	0.1	0.2	0.3	0.4	0.5	0.6	0.7	0.6	0.5	0.4	0.5	0.6	0.7	0.8	0.7	0.1
Levy (high)	0.5	1	0.5	1	1.5	2	2.5	3	3.5	3	2.5	2	2.5	3	3.5	4	3.5	0.5

* Phases shown in Table 3.3 reflect classification of the previous year in Table 2.2. The time lag recognises that it would often be necessary to wait until near the end of a year before deciding how to classify it, so rates could not be adjusted until the beginning of the next year. In the table, T = trough, P = pause, R = recovery, B = boom, D = downturn. For the purposes of Figure 3.4, CGT rates are assumed to rise by 5% per year in recovery or boom years, fall by 10% per year in downturn or trough ones, and remain unchanged in pauses, subject to a minimum of 10% and a maximum of 60%. The Vacant Sites Levy is also assumed to rise in uniform steps in recovery or boom years, subject to a maximum of 4%. In pause years, it is assumed that the rate would decrease in uniform steps, as a way of reducing out-of-pocket costs to developers in uncertain market conditions.

FIGURE 3.4 NET LAND PRICES PER SITE UNDER THREE CGT & LEVY SCENARIOS, 1988–2009

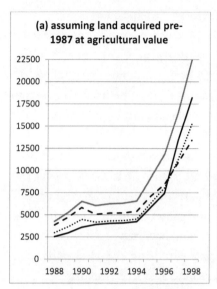

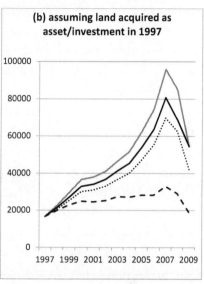

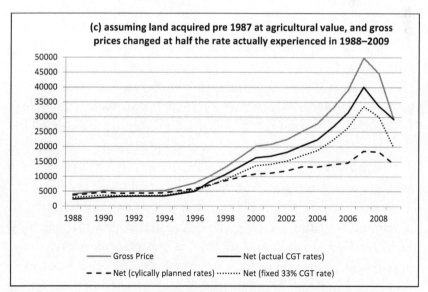

Source (for gross land prices in Figure 3.4): Department of the Environment/DKM Construction Industry in Ireland Review and Outlook series.

already being developed. The simplest way of achieving a cyclically variable version of CGT as outlined in Box 3.6 would be to modify the existing CGT system in so far as it affects development land.

While this is the obvious option, it is worth considering more complex alternatives as well. Past variations to the CGT code to address development land issues have typically been temporary ones, followed by reversion towards the mainstream version. Cyclically variable rates would not fit comfortably into standard CGT practice, and might be even more vulnerable to this.

The proposed LVS system, though further removed from the approach discussed in Box 3.6 in terms of method, is specific to development land, and thus less exposed to that risk. Also, revising the LVS system on CGT principles could allow development land gains to remain subject to a single tax on those gains, and avoid the same land becoming liable to both CGT and LVS. It may therefore be worth exploring the alternative of an admittedly drastic modification of the proposed LVS system.

A cyclically variable version of land value sharing

An initial 'General Scheme' outlining the content of a future LVS bill was published in December 2021, and an amended one in April 2023. These seem to have had three main objectives. Firstly, they aimed to recover a higher proportion of the betterment or uplift in values which results from zoning of land, with around 50% of it recovered from land zoned residential, via a 30% levy and the 20% transfer of the site under Part V.[45] In the 2023 version, the levy applied to existing zoning as well as newly zoned land, and to land zoned commercial and industrial as well as residential.[46]

Secondly, they aimed to do this while minimising adverse effects on development viability. Uplift is to be calculated after the making of each Development or Local Area Plan, as the difference between existing use value and its value in the use for which it is zoned. The levy on this uplift would then become a fixed charge on the land, payable prior to commencement of development. It was assumed that certainty on the amount due will lower landowners' asking prices and developers' bids, and that this would make it more likely that the levy would be 'passed back' to landowners, rather than 'passed on' to purchasers.[47]

Thirdly, the proceeds of LVS levies were to be applied to the funding of better and more timely physical and social infrastructure,[48] particularly in new housing areas and UDZs.

The second aim is not easily achieved. While the 2023 General Scheme did make provision for voluntary payment of the levy at earlier stages, compliance with the condition attached to the planning permission requiring payment only becomes obligatory when development is about to commence. The levy would thus normally be paid by developers.

In principle, it could be absorbed by them in the form of reduced margins, or passed on to house buyers, through reduced output and increased prices, or passed back to landowners, via reduced land purchases and lower bids for sites. It could often have more than one of these effects, and the mix is likely to vary according to local market conditions and timing.

LVS in its April 2023 form would tilt the balance towards passing it on to purchasers, in practical situations in which developers are likely to find themselves, such as:

(a) The site is part of a long-term land bank, bought well before it was zoned, at prices similar to current existing use values. The developer may absorb the cost of the levy or pass it on, but there is no one to whom it can be passed back.

(b) The site is bought before it is zoned, but after its zoning becomes probable. In this case, its price will normally include 'hope value' as well existing use value. This hope value will form part of the uplift above existing use value to which the levy will apply, and developers will have to pay the relevant percentage of this part of the uplift, even though they are not the beneficiaries. As with (a), they can absorb it or pass it on.

(c) The site is bought after zoning. Despite its emphasis on certainty, the 2023 scheme included (s.31BD, s.5) provisions allowing variation in the rate between 20% and 30% and requiring a review of its operation within five years. Competitive bidding for development sites favours optimists, which in an LVS context may include those who hope to benefit from these provisions, or from the wider tendency to frequent change in legislation affecting housing. Developers who underestimate the cost of meeting their LVS obligations may wait for the situation to change, or prices to rise. If enough of them do this, prices probably will rise, thereby passing on the levy to purchasers.

(d) The developer has already bought a zoned site. While the first version of the General Scheme exempted land which had already been zoned before LVS came into effect, on the basis that its development value due to zoning may already have been capitalised into its price, the second version extended the levy to land which was already zoned. This exposes developers who have already bought land at prices which reflect its development value, to a levy on uplift from which they have not benefitted. As with (a) and (b), they can absorb it, or pass it on.

In cases (b), (c) and (d), previous owners would realise part of the uplift, on which developers will be charged the relevant percentage. These owners would thus have passed on any LVS liabilities that might in principle have applied to their gains. LVS in this form was as likely to add to developers' costs and house prices as any other form of development land tax, and its main distributional effect within the development pipeline was unlikely to be reduced net gains to landowners. Recovery of landowners' windfall gains on development land is a worthwhile objective, but LVS as outlined in the 2023 General Scheme is not likely to promote it effectively.

Combining an annual vacant sites tax with a CGT type version of LVS, with both paid at rates which varied cyclically in the manner outlined in Box 3.6, would reduce dependence on the levy being passed back. In cases where successive stages in a site's passage through the development pipeline were associated with different owners, each successive owner would be charged directly, in proportion to the uplift they themselves had realised. Where most of the uplift went to landowners, they would pay most of the tax. These payments might still be passed on or passed back, but the balance would be tilted more towards passing back. The bargaining position of each vendor would be weakened, because net gains from holding land back from development in a rising market would be reduced, and annual levies would progressively increase the risk of cumulative net losses in the event of a downturn.

However, it would complicate matters if development land was subject to both a CGT type version of LVS, and conventional CGT. Proposals for LVS have made no reference to existing methods of taxing increases in the value of development land, such as Corporation tax and CGT, and seem to involve a preference for duplication rather than consolidation. Presumably the intention is that all three should operate in parallel. A consolidated development land tax would remove this duplication.

The proceeds of a consolidated development land tax, which combined LVS obligations with those currently arising under the CGT and Corporation tax codes, could be applied to raising the standard of infrastructure in new development, by transferring some of them to the Development Contributions funds of the relevant local authority, or to any separate Development Contribution scheme/fund specific to particular SDZs or UDZs.[49] Unlike existing CGT and Corporation tax revenues, those from a consolidated development land tax would all arise from specific blocks of land in specific places, facilitating their transfer back to those places.

Unlike development contributions, a substantial part of these revenues would arise in advance of the construction projects which gave rise to them, rather than at the same time, as many of the land transactions on which tax would be levied would occur well before development on that land commences. This is usually true of developers' land purchases, and still more so where investors buy from the original landowner. Such upstream revenues would make it easier for local authorities to provide advance infrastructure for large-scale development, and less dependent on borrowing to provide it, in the hope that it will collect enough contributions from its subsequent progress to repay the loans.

It would also be easier to apply the cyclically variable approach outlined in Box 3.6 via a consolidated tax, which combined obligations under LVS with those arising from disposals of development land under CGT and Corporation tax. This would recover more betterment, because rates would rise when values were high. A consolidated development land tax, which would be more effective in sharing land value than the LVS system proposed, might be described as 'cyclically variable land value sharing'. Box 3.7 outlines how such a tax might work.

Box 3.7 The Case for Cyclically Variable Land Value Sharing (CVLVS)

A cyclically variable form of LVS could apply to all increases in land value above its existing use value until a commencement notice was lodged immediately before the start of development. If there were changes of ownership prior to development, a share of the increase in value within each individual period of ownership would be levied on each pre-development disposal, as well as on the increase between the last such disposal and the start of development.

This approach allows for the possibility of the initial zoning being changed in a subsequent plan, and the initial planning permission being replaced by a revised one.

The levy would apply to companies as well as individual taxpayers, and the gains shared in this way would be exempt from CGT and Corporation tax. Corporation tax is charged at a lower rate on profits arising from sales of fully developed land than on those from sales of undeveloped or partly developed land, and more favourable treatment of those who actually develop land could be retained, by giving them a partial rebate on their CVLVS payments once their completed development had been sold or occupied.

The percentage share recovered by the community would be at a cyclically variable rate, as outlined in Box 3.5. The rate would thus be high when land values and the volume of transactions were high, and so would maximise the share of gains recovered by the community over the cycle as a whole. However, in the recovery phase, when it is particularly important to minimise any tendency to hold land back in the expectation of future rises in after-tax value, it would be relatively low initially, but would rise in annual steps – and be known in advance to be due to continue to do so – as the volume of development increased.

Tax increases are liable to cause some landowners to hold their land back from development, typically reducing supply, raising prices and causing some or all of the tax increase to be passed on. This happens because an increased tax will definitely reduce net gains at the time it is introduced, but is less certain to do so in the medium or longer term. The natural reaction of landowners to the tax may in itself produce an offsetting rise in value, or the next government may change policy again in a few years' time. Raising rates in steps reduces expected future net gains as well as those immediately available, and allows lowered expectations to be reinforced on an annual basis. This should reduce the tendency to hold back land and pass on increased taxes.

This approach does not conflict with developers' need for certainty, or, more realistically, reduced uncertainty. Unpredictable swings in raw land values should be moderated by compensating changes in CVLVS rates. There may be a wider range of possible future tax rates, but there should be a narrower range of possible future net land values, and more certainty on how those values will affect the profitability of specific developments.

As indicated above, part of the proceeds of such a tax could be returned to the relevant local authority by the Revenue Commissioners, and ring fenced for infrastructure purposes. Where they arose in designated UDZs and SDZs, they could be channelled to ring-fenced accounts for infrastructure in those areas.

REDUCING THE RISKS OF COMBINED USE OF CVLVS AND A VACANT SITES LEVY

The construction industry would be concerned about the effect of the above taxes on the viability of development. In some cases, viability is marginal, and depends on specific conditions in the immediate neighbourhood of the development site, as well as on wider market conditions. It may be necessary to wait for these to occur, and part of the skill of a developer consists in being able to identify when, as well as where and how, a project becomes viable.

In relation to concerns on an annual vacant sites levy, the obvious answer is that if and when development is not viable, this should be reflected in a low land value, and the amount of any levy payable then would, therefore, also be very low.[50] However, as the Joint Oireachtas Committee pointed out in the 1980s, land is quite often bought by non-developers on the basis of long-term expectations of its future worth, and their bids may be unrelated to calculations on the viability of its development in the short to medium term. Inflated values could thus lead to inflated tax costs to developers.

The availability of partial rebates for developers on both CVLVS and annual payments on vacant land suggested in Boxes 3.5 and 3.7 would dilute the additional tax liabilities on the viability of their developments, and the remaining effects should be counterbalanced by lower development land prices due to reduced competition for sites, as purchase for investment reasons and holding land back from development would become less attractive.[51] Lower land prices and better availability would benefit smaller builders who tend not to land bank or hold land for longer-term projects, as well as larger ones that do. Developers who had already bought land when the relevant legislation was published could benefit from a lower annual levy, as suggested in Box 3.5(b).

At the same time, the suggested tax measures would still give all developers a stronger motive for developing sooner rather than later, and for developing earlier in the cycle, rather than waiting for prices to reach their peak.

There would be other significant risks. Landowners might doubt whether governments would be able to keep raising CVLVS rates on development land in a rising market. The conventional view is that supply is stimulated by reducing taxes, and increasing them, even on a step-by-step basis, would reduce it. The jump in Capital Gains Tax receipts which followed reduction of the general CGT rate to 20% in 2000 is often cited as evidence of the beneficial effect of such cuts on disposals and revenues. Such prophecies could be self-fulfilling, as the reforms would not succeed unless they influenced landowners' expectations.

This credibility problem could be reduced if the system in Boxes 3.5–3.8 was applied in combination with additional forms of compulsory acquisition at or close to existing use value, as outlined in the first part of this chapter. For instance, vigorous development of new towns on sites acquired at such prices, and widespread use of advance acquisition under Part V (as outlined in Boxes 3.2 and 3.3) would reduce dependence on the willingness of landowners and developers to supply development land voluntarily. They would have less reason to expect the system to be put into reverse and, to the extent that they still did, their scepticism would matter less because there would be safety valves.

A more drastic approach would be to use implementation of the system outlined in Boxes 3.5–3.8 in the short term, to pave the way for implementation of the Kenny report in the medium term. If the intention to implement both were announced at the start of a recovery, the effect of the two measures on landowners' expectations would be mutually reinforcing. Waiting for CGT/CVLVS increases to be reversed would be a less plausible strategy for landowners if there was a realistic prospect of compulsory acquisition close to existing use value in the medium term.

Rising CVLVS rates (which would not go into reverse in a downturn in a Kenny-based scenario) would progressively reduce the proportion of development gains retained by landowners, bringing net open market land prices closer to those based on existing use values, which would apply to post-Kenny acquisitions. Reducing this gap would have two important benefits:

(i) The transitional disruption involved in the move from market-based land prices to existing use-based ones would be less.

(ii)   It would reduce the difference between existing use value-based prices and after-tax open market prices in the dual land market likely after implementation of Kenny. A situation in which there were two widely divergent sets of net prices would be unlikely to survive for long.

THE 2023 VACANT HOMES TAX

Despite previous official scepticism, this tax was introduced in Budget 2023 and s.96 of the subsequent Finance Act. A 2018 report by Indecon commissioned by the Department of Finance considered the possibility of identifying vacant housing by requiring its owners to declare it in their annual RPT returns and listing them in a register of vacant property, but recommended against this, as

(a)   Setting up such a register would involve substantial initial administrative costs;

(b)   The percentage of dwellings vacant long term (rather than for medical reasons, refurbishment, sale etc) was low;

(c)   Vacant properties are in a state of flux, not static like normal residential property;

(d)   Derelict properties may fall outside the RPT remit;

(e)   A survey of auctioneers suggested a levy of €2–3,000 a year would be needed to alter the behaviour of owners in Dublin (Indecon, 2018, p.ii–iii, vi, 33–34, 38–39).

This view seems to have been accepted initially, but Housing for All indicated (2021, p. 109) options on a vacant buildings tax were being considered, and legislation was introduced providing for immediate implementation of the option selected, in the form of a Vacant Homes Tax (VHT), following Budget 2023. This creates an obligation on owners to declare vacant housing, and if required, to submit a return stating whether the house in question was occupied for less than 30 days in the previous year. The need for a separate register of vacant property constantly in need of revision – problems (a) and (c) – is to some extent sidestepped by it being maintained by the Revenue Commissioners for their own information, rather than a public register subject to submissions and appeals in the manner of the RZLT. VHT is set at three times the RPT rate which would apply if the house was occupied. As RPT has been charged at around 0.1% of value from 2021 on, VHT has been set at around 0.3% of value.

This is not necessarily the end of the process. VHT could develop further, but it could also atrophy. Previous scepticism on the need for such a tax might well reassert itself, if experience with VHT suggested it was only having a marginal effect. This is a risk, because vacant residential property is a moving target, which is more of a problem at some times and in some places than others.

However, pointing to times and places where it is not a serious problem as a reason for inactivity, leads at best to belated, reactive legislation in those when it is, and at worst to passivity and lack of awareness even then. The most disastrous example of the latter was the widespread tendency for purchasers of new houses and apartments to hold them vacant while their capital value appreciated in the 2003–7 period – the 'buy to hold' phenomenon. This contributed to the 2008 crash, by preventing excess supply from moderating price rises and market exuberance at an earlier stage. There were no measures in place to discourage this practice, as the Bacon demand-side ones had been set aside by then.

The problem is not on the same scale in the current cycle, but is not insignificant either. An article by Killian Woods in the *Sunday Business Post* (20/6/21) cited two developments in Dublin controlled by US fund Kennedy Wilson, containing hundreds of luxury apartments lying empty, and a survey by urban design consultants Anois, which identified over 400 properties in Cork city which had been vacant for more than two years. The Indecon report noted (p. 17) there were 5,300 units categorised as new, unused residential property for RPT purposes nationally in 2016, and that this was distinct from the 12,300 in a separate 'unsold by the builder' category. These unused new units were temporarily exempt in 2016.

VHT is more likely to become firmly established if it deals effectively with the issues raised in the Indecon report and listed at (a) – (e) above. Box 3.8 suggests ways in which legislation could be strengthened, so as to make this more likely.

Box 3.8 Vacant Residential Property and Local Authorities

A legal obligation could be created for owners of vacant residential property to declare it, in the same way as they are obliged to declare their income. As with income tax, the Revenue Commissioners could impose penalties and interest on taxpayers who failed to declare it.

Instead of compiling a register of vacant residential buildings, which would encounter the problems cited at (a) and (c) above, local authorities could be required to submit a list of vacant residential properties known to them to the Revenue Commissioners each year.

Local authorities would need to have a sense of ownership to be likely to do this efficiently, and also to keep the register of vacant land referred to in Box 3.7 accurate and up to date. If 100% of all revenue collected from these levies was transferred back to them, this would obviously help. They could also be given wider discretion on the standard rate to be charged on vacant residential property in their area than they are for RPT on occupied residential units, and thus be able to respond better to variations in local property market conditions.

Housing for All promised (p. 109) to introduce legislation allowing local authorities to charge full rates on vacant (non-residential) buildings. If the principle were adopted that all urban property should be subject to rates or RPT or a development land levy, unless explicitly exempted from the relevant tax, and exchange of information between the Revenue Commissioners and local authorities on these facilitated, this would reduce evasion. The main aim would be to discourage vacancy: raising revenue would be secondary.

LESS PLANNING AND LOWER TAXES?

A more general difficulty, affecting most of the suggestions put forward in this chapter, is that they involve relatively technical solutions. Reforms are more likely to attract support if they involve a single, overarching principle, which can be clearly stated and easily understood. This applies particularly to reforms which require mobilisation of public opinion if they are to prevail over opposition from powerful interest groups. The only reform discussed in this chapter which might satisfy this criterion is one based on the Kenny report, and, even in that case, the complications involved in phasing it in (e.g. as outlined in Box 3.1) would dilute support for it.

While Kenny envisaged a greatly increased role for the state, there is a rival view at the opposite end of the spectrum, which could also gain such support, and can also be clearly stated and easily understood. This sees high land and house prices as due to too much state intervention, and avoidable by reducing planning controls and taxes on land sales and development so as to allow extra supply to reduce prices.

This view has empirical support. Morley et al. (2015, p. 16) found that 'the vast majority of the literature on land use regulation' considers that it restricts the supply of new housing and raises house prices, noting that much of this literature involves comparison between different parts of the United States. They also comment that 'the nearly exclusive focus on prices is problematic because difficulties then arise in determining whether higher price increases are due to higher demand or lower supply'. For instance, local authorities may be more likely to have strong planning controls in areas where development pressures are greater. An OECD study (2011, pp. 8–9) found that housing market responsiveness tended to decrease as population density increased.

As an example of the relationship between responsiveness and prices, the OECD study cited the very large price increases in the UK and the Netherlands, 'where the responsiveness of new housing supply to housing prices is noticeably low'. However, 'the flip side is that in flexible-supply countries' more rapid adjustment to 'large changes in demand ... contributes to more cyclical swings in economic growth, as witnessed by recent developments'.

This latter point was particularly relevant to Ireland. A loose planning regime provides the widest incentive for increased supply at the height of a boom, but it is not necessarily helpful at that point. Oversupply of new houses and development sites in the run-up to the 2008 crash was proportionately much greater than would have been possible under the more restrictive planning regime in Britain. This is a key weakness in attempts to apply the well-developed arguments for looser planning controls in Britain to Ireland. Irish planning controls have always been looser than British ones anyway, and the 2008 crisis showed that, in some conditions, this looser Irish stance could do a lot of harm.

Lower house prices are not likely to be the only effect of a loose planning regime, and not necessarily even the main one. In North American cities with loose planning controls and low house prices, densities are presumably also low in most cases. Bramley et al. considered (1995, pp. 149–58) British planning controls may have more effect on density than price: house prices 'may not be that much higher as a result, but people have a lot less space for their money'.

Planning regimes vary not only in how restrictive they are, but also in how firmly established their current character is. Where they have not changed much in the recent past and are not expected to change much in future, current incentives and future expectations will be aligned with each other, and have similar, mutually reinforcing effects.

It would take some time for a much looser planning regime to develop this sort of stability in Ireland. There would be inevitable uncertainty on whether the change in the planning regime was permanent, or would be reversed by another government, due to an environmentalist or nimbyite reaction. Also, as an EU member, Ireland is more subject to existing and future EU directives which affect planning policy than individual American states are to federal level interventions of this type. A regime of minimal controls in Ireland would need to survive intact for the terms of two or three governments for it to become established enough to shape expectations effectively.

In the meantime, owners of well-located land which would be zoned under almost any planning regime would have a motive for waiting to see if any reduction in prices due to increased supply was temporary. This would be balanced by the incentive to develop quickly land which would be unlikely to get planning permission in normal circumstances, but the shift of development from more to less suitable areas would provoke opposition.

Greatly increasing the amount of theoretically developable land would further destabilise the current system of servicing. The greater the uncertainty on which land will be developed, the less economic it is to provide services at public expense. This would probably result in developers being expected to provide more of their own services. To some extent, this is what happened in the pre-2008 boom, but it led to a proliferation of small, estate-specific pumping stations, treatment plants and well-based water supply schemes, and their high operating and maintenance costs becoming a public responsibility when they were taken in charge.

An analogy can be drawn between land supply, and water supply via older networks where half the water is lost through leaks, leaving the operators with a choice between increasing the raw supply, and reducing the leaks. Zoned land is also subject to large-scale leakage, much of it being unserviced, or withheld from the market by its owners, or acquired for speculative purposes or as a longer-term investment asset. As with water, increasing the raw supply of development land sounds simple, but there is a risk that much of the extra supply will also leak, and it is the more wasteful option, environmentally and in terms of physical resources – not characteristics which recommend themselves at present. Also, development land needs are much more cyclical than water supply ones, and less easily matched by simple removal of quantitative constraints.

This chapter has focused more on better management of the system we have than on radical departures from it. In the development land market, the behaviour of landowners and investors is strongly influenced by expectations, so the suggestions in Boxes 3.5–3.8 involve managing these expectations so as to bring their contribution to land supply more into line with need in the various phases of the cycle. Because of the importance of lead times and expectations, this cannot be done merely by interventions designed to change current behaviour. It also requires a system of incentives and disincentives, which will respond to the various possible future phases of the construction cycle in a way that can be predicted in advance.

Managing expectations will not be enough by itself. The construction industry complains about planning delays, which do indeed affect supply, but makes no reference to landowner, investor and developer ones. The power to acquire land compulsorily at existing use value is needed to reduce dependence on the timing preferences of these groups, particularly in relation to the lower half of the housing market. The existing Part V system could provide this, if amended to allow acquisition of the 20% to be transferred in advance of a planning application.

CONCLUSION

The three approaches described in this chapter will probably continue to be pursued in Ireland for the foreseeable future. The purpose of the chapter has been to suggest versions of these generic approaches which have four basic features.

Firstly, with the exception of full implementation of the Kenny report as outlined in Box 3.1, the suggestions are targeted, their scope is limited, and the financial and personnel requirements are modest. Buying land for new settlements (Box 3.2) and land due under Part V in advance (Box 3.3) involves buying a small fraction of land likely to be developed over the next ten years, rather than most of it, as envisaged in the Kenny report. Confining such purchases to the cities and their commuting hinterlands limits their scope further. Active management of the development of neighbourhoods through local contribution schemes equalised to take account of differences in public facilities provided (Box 3.4) requires much less intervention than, say, pooling and re-dividing the land on the Dutch or German models.

Secondly, the suggested versions involve systems designed to stay in place and remain politically acceptable throughout the economic cycle. The CVLVS, development land and vacant building rates outlined in Boxes 3.5–3.8 would all vary upwards and downwards in line with the cycle, making it less likely that they will be allowed to fade away as irrelevant or inappropriate or unduly onerous in some phases. The relatively low cost of acquiring land at close to existing use value for new settlements, and in advance for Part V purposes (Boxes 3.2–3.3), should make it possible to continue doing these things in the trough phase of the cycle, when public funding is tight.

Systems need to stay in place because of the problem of lead times. This applies not only to specific interventions in the land market, but also to any institutional changes in the public sector they may make necessary. Typically, half a decade will elapse from the time new institutional arrangements are first announced until the legislation, personnel to operate it, and procedures to be used in applying it are all fully operational and producing worthwhile results on the ground. If we wait until there is an immediate problem, it will usually be too late.

Thirdly, while the suggestions in Boxes 3.2–3.4 (new towns, advance use of Part V, equalised contribution schemes) are alternatives to Box 3.1 (the Kenny report), the suggestions in this chapter are otherwise mutually compatible, and capable of being implemented in parallel.

Fourthly, all suggested versions are designed to anticipate rather than react to successive phases of the cycle. The suggestions on CVLVS and development land taxation (Boxes 3.5–3.8) address this task directly, and are quite complicated as a result. But some way of rebalancing incentives is needed so it becomes more attractive to sell land earlier in a recovery, and less attractive to delay until a boom is close to its peak. Landowners, developers and investors have expectations, accurate or otherwise, and these influence their behaviour. Pre-announcing what CVLVS and levy rates will apply under a variety of future circumstances is a way of changing those expectations. Systems explicitly designed to cope with such changes are also more likely to benefit from belief in their permanence, whereas initiatives designed to respond to a current problem are more likely to be perceived as transient.

Publicly owned land, whether under the management of the LDA, or acquired for new settlements or in advance under Part V (Boxes 3.2–3.3) will be of most value in anticipating the cycle if acquisition is complete and plans for it reasonably advanced, at the point when a trough is ending and a recovery about to begin. This, unfortunately, is the point at which funding is least likely to be available. However, recoveries spread outwards, starting in Dublin, then affecting the other cities, and then gradually moving outwards through their commuting areas. It should be possible to take account of this sequence in applying such limited funding as is available for land acquisition during the trough and early recovery phases.

As indicated in Figure 3.1 at the start of the chapter, the supply of development land is only the first stage in a longer development process. Zoning of land, and its transfer from landowners or investors to developers does not lead to practical results unless it is also serviced. To the limited extent the argument for trying to moderate development land prices by increasing zoned land has merit, it applies primarily to the supply of serviced land. Unlike zoning, providing the necessary infrastructure is far from costless and has, in some periods, been damagingly inadequate. Provision of infrastructure is discussed in the next chapter.

CHAPTER 4

INFRASTRUCTURE

Summary: Funding for local infrastructure comes mostly from specialised government agencies. These also have other responsibilities, which can lead to local infrastructure being under-funded, as it did in the 1990s. The Serviced Land Initiative (SLI) was set up in response in 1997 (abolished in 2009). Adequate serviced land requires funding for different types of local infrastructure to be coordinated, in space and time. A permanent successor to the SLI is suggested to help fund and coordinate infrastructure on selected land via contracts with the relevant agencies which control timing. It could also help maintain a 'floor' level of investment in recessions, so there is enough serviced land to meet demand in a recovery, without delays due to lead times.

Infrastructure projects are affected by queuing which, for a given level of funding, leads to more areas and time periods in which infrastructure is inadequate. Selecting higher cost ways of resolving deficiencies lengthens queues. A coverage-friendly option which would best achieve the basic aim of a project at close to minimum cost could be developed, in parallel with development of a conventional 'preferred' option designed to maximise net economic benefits. This extra option would increase flexibility, particularly in cyclical downturns, when it would be a way of continuing to meet a reasonably wide range of infrastructure needs, despite reduced resources.

Actual development of land requires a number of different types of local infrastructure (as well as a landowner willing to sell it to a developer who wants to construct buildings on it). Some of these – particularly water supply and sewerage – have to be in place already for development to be possible,[1] and thus directly affect land availability. In new housing areas, in particular, these need to be supplemented by other types of infrastructure to provide reasonable living conditions for residents, including primary schools, public transport, pedestrian and cycle links, any necessary local road improvements, parks and local shops. These should be provided in parallel with development, but, in practice, there has often been a long wait for them.

The various types of publicly provided local infrastructure are funded in different ways by different public sector organisations. Provision of whatever services are lacking therefore needs to be coordinated, as otherwise the various organisations involved are unlikely to provide or fund their type of infrastructure for the same land at the same time, and a lot of resources may be spent producing partially serviced land which cannot be developed until other infrastructure is added, or which will be poorly served if it is. The first part of this chapter therefore deals with this coordination issue.

Coordination of local infrastructure is particularly important where substantial blocks of greenfield land are being developed. Land which has already been developed once and then cleared – 'brownfield land' – usually still has the infrastructural services which allowed it to be developed in the first place, though these may need modernising. Infrastructure in existing urban edge development may also have enough spare capacity to serve some adjacent greenfield land, via low-cost extensions to pipe and transport networks. However, this is less likely to be the case with greenfield development of relatively large new neighbourhoods, as recommended in the 2004 NESC report.[2]

Local development occurs primarily as a result of urban growth, and this, in turn, requires good quality infrastructure at other spatial scales: larger suburban areas, towns and cities, sub-regions and regions. Funding for infrastructure – both at local and at other levels – comes mainly from the state's public capital programme, and is, to a considerable extent, channelled through the same central government departments and agencies, so projects, project types and geographical areas are, to some extent, in competition with each other for this funding. This competition doesn't necessarily result in adequate coverage of less local infrastructure needs at town, city, regional or sub-regional level. The second part of this chapter deals with improving coverage.

A. COORDINATION OF LOCAL INFRASTRUCTURE

In the past half century, coordination of infrastructure has been sought in a variety of ways. The tension between local coordination of different types of infrastructure, and dependence on separate, functionally defined central government departments and agencies for funding, was recognised at an early stage by the 1971 White Paper on the Reorganisation of Local Government (pp. 10–11):

> *Central government is organised on functional lines while local authorities are multi-purpose bodies. As a result, responsibility at national level for the different services which local authorities provide must inevitably be divided between several Departments of State.*

In response, there needed to be one central government department with responsibility 'for coordination between the activities of local authorities and those of other public authorities and for maintaining consistency and continuity in the relationships between the different branches of the central government and the local authorities'.

In parallel with this aim of horizontal coordination at central government level, the White Paper emphasised (p. 18) the primary role of local authorities in coordinating development:

> *The various functions of local authorities (especially relating to roads and road traffic, sanitary services and planning and development) are interrelated: all are concerned with the physical environment and must be considered as part of the overall development of an area. At that level, the need for coordination between the various services is of paramount importance. The most effective way to ensure that is to entrust them to a single multi-purpose authority having*

exclusive jurisdiction in the area and operating in accordance with a comprehensive and integrated plan.

However, capital expenditure by local authorities needed (pp. 54–5) to remain under central government control, and 'be attuned to the state of the economy and to the Government's economic and social policies'.

The actual system of funding for sewerage and water supply in the 1970s and 1980s involved local authorities seeking sanction from the Minister for the Environment to borrow for capital works. If the relevant section within his Department reported favourably on a proposal for such works, sanction would be forthcoming, and a proportion of the loan charges on this borrowing (usually 40–50%) would be paid for by central government grant. While investment and maintenance of national primary and national secondary roads was 100% centrally funded, local authorities had a block grant for other roads. Some contributions towards works which facilitated particular developments were raised from developers as a condition of planning permission (Roche, 1982, pp. 181–3, 251–2, 258–9).

In theory, this was a fairly 'horizontal' system, with most local infrastructure part funded by the Department of the Environment and implemented by multi-purpose local authorities. It was less horizontal in practice, as most central-local interaction was between the specialist local authority sections and the corresponding sections in the Department of the Environment, whose approval and funding recommendations were necessary for investment in sanitary services[3] and national roads. National roads were/are relevant to local development because they naturally converge on the main urban areas, so new bypasses and relief roads there may be classified as national roads.

Coordinating public transport with other infrastructure was more difficult, as funding of the former was decided at national level, and was outside the control of local authorities or the Department of the Environment. Once the recession of the 1980s bit, proposals for a shift from road investment to public transport in plans such as the 1978 Cork

Land Use Transportation Study (LUTS) simply went unimplemented (Mansergh, 2001, pp. 499–505). However, local authorities also had insufficient funds then to even maintain the existing road network, and so were not well placed to expand it in developing areas, or even provide more basic facilities, such as missing sections of footpaths and street lighting[4] on existing roads in such areas.

WATER SERVICES AND THE BOOM

At the end of the 1980s, there were two significant changes in the funding of sanitary services. In 1988, the system whereby the state paid part of the loan charges on local authority investment in them was replaced by 100% state grants, with no local authority contribution required. This change was questioned by Coughlan and de Buitleir (1996, p. 90), on the basis that it left local authorities with 'no direct financial incentive to appraise or prioritise projects', and risked them 'seeking to have as many projects as possible approved … for its area without the level of appraisal which would occur if costs as well as benefits were being fully weighed against each other'.

Local authority officials were naturally under pressure from elected members to improve local services in as many areas as possible, and had less incentive to resist inclusion of lengthy and unaffordable lists of projects in development plans. This may have weakened their commitment to coordinating provision of local infrastructure in places where substantial amounts of development were likely to happen, and increased the need for the Department to fulfil that role.

However, the Department became less able to fulfil it in the 1990s, as Ireland benefited from very generous EU funding in that decade, for investment which qualified for support under the Structural and Cohesion Funds. As a consequence, investment in sanitary services shifted towards environmental and employment-related projects, which qualified for EU support, and away from the servicing of housing land, which did not. The sanitary service objectives of the 1989–93 National Development Plan (NDP) made no reference to the latter, and prioritised (p. 58) the 'achievement ... of proper quality standards for water supplies and the prevention of pollution', and 'capital investment to support development policies in the key sectors of the economy'. The 1994–9 NDP's main policy priority (pp. 115–6) was the need to increase:

investment in water and sanitary services in the period up to the year 2000 so as ... to

- ensure that stringent quality standards for drinking water are fully ... met;

- eliminate untreated sewage discharges from major coastal towns; and

- eliminate all pollution of inland waters by sewage discharges

These objectives are reinforced by requirements of EC environmental legislation ... Investment in environmental services will be continued and intensified during the 1994 to 1999 period, maintaining the economic objectives of the current Water, Sanitary and other Local Services Operational Programme with an even greater emphasis on the environmental aspects of service provision.

Following the surge in housing demand and prices from 1996 onwards, the 1998 Bacon report identified (p. xiv) water/sewerage and road infrastructure as key constraints on housing supply in Dublin, and linked

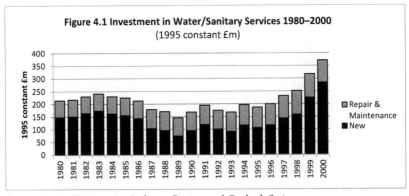

Source: DoE, Construction Industry Review and Outlook Series

these constraints to the predominantly environmental priorities influencing investment in the former:

> *EU funding for water and sewerage services is directed primarily at providing improved waste water treatment and collection, as required under the Urban Waste Water Treatment Directive and improving the quality of drinking water supplies to meet EU drinking water standards. While the provision of these services is enabling statutory, environmental and public health objectives to be met, a lack of flexibility in the use of EU funds and the limited exchequer funds that have been available has meant there has been no specific targeting of funds at providing services to open up land for residential development. Any land which has been made available over the last few years can be considered as a beneficial spin off from investment in water and sewerage services, rather than the result of a specific objective of the investment.*

As Figure 4.1 shows, for most of the 1990s, investment in sanitary services was actually lower in real terms than it had been in the depressed 1980s. EU funding was being used to substitute for Irish funding, rather than to add to it, and the pattern of investment was changed partly for financial management reasons so as to maximise eligibility for that funding.

However, once the scale of the surge in housing demand became apparent, priorities were revised. The Serviced Land Initiative (SLI) was announced in late 1997, to provide 40% central funding for water service projects which would open up land for new housing, with local authorities providing the remaining 60% (Gleeson, 2002, p. 215). The Bacon report (April 1998) recommended increasing SLI funding, and also commented (p. xv) that:

> *In some limited cases the main constraint would appear to be the provision of road infrastructure which, up to this, has not been recognised as a specific objective. Where action needs to be taken and cannot be funded through the current non-national roads programme additional resources should be made available to local authorities on a similar basis to the existing Serviced Land Initiative.*

The government added a 'Developing Areas Initiative' to the SLI in 2008, as:

a new mechanism for the Department and local authorities to support work at central and local government levels to secure better co-ordination and timely delivery of key infrastructure and services in fast-growing developing areas in parallel with housing development.[5]

This was due to social infrastructure, which should have been provided in parallel with new housing, lagging far behind. The highest profile problem was insufficient primary school places in rapidly expanding suburbs. In response, the Departments of Education and the Environment published a code of practice in July 2008 – 'The Provision of Schools and the Planning System'.

The various measures on servicing of development land undertaken from 1997 on did not develop into a permanent system, and instead went into reverse after the 2008 crash. The SLI was abolished in 2009. Investment in water services fell by 40% between 2009 and 2012, and the (national) Water Services Investment Programme for 2010–12 reverted to pre-SLI priorities:

With the changed economic climate and the finalisation of the first cycle of River Basin Management Plans, the new programme aims to prioritise projects that target environmental compliance issues. It also fully supports economic and employment growth as envisaged in the Government's policy document 'Building Ireland's Smart Economy – A Framework for Sustainable Economic Revival'.

LIHAF (2016)

While there were no special mechanisms to coordinate funding of local infrastructure in the 2010–15 period, a Local Infrastructure Housing Activation Fund (LIHAF) was introduced in 2016. This was in response to a new housing crisis in cities, due to economic recovery, the lack of new construction, and the loss of construction capacity after the 2008 crash.

LIHAF sought to coordinate infrastructure investment with the actions of developers. To ensure LIHAF funding led to actual development of affordable housing, applications for LIHAF funding had to include commitments by developers to produce affordable housing, within a specified time frame, with provision for clawback if these were not honoured.[6] This reflected weakening of the assumption that most development land, once serviced, would be developed without undue delay. This was not the case during the post-2013 recovery, so a way of identifying land which would be developed fairly quickly once serviced seemed necessary.

The government was concerned that construction of 15–20,000 houses was being prevented by infrastructure blockages, or because funding of missing infrastructure by house-builders would make their developments uneconomic.[7] LIHAF could fund off-site infrastructure normally funded by local authorities, such as local roads, footpaths, street lighting, and storm water disposal. It had funding of €200 million, with €50 million of this coming from local authorities.

A Serviced Sites Fund was introduced in 2018, with a narrower remit – to fund infrastructure works on local authority owned lands, so that they could be developed for affordable housing.[8] A sum of €310 million was to be made available over the 2019–21 period, subject to maximum expenditure of €50,000 per house, allowing construction of 6,200 houses, though only 400 of these are expected to be delivered by 2022 (Hession, 2019, pp. 10–16; O'Connell, 2021).

IRISH WATER

LIHAF did not include investment in local water supply and sewerage, on the basis that these would be funded via Irish Water's strategic investment plans. Irish Water was established in 2013 as a national agency, which would take over responsibility for managing and investing in water services from local authorities and the relevant sections of the Department of the Environment. As in the 1990s, policy was influenced by financial management considerations – in this case, to convert investment in water services from government expenditure, subject to EU controls on maximum government deficits, into commercial investment by a semi-state body funded mainly by user charges, with extra revenue from water charges for residential users.

These aims were not achieved, due to public resistance to residential water charges. However, the establishment of Irish Water had an important side-effect in that local funding and implementation decisions on water services were no longer under the direct control of the government department and local authorities responsible for planning and housing. This increased the need for coordination between separate agencies.

This was, to some extent, met by increased emphasis on coordination of local infrastructure through plans. The 2018 National Planning Framework envisaged (p. 148) water services for future development being coordinated with other infrastructure through plans at national level:

Investment in water services infrastructure is critical to the implementation of the National Development Plan. The current Water Services Strategic Plan by Irish Water will be updated in the light of the policies in the National Planning Framework addressing the requirements of future development, while also addressing environmental requirements such as obligations under EU Water Framework Directive mandated River Basin Management Plans.

Servicing of development land will continue to be in competition for funding with Irish Water's other responsibilities. The 2021–30 version of the NDP lists (pp. 134–5) 23 activities, of which 15 relate to water quality and conservation, and to maintenance, management and remediation of existing systems, four to servicing new urban and two to servicing new rural development. The Irish Water Investment Plan 2020–4 proposed expenditure of €4.8 billion over that period (i.e. around €1 billion a year), of which 70% was allocated under water quality, conservation and system maintenance heads, 15% to the Greater Dublin Drainage and Eastern and Midland Region Water Supply Projects,[9] due for completion by 2029–30, and 13% to the shorter term servicing of other new development.

A CIF submission (August 2021, p. 29) recommended an increase in the capital allocation for Irish Water by €2 billion per annum, arguing that in some areas there was less than two years' supply of zoned and serviced land, and that 'provision of water and wastewater infrastructure is currently the slowest moving part in the provision of state controlled infrastructure'.

The subsequent 2021–30 NDP increased the 2021–5 capital allocation to Irish Water to €6 billion, but even if all of this increase was used to boost shorter-term servicing of new development, aggregate investment under this head would still only average around €350 million per annum in those years.[10]

Regardless of whether the current real need is closer to the NDP or the CIF's estimates, there is an ongoing risk of funding for water services infrastructure on development land being squeezed by Irish Water's other responsibilities. Temporary increases in funding to Irish Water, or temporary schemes based on the SLI or LIHAF model, are not an adequate response to periodic re-emergence of shortfalls in the amount of serviced land, because of the problem of lead times. By the time it is clear action is needed, it will be too late.

IMPLICATIONS FOR TIMING AND COORDINATION OF LOCAL INFRASTRUCTURE

The main implications of the ebb and flow of government interventions in the servicing of development land – from 1989 onwards – seem to be as follows:

(a) Switching the emphasis back and forth between environmental or employment-related aims, financial management, and servicing of development land is a risky way of dealing with the latter. The lead times involved in designing, approving, tendering for and implementing infrastructure projects are longer than the period over which property market conditions can be foreseen with reasonable accuracy. The relevant authorities can therefore not afford to wait until shortages become evident, and then step up servicing of development land. Peter Bacon not unreasonably responded to critics complaining about the length of time before the measures he proposed took effect, by saying 'two years is not a very long time given the kind of delays that exist in relation to resolving the supply issues' (*Construction*, Sept. 2000, p. 25). Two years may however be long enough to allow loss of control over property markets. House prices rose by 54% nationally between the announcement of the SLI late in 1997, and Bacon's comment in 2000. Even if the SLI had been announced in late 1995, this would still have been too late to complete enough extra infrastructure projects to significantly dampen prices rises of 36% between Q4 1995 and Q4 1997 (50% in Dublin).[11]

(b) To cope with this, we need a 'floor' – a minimum level of investment in the servicing of development land, regardless of current market conditions, or a 'buffer' (maintaining a stock of undeveloped serviced land sufficient to meet unexpected demand, in the interval before extra investment in response can take effect), or some mixture of the two. A floor would be preferable, as it could maintain a continuous flow of work, whereas investment to maintain a given buffer would be more of a stop–start process.

(c) Funding of this floor needs to be separate from funding of other investment currently under the same remit, so it does not compete with other policy aims (e.g. water quality versus servicing of development land) for its share of a generic item in the national budget. This would not prevent the same agency (e.g. Irish Water) from implementing both types of project, providing sufficient funds were ring-fenced for the former.

(d) The Departments of Finance and Public Expenditure would resist a floor which had to be maintained regardless of the state of the public finances. However, the financial destabilisation and costs caused by loss of control over the property market from the late 1990s on vastly outweighed any benefits from moving this type of funding back and forth between different aims.

(e) Development land requires a number of different services, so an SLI-type fund needs to be capable of funding several different types of infrastructure, and to distribute funding so that they coincide with each other and existing infrastructure on the same land.

(f) Under some market conditions, it may be necessary to coordinate the actions of landowners and developers with those of infrastructure providers, so the activities of the latter result in actual development of land reasonably quickly.

Box 4.1 suggests a way of responding to the above points.

Box 4.1 A Coordinated Local Infrastructure Investment Fund (CLIIF)

A single permanent source of funding for the infrastructure needed on development land could be established, and managed by a section within the government department responsible for housing, planning and local government. This section could enter into contracts with specialist central government agencies, local authorities, or private sector developers to provide specified infrastructure projects. Coordination of provision of services for a particular area or block of land could be achieved by several contracts – one for each service needed – with timing clauses. Such mutually supportive cross-compartment packages could apply to a small local area, or to a substantial segment of a metropolitan or other urban area.

Preferably, CLIIF grants would be less than 100% of project cost, and would be supplemented by matching funding from local authorities and/or the agencies which would otherwise have been responsible for this. As with the SLI, matching funding could be used to encourage realistic prioritisation. Contracts could provide for interim management of completed pieces of infrastructure by the implementing body, subject to longer-term arrangements for them to be taken in charge by the normal agency or local authority. As with the SLI, CLIIF supported projects would supplement rather than displace the normal method of provision.

One function of the CLIIF section would be to define how a 'floor' level of infrastructure investment was measured, ensure it was maintained, and publish data demonstrating this. During recessions, this minimum investment should be concentrated in and around Dublin and other cities, where the property market recovers first, and where reacting to a recovery by increasing the rate of investment is least likely to be in time to prevent shortages and price surges in the housing market. Once a recovery was underway, funding could extend to other urban areas, where substantial increases in demand seemed likely.

Priority could be given to servicing land whose owners had committed themselves to develop, on a given basis and timescale, in return for a reciprocal commitment on provision and timing of specified infrastructure. This would put the principle behind LIHAF on a permanent basis. However, coordinated funding should not be limited to such land. The movement of land needs to be encouraged along the full length of the development pipeline, not just at the delivery end of the pipe, as a hand-to-mouth response to periodic housing shortages. This means some land will have to be serviced well in advance of development. If an effective vacant land and cyclically variable development gains tax regime were in place, as outlined in

Boxes 3.5–3.7, there would be other incentives to keep moving land through the pipeline.

The consolidated tax on development land suggested in Box 3.6 (CVLVS) would be an appropriate source of revenue for CLIIF, and a specific percentage might be allocated to it. This income would be highly cyclical, so there would be a need for arrangements for holding back some of it in the upper part of the cycle, so it would available to maintain a floor level of local infrastructure investment in the lower part. From a macroeconomic point of view, there would be advantages in raising revenue from development land – the most cyclical component in a highly cyclical sector – during booms, and holding it back for investment within the same sector in the subsequent trough.

CLIIF AND THE HIERARCHY OF PLANS

The need for the suggestions in Box 4.1 may be questioned, on the basis that effective ways of coordinating servicing of land already exist, and are currently being strengthened, by incorporating it more explicitly into the hierarchy of plans which has been developed and refined from the 2000 Planning and Development Act on. This involves formal plans at national, regional, local authority and local levels, with vertical and horizontal coordination of the activities of the various public sector organisations involved in the development process happening primarily through mutual alignment of these plans, at these different levels.

At national level, the 2018–40 National Planning Framework (NPF) made a point (pp. 11–12, 131) of its alignment with the National Development Plan (2018–27) as giving the NPF greater credibility than previous attempts at more balanced regional development.[12] As noted above, it is also intended to align a revised version of the Water Services Strategic Plan with the NPF.

The three regional assemblies have Regional Spatial and Economic Strategies. In addition to local authority Development Plans and Local Plans, a new, metropolitan level has been added,[13] in the form of Metropolitan Area Strategic Plans (MASPs), supplemented by parallel Metropolitan Area Transport Strategies.[14] The 2018 National Planning

Framework (pp. 134–7) saw MASPs as addressing 'high level and long term strategic development issues' for the five cities in the Republic and their surrounding areas and also as working out 'a sequence of infrastructure prioritisation, delivery and coordination'.

Plans normally end with proposed arrangements for their implementation. These typically include phasing programmes, and committees on which the relevant agencies are represented. This is supplemented at local level by communication between the various functional sections within local authorities, and coordination by local authority management.

These arrangements, while apparently comprehensive, are not adequate by themselves. For the purposes of coordinating agencies, plans are a blunt instrument. They naturally focus on substantial projects, and may deal cursorily or not at all with minor actions or details which may determine whether particular blocks of land are available for development. Most assume funding will be higher[15] and project costs lower than they subsequently turn out to be. This is often necessary to achieve consensus, as the greater selectivity and reduced levels of service that a more strictly realistic approach might require may be unacceptable to some stakeholders. Plans are also liable to disruption by unforeseen factors, including institutional and policy changes at national or EU level, difficulty in obtaining regulatory approval and legal challenges, as well as the economic cycle. It is thus quite rare for a plan complex enough to contain multiple, diverse projects to be carried out as originally intended.

As this gradually becomes apparent during the life of a plan, functional organisations which control detailed allocation of funding for particular types of project can decide which parts of the plan are actually implemented, and in what order. The projects agencies implement are part of the plan, which was accepted by other participants, and the resource constraints they face are real, so they can do this without attracting much criticism. Plans and phasing programmes become a menu, from which some items can be selected for immediate implementation, and others deferred, or tacitly abandoned. Alignment between parallel plans, or parts of the same plan due to be carried out by different agencies, are likely casualties of this process.

Plans are a necessary condition for coordinated action by different bodies, because they create an agreed context in which this can take place, but not a sufficient condition. Public bodies face a variety of incentives and disincentives, and being able to show they have fully discharged their responsibilities under an adopted plan, at the appropriate time, or have fully coordinated their actions with other public bodies, are rarely the most powerful ones. CLIIF-type funding would modify these incentives, by allowing the relevant public bodies to meet their obligations to service development land in line with agreed plans, at reduced cost to themselves.

Consider, for instance, the incentives faced by Irish Water, where circumstances had changed relative to expectations in the relevant plan, making some modifications unavoidable, and its resources were constrained. It might understandably then defer:

(a) Servicing an area involving above average costs for them, but included in a plan due to below average overall costs (e.g. because the transport system has spare capacity there);

(b) Extending water supply and sewer networks to serve substantial blocks of development land for complete new neighbourhoods, as these will usually be developed over quite a long period, and Irish Water would have to carry costs in the interval before the area is fully developed and they are fully recovered through connection charges.

(c) Implementing plan proposals on servicing of development land during recessions, when there was no immediate need for it, as they would have to carry the costs until demand recovered, and they may have more urgent alternative needs for the funds.

CLIIF-type funding could ease these misalignments of incentives, by contributing to above-average water services costs under (a), and investment during recessions under (c), providing, of course, that these contributions were part of packages which resulted in fully serviced land. Where type (b) blocks of land are in multiple ownership, and there is no single developer who can be charged for the costs of a network extension, the local authority could construct and be the interim owner of such extensions, supported by CLIIF funding. Under its connection charging policy, Irish Water could still charge for connections to individual developments and premises, and could pass some of this income back to the local authority as it arose, to offset costs incurred as its agent.[16]

The underlying point can be summarised by describing plans as agendas, whose effectiveness depends on the tools in place to ensure they are acted on. CLIIF is a suggested extra tool, given the limitations of existing means of implementation.

CENTRALISATION AND LOCAL AUTHORITY DEVELOPMENT CONTRIBUTIONS

The context in which the current system for provision of local infrastructure has evolved is one of increasing centralisation. The creation of new national agencies – the National Roads Authority in 1993, the National Transport Authority in 2010, and Irish Water in 2013 – has strengthened vertical relationships on a function-by-function basis. Each of these national agencies is typically linked to a corresponding section within the main local authorities, which they supervise and fund, on the lines summarised in Table 4.1. The new agencies have also led to greater institutional separation of closely related functions, both in the case of water services, and by separating national and regional road construction.

For the purposes of this chapter, I have assumed that centralisation is part of the DNA of the Irish state, and that no practical purpose would be served by, say, arguing for a general return to the world envisaged by the 1971 White Paper, with local infrastructure being coordinated mostly by and within local authorities. As that White Paper noted, central gov-

TABLE 4.1   CENTRAL AND LOCAL GOVERNMENT ROLES IN THE PROVISION OF LOCAL INFRASTRUCTURE

Level of Government:	Public provision of:						
	Foul sewerage	Water supply	Regional & local roads, footpaths, storm drge.	Cycle routes	Bus & rail services, bus priorities	National roads	Schools
NATIONAL:							
Department	Housing and Local Government			Transport			Education
Funding/Supervisory Agency/Service Provider	Irish Water			National Transport Auth. (NTA), Bus Éireann, Iarnród Éireann		Transport Infrastructure Ireland (TII)	
REGIONAL AUTHORITY							
LOCAL AUTHORITY:							
Departments/ sections/ offices:	Water Services Investmt. Programme		Road Design Offices/Transport Planning/ area engineers			National Roads	Planning

ernment is organised on functional lines, so centralisation and segmentation by function go together.

CLIIF is thus suggested as a way of selectively compensating for this segmentation, to improve the coordination of local infrastructure. However, it requires the active participation of local authorities, as they have a strong motive for making sure coordination is effective, and detailed local knowledge on how to achieve it. While it is desirable that they match funding from central government sources, as with the SLI, this raises the question of how far they can afford to do this. Local authorities have borrowing powers which can be used to invest in projects likely to increase future revenues through the rates and residential property tax system, but there are prudential limits to such borrowing, and it is subject to central government approval.

Local authorities levy contributions towards the cost of works facilitating development, but the contributions system was only fully effective for a brief period in the early 2000s. Prior to that, under the 1963 Act, contributions towards works facilitating a particular permission could be levied, but only if those works had been carried out in the seven years before the date of permission, or in a specified period after it (usually also seven years).[17] The amounts charged were modest, partly because An Bord Pleanála was inclined to interpret these provisions conservatively. Total planning contributions raised were 1.5% of the value of new private residential and commercial construction output in 2000.[18]

The 2000 Act replaced this system with a requirement for each local authority to produce a General Contributions Scheme, involving standard rates to be charged to each class of development, based on anticipated investment by the local authority in public infrastructure and facilities, including investment funded by state grants.[19] It was no longer necessary to show which particular infrastructure projects benefited a particular development, though additional Special Contributions could still be charged for 'specific exceptional costs not covered' by the general scheme and benefiting that particular development. The new system came into force in 2002–4, and had raised contributions to 3% of new private residential and commercial construction output by 2006.[20]

This improvement was not sustained, mainly due to changes to the status of investment in water services. The EU's Water Framework Directive, 2000 required (art. 9) capital investment in water services to be financed from (current) user charges by 2010, though with some provision for derogations, so development contributions for water services were due to be phased out. The subsequent transfer of responsibility for them to Irish Water meant that local authorities could no longer charge contributions for water services; instead, Irish Water were allowed to charge connection charges, at levels set by a regulator. This typically reduced the amount local authorities could charge through the contributions system by a half or more.

In the depressed period following the 2008 crash, the IDA and the government also became concerned that high contributions were discouraging new employment-generating projects. This concern resulted in the 2013 Development Contribution Guidelines, which required a variety of reductions and exemptions in the relevant levies. Concerns on the effect of contributions on housing output led to the announcement of a Development Contribution Rebate Scheme, which refunded 80–100% of contributions paid in respect of housing developments of 50+ houses costing €300,000 or less in Dublin and €250,000 or less in Cork, though government did compensate local authorities for the cost of these rebates.

The resources available to a local authority through the contributions system have thus been depleted by centralisation, and further weakened by the expectation that they keep contribution rates as low as possible.[21] There seems to be some uncertainty on whether development contributions will even survive, as no specific provision for them was included in the Draft Planning and Development Bill in January 2023. This would reduce or remove their capacity to part-fund local infrastructure and influence investment under a CLIIF-type scheme.

There are several ways in which this capacity might be rebuilt. Firstly, as suggested in Chapter 3, a percentage of the revenue from a consolidated development land tax or CVLVS might be channelled into the Development Contribution Scheme for the area in which it arose. Secondly, the transfer of local authority water services to Irish Water might be partially reversed, on the basis outlined in Box 4.2.

Box 4.2 Decentralisation of Responsibility for Network Infrastructure

Irish Water, in their 2019 Connection Charging Policy, distinguish (pp. 8–10) between network infrastructure, such as water mains and collection sewers, and treatment infrastructure, which produces potable water to feed into – and treats effluent from – these pipe networks. The following case can be made for transferring responsibility for networks (and their extension to serve new development) back to local authorities:

(1) It would allow local authorities to resume recovery of costs of network extensions via development contributions, and responsibility for connecting new developments to networks. Current Irish Water connection charges are based on these costs, except in cases where treatment works have been upgraded or advanced to facilitate a specific development. Treatment improvements to meet general growth in demand are funded through Irish Water's Capital Investment Plan, not from connection charges.

(2) It would also allow Irish Water to concentrate on treatment infrastructure. This would separate water quality, health and environmental issues, which are primarily related to treatment, from network extension issues related more to the availability and location of usable development land, thereby reducing the risk that the funding needs of the former would lead to the latter being under-resourced, as in the 1990s.

(3) Water and waste water treatment projects are often on a large scale, and will arguably be carried out more efficiently by a specialist national agency. This was one of the main arguments for establishing the NRA for major road projects in the 1990s. Conversely, detailed local knowledge is more critical for the extension and maintenance of pipe networks, and local authorities are more likely to have this than a national agency.

(4) Separating responsibility for treatment from responsibility for networks is arguably less undesirable than separating responsibility for local roads from responsibility for water pipes and sewers, which are mostly

under or alongside them. Where extensions to the pipe network coincide with extensions to the local road network, there are likely to be economies in carrying them out in tandem. Local sewers, water pipes and roads are the core of local infrastructure systems, and are in particular need of coordination.

(5) If local authority contributions were reintroduced for network investment only, any tension with the Water Framework Directive and the polluter pays principle would be minimal. The costs of creating extra treatment capacity are more directly related to the volumes treated than the cost of different foul sewer and water pipe sizes. Moving up or down to the next available pipe size has much more effect on capacity than on cost. Any departure from the polluter pays principle would be very minor in comparison with the absence of water charges for residential users.

Thirdly, the risk that the contributions system may discourage development in depressed conditions, and recover too small a fraction of development gains during booms could be reduced by changing indexation provisions in Contributions Schemes, as outlined in Box 4.3.

Box 4.3 Indexation of Contributions in Line with House Prices

At present, the consumer price index or capital goods (building and construction – materials and labour) index is sometimes used for indexation purposes, but national or local house price indices could be used instead for residential developments. While construction costs vary cyclically, they do so less than house prices, as the latter include variations in land values and the developer's profits as well, and both are very volatile. If contributions were indexed in line with house prices, they would respond to the pressure to lower contributions during recessions, while raising them again automatically as the economy and housing market recovered.

Under s.48.1 of the 2000 Planning and Development Act, contributions are levied towards the cost of 'public infrastructure and facilities benefiting development in the area of the planning authority' and the extent of this benefit – in terms of gains to the landowner and profits to the developer – varies widely over the cycle. While contributions should reflect the 'actual estimated cost' of servicing development in the area (s.48.3(b)), this is on an aggregate basis. Local authorities have discretion on how this cost is allocated, and an explicit power to apply reduced contributions 'in certain circumstances' under s.48.3(c). Indexation which reflected cyclical variations in the gains from development would be consistent with the Act as it stands.

Indexation on this basis would make it less likely that contribution rates would be depressed throughout the cycle, in order to avoid discouraging housing development in the lower part of it. As contributions income would rise during booms, and fall during recessions, financial management would be needed to smooth the rate of investment. Provision for building up a surplus in booms to help fund investment in other parts of the cycle would need to be written into Development Contributions Schemes.

Some empirical support for the suggestions in Boxes 4.1–4.3 can be derived from experience in the 2003–7 period. Box 4.2, in effect, suggests restoring a contributions system similar to the one in force then, and Box 4.1 a revived and extended version of the SLI. These systems worked well enough to allow ample – indeed excessive – amounts of residential and commercial development to take place in that period.

B. INFRASTRUCTURE COVERAGE AT OTHER SPATIAL LEVELS

Adequate local infrastructure is usually a necessary condition for the growth of larger areas – regions, sub-regions, cities, large component parts of those cities (e.g. the 'northside'), and towns – but not a sufficient one. Many project types work best when the volume of users falls within a certain limited range, and become increasingly inefficient when user numbers fall outside this. Depending on the density of population and employment in the area, efficient ranges correspond to efficient spatial scales. Infrastructure projects become progressively less local as the populations they serve rise above a few thousand people.

Economic growth in these larger areas requires a combination of factors. While there may be some spill-over – high quality infrastructure of one type or in one area may, to some extent, compensate for poor quality of related types or in neighbouring areas – coverage is nevertheless an important issue, because of the number of different types of infrastructure which need to be provided and the number of areas which need to be served. Physical infrastructure also needs to be complemented by social and 'soft' infrastructure, and non-infrastructural factors:

> *The growth literature shows that while there are many drivers of growth, each one is a necessary but not sufficient condition of growth, and instead a combination of factors is required. Thus, for example, infrastructure on its own is unlikely to change the economic circumstances of a lagging region and may indeed have negative effects if it facilitates firms from outside the region to compete within the region.* (Morgenroth, 2012, pp. 9–10)

Covering a broad range of needs is thus likely to promote growth more effectively than concentration on a few of them. But coverage occurs in time, as well as in space and by type of need. If needs are classified by type and by area, coverage of the resulting matrix can be treated as the proportion of a given time period in which the needs within it are satisfactorily met. It is easy to neglect the time dimension: knowing a project to address a particular deficiency is planned distracts attention from the length of time likely to elapse before it is operational.

The interval between emergence of needs and completion of projects to address them depends on the balance between planned investment and the actual flow of funding available. If the former exceeds the latter, queues will form, or lengthen if there is already a backlog of projects.

CYCLICALITY, THE RATCHET EFFECT AND QUEUING

Cyclicality creates favourable conditions for a ratchet effect. In the upper part of the cycle, employment, population, the demand for transport, and other forms of infrastructure are all growing rapidly. These conditions make ambitious, state-of-the-art projects which benefit as wide a group as possible seem both more necessary and more feasible. In theory, this will be balanced by more cost-conscious design of adequate, more narrowly targeted facilities in the lower part of the cycle, but, in practice, there is likely to be an imbalance. New projects are less likely to be designed at all in the latter part of the cycle, and sponsoring agencies are more likely to react to a downturn by suspending work on high-cost projects, rather than by abandoning them.

This is likely to promote queuing of infrastructure projects. Such queuing appears widespread in Ireland, but it is not easy to quantify it, and some fairly drastic simplifying assumptions are needed even to define when it is happening, in a way which can be applied in the real world. If we start from the desirability of avoiding gaps in coverage, this implies anticipating the point at which the adverse economic, environmental or social effects of an unmet need become seriously damaging, early enough[22] to allow the project to be complete by the time that point is reached. If projects are planned but not completed (or started) by then, this may be regarded as evidence of queuing.

The standard solution to project queuing, particularly favoured by the construction industry, is to increase public capital investment. However, even if this is possible, it is not necessarily effective, as increased funding may lead to the selection of higher-cost solutions to particular deficiencies, as well as improved coverage. For instance, in the late 1990s, improvement in the public finances led to replacement of the 478 km of basic dual carriageway recommended by the NRA 1998 Road Needs Study (1998, Ch.8) for the M/N 6, 7, 8 and 11 corridors west and south of Kinnegad, Portlaoise, and Bray, by motorways. Few now doubt this was the right decision, but the additional 216 km of basic dual carriageway[23] which could have been built with the funds released if the lower-cost option had been selected may not be factored into this assessment.

It is possible to reach the end of a long boom in which there has been ample infrastructure investment with many needs unmet. A report on infrastructure delivery by the Irish Academy of Engineering (IAE) and Forfas in 2011, when the motorway network was more or less complete, said (p. 6) that despite major investment in the previous decade, there was 'a requirement for sustained investment in critical infrastructure to permit essential economic growth'.

The 2018 NDP illustrated the effect of economic recovery on investment aims, being, according to NESC (2019, p. 56) 'intended to move Ireland close to the top of the international league for public investment'. Surprisingly, it seems to have been assumed that this would make the sector less rather than more vulnerable to cyclical disruption, as the NDP would also 'provide clarity to the construction sector, to allow it to provide the capacity and capability required to deliver the Government's long term investment plans'.

It is more likely Irish infrastructure investment will continue to fluctuate. As Figures 2.2–2.5 indicate, the only period in which it enjoyed relative though depressed stability was from the mid-1980s to the mid-1990s. There are no periods in which it has been both high and stable: even the peak of 1981–2 followed a 60% real increase in the public capital programme since 1976.

THE EFFECT OF CENTRALISED FUNDING

Cyclicality is not the only factor likely to tilt project design towards state-of-the-art facilities benefitting as wide a group as possible, rather than containing individual project costs to allow a wider range of infrastructure needs to be met reasonably quickly. Centralised control of public investment in Ireland is likely to reinforce this effect.

If infrastructure was locally funded by city and county councils from local taxation, support for high-cost options would be balanced by awareness that this could result in extra local taxation, or delays to other local projects, with local decision makers and the local population knowing what specific projects were likely to be affected. Widespread reliance on 100% central government grants has the opposite effect. It means benefits seem far more real than costs for those within project catchments. They gain the benefits, but the costs are carried by the state as a whole. They thus have a motive for enlarging the scope of projects and seeking the highest level of service.

This is not balanced by cost considerations, as they will not expect the costs of the project to significantly affect national tax and debt levels, or state funding of other projects in their area. Public support on this basis is particularly relevant for transport projects, where awareness of the effects of different options on levels of service and access to improved facilities is greater.

Queuing enables the central government agencies which allocate funding to cope with the accumulated pressures for extra investment. The queues may be modest and orderly, with projects carried out in a planned sequence set out in a programme of investment, to be completed in a specified time period. Often they are not, because it is not possible in practice to carry out all the projects in the programme in that time period. Those which cannot be implemented within it are included, as a way of promising they will be funded eventually. A popular variant on this is to schedule the start of high-cost projects right at the end of the relevant time period, with most of the expenditure falling outside it. This effectively extends the time covered by the programme.

These techniques defuse the issue of coverage, by converting it into one of priority or timing. They thus reduce the need to look more closely at high-cost solutions, or seek less costly ones. There are limits in terms of how far these techniques can be used, as infrastructure programmes need to retain credibility. However, the supporters of projects which are not included in them can be mollified by the suggestion that they may be included in future programmes.

The net effect is to detach arguments for high-cost options from consequences for coverage. Most projects need some public and political support, and this often leads to inclusion of additional elements not strictly necessary to achievement of the main objective, which will help attract this, or at any rate neutralise opposition. It is difficult for coverage arguments to compete with this, as, in the absence of local capital budgets, they are based on delays to funding to unspecified projects somewhere else, and may sound nebulous and penny pinching. Calling for 'value for money' is not particularly helpful, as it is not the same thing as coverage: a megaproject may be excellent value for money, but preferring it to a lower-cost alternative which may be equally good value for money can still delay other projects.

The imbalance between pressures for higher-cost projects and coverage considerations may be endemic, as the underlying causes – cyclicality and centralisation of the public sector – are unlikely to go away. However, the project evaluation process could help redress this if it had to include coverage-friendly options, and the most promising of these was given a high profile. Coverage-friendly options may take several different forms, so some relatively high-profile transport projects currently being designed or evaluated are used to illustrate the possibilities.

COVERAGE-FRIENDLY OPTIONS: EXAMPLES

(1) Tipperary and the N24 – the absence of an incremental option

The proposed bypass for Tipperary town illustrates coverage issues and the importance of the time dimension, as selection of a high-cost option there may have contributed directly to delay in removing the infrastructure deficiency that project was intended to address. The County Council identified a need for a bypass for the town in the early 1990s, and plans to provide one reached the public consultation stage in 1999–2000. A 'preferred route' was put on public display in 2001,[24] and selected in 2003, but progress towards implementation was suspended for financial reasons in 2011. A new design process – 'starting from a blank canvas' – started with a fresh public consultation round in January 2021.[25]

The 2001 preferred route was 30.5 km long, as it bypassed the villages of Bansha, Oola and Monard as well as Tipperary town on their northern side, before crossing the existing N24 between Oola and Pallasgreen and bypassing the latter on its southern side. Even in 2000, at the time of the first consultation process, it was clear that the road being designed would be five or six times the length necessary to bypass Tipperary town itself, and this raised the question of what would happen if finance for 20–30 km of new road was not available. The implied answer was that we would just have to wait until it was. The NRA may not have taken the possibility of funding difficulties seriously, as it decided, in 2007, that the entire length of the N24 should be dual carriageway,[26] and, in 2008, that the scheme for the Bansha to Pallasgreen section of the N24 should be amalgamated with the one for the adjacent Bansha to Cahir section.[27]

Tipperary town has declined economically in recent years, partly because of lack of industry, but retail businesses on the Main Street have also suffered severely, with adverse effects of N24 traffic and associated congestion being an important contributory factor. By 2018, this decline had prompted 'March4Tipp' demonstrations on the Main Street, attended by around 5,000, with the not unintended effect of bringing traffic on the N24 to a halt. Tipperary has become a high-profile example of the decline of medium-sized country towns in the national media.

These problems might have been reduced if the new route of the N24 had been capable of incremental implementation, allowing urgent sections to be constructed first. A new route which crossed or came close to the existing N24 on either side of Tipperary would have allowed the new section bypassing the town to reconnect with the existing N24 on each side of it. An incremental option could have been treated as the 'coverage-friendly' one, and its merits could have been compared with the second-round options considered in 2000, and the preferred one in 2001. It might or might not have performed well, but at least an alternative which did not lock the Tipperary area into an all-or-nothing solution would have been explicitly evaluated.

A second opportunity to apply an incremental approach arose in the fresh design process undertaken in 2021. There was worthwhile political support for this. Tipperary County Council unanimously passed a motion in May 2021, calling both for the overall N24 scheme to be

Figure 4.2 N24 Improvement Preferred Routes (2001 and 2022)

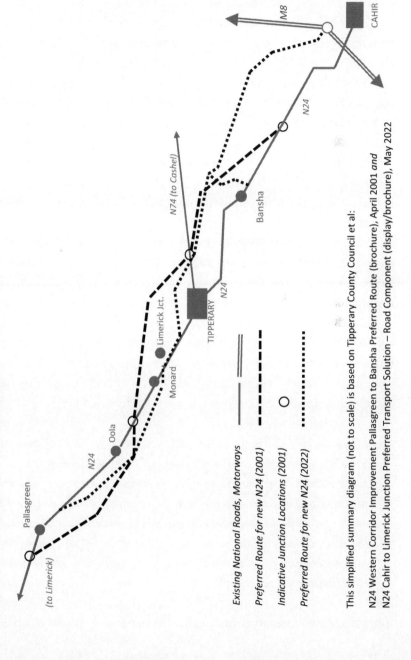

Existing National Roads, Motorways

Preferred Route for new N24 (2001)

Indicative Junction Locations (2001)

Preferred Route for new N24 (2022)

This simplified summary diagram (not to scale) is based on Tipperary County Council et al:

N24 Western Corridor Improvement Pallasgreen to Bansha Preferred Route (brochure), April 2001 and N24 Cahir to Limerick Junction Preferred Transport Solution – Road Component (display/brochure), May 2022 brought forward, and for the section bypassing Tipperary town to be prioritised within that scheme, and Transport Minister Eamon Ryan was quoted as being in favour of building a bypass for Tipperary town first, with this connecting to other improved sections later (*The Irish Times*, 4 October 2021).

These calls seem to have had limited effect. The new preferred route announced in May 2022 still requires around 25 kilometres of new road to be constructed in order to bypass Tipperary town, as the section south east of it does not cross the existing N24 at any point[28] (see Figure 4.2).

(2) *The Cork-Limerick motorway: Uncosted and coverage-friendly options*

Evaluating a coverage-friendly option has to involve comparison of its costs with those of alternatives. Phase 1 of the evaluation process on the proposed new N/M20 motorway connecting Cork and Limerick resumed in 2020 (as in Tipperary, a previous design process had been suspended in 2011), and included several coverage-friendly options, but this was of little value, because they were eliminated prior to any discussion of costs. Phase 1 involved subjecting seven new road route options to a Multi-Criteria Analysis (MCA), with the use of this technique being justified on the basis that it was identified in:

> the Department of Transport Common Appraisal Framework as being required in establishing preferences by reference to an explicit set of objectives. It is particularly suited to larger transport projects where there is a range of potential beneficiaries and where benefits can be both quantitative and qualitative. In the MCA process, project objectives are determined ... in advance of identifying alternative solutions. The analysis is then based on appraising the performance against the objectives, so that overall best performing scenarios can be determined. (Barry et al., 2020, p. 1)

The M20 MCA scored these options in accordance with six generic criteria:

Figure 4.3 Limerick – Cork Motorway, Phase 1 Options (A-G), 2020

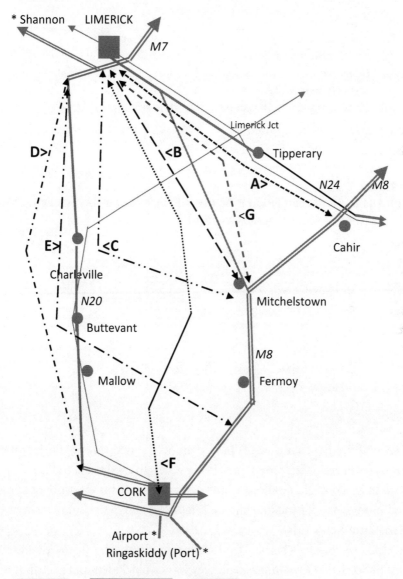

Existing Roads, Dual Carriageways, Motorways, Rail lines

This simplified summary diagram (not to scale) is based on Barry Transportation *et al* 'N/M Cork to Limerick Road Improvement Scheme, Phase 1 Multi Criteria Analysis', Feb. 2020, Figures 1–7.

(1) Economy objectives (including connectivity, reliability and regional growth)
(2) Safety
(3) Environment (including length of new road required)
(4) Social inclusion (benefits to deprived urban area)
(5) Integration with other objectives (including sustainable development and planning policy)
(6) Physical activity (walking and cycling opportunities in towns)

These criteria were applied to the new road route options listed in Table 4.2, and shown in Figure 4.3.

TABLE 4.2

OPTIONS EVALUATED IN PHASE 1 OF THE MULTI-CRITERIA ANALYSIS REPORT ON THE N/M20 PROJECT (FEBRUARY 2020)

Scenario	Road:	From	To	Length	Time*
A	Spur NW from M8	Cahir	Limerick (SE edge)	54 km	88 mins
B	Spur NW from M8	Mitchelstown	Limerick (SE edge)	53 km	71 mins
C	Spur NW from M8	Mitchelstown	Limerick (SW edge)	57 km	73 mins
D	Cork to Limerick	Cork (NW edge)	Limerick (SW edge)	80 km	64 mins
E	Spur NW from M8	Fermoy	Limerick (SW edge)	73 km	78 mins
F	Cork to Limerick (with spur to M8)	Cork (N edge)	Limerick (SE edge)	105 km	68 mins
G	Spur NW from M8	Mitchelstown	Limerick (SE edge)	54 km	73 mins

* Travel time by car between Cork and Limerick city centres

The 'preferred' scenario was (D), chosen on the basis of shorter journey times; fewer accidents; provision of better access to and greater traffic reductions in Mallow, Charleville and Buttevant; more benefits for deprived areas and more scope for walking and cycling there; and better connectivity to Kerry and West Cork.

The question of whether these secondary advantages justify the extra cost of Scenario D was not asked. Cost was not included under 'economy objectives' or referred to elsewhere in the MCA, even though Scenario D involves a route 50% longer than the shortest alternative (B). Instead, the Phase 1 MCA was treated as conclusive, and all the shorter route scenarios

(A–C, G) were excluded from further consideration in Phase 2 of the consultation process: 'The MCA framework demonstrates the best performing road based scenario is Scenario D. The preferred road based scheme and the two rail based scenarios will be carried forward to Phase 2 Option Selection.'

The comparisons in Phase 1 would be more realistic if options were packaged to include complementary improvements they made necessary – and economies they made possible – elsewhere. M8 plus spur options could be combined with local bypasses for Buttevant and Charleville, making them more comparable with Scenario D, with fewer accidents and more scope for walking and cycling in those towns. The MCA emphasised Scenario D's role in improving access to Cork Airport and Port, so it should be packaged with the higher standard Cork northern ring road needed to achieve this,[29] which spur options would not need.

In the Phase 2 public participation exercise launched in November 2020, the options to be considered were confined to the Cork–Mallow–Charleville–Limerick corridor, with the main ones being six alternative alignments of the same route. New options were also introduced at that stage, including a new rail spur, and 'targeted' local improvements to the existing N20 ('T1'). The inclusion of the latter may reflect the increase in the anticipated cost of a Cork–Limerick motorway, from €8–900 million in 2010, to almost three times as much in 2021.[30]

The 'preferred route' announced in March 2022 was a version of Scheme D – an 80-km motorway or dual carriageway from Cork to Limerick, 30–40% of which would involve upgrading of the existing N20,[31] with the rest running parallel to it. The scope, cost and potential support for the scheme are increased by including proposals for an 80-km cycleway to run alongside the new road, and a direct hourly rail service between Cork and Limerick, which avoids the need to change at Limerick Junction.

Recent press comments from the design team have emphasised the high accident rate on the N20. Motorways are much safer than two lane inter-urban roads, because they separate opposing vehicle movements and different types of road user, and have no frontage access. A spur NW from Mitchelstown would not pass close to any substantial intermediate town, so traffic volumes on it would be low enough to avoid a need for it to be a motorway, and possibly low enough to be consistent with a 2+1 road. A purpose built[32] 2+1 spur road would segregate opposing flows and would not allow frontage access or right turns, like a motorway, with similar safety advantages. In combination with the M8, a motorway or 2+1 spur would provide a fully segregated route between Cork and Limerick. Partial segregation for more local traffic on the existing N20 corridor could be achieved by bypasses to Charleville and Buttevant.

There are thus coverage-friendly alternatives to the Cork–Mallow–Limerick motorway option. While the safety benefits of the latter might be greater once it was in full operation,[33] this could happen considerably later than it would for a less expensive option. If so, somewhat lower eventual accident rates may have to be balanced against higher ones in the intervening period.

Interaction between Examples 1 and 2: A grouped approach to transport projects

High-cost versions of large projects in the same general area are more likely to be in competition with each other for funding or priority. In a 2017 submission to the NPF, Tipperary County Council argued for an M24 to connect Limerick, Waterford and Cork, with Cork being connected to the first two via the M8 and a junction with the M24 at Cahir. The submission estimated the M24 by itself would cost €1.02 billion, but if the N20, N25 and N24 (shown diagrammatically on Figure 4.4) were all replaced by motorways, this would cost a total of €2.75 billion. Costs of up to €1.7 billion could thus be avoided, or at any rate deferred.

As with the 'spur NW from Mitchelstown' scenarios in Table 4.2, this proposal reduces motorway length by 'canalisation', which combines more than one inter-city movement on a single motorway, and accepts less direct routes. However, this principle does not necessarily lead to the conclusion favoured by Tipperary County Council. If routes to the three Munster cities converged at Mitchelstown rather than Cahir, this would

Figure 4.4 Possible Canalisation of Inter-Urban routes in Munster

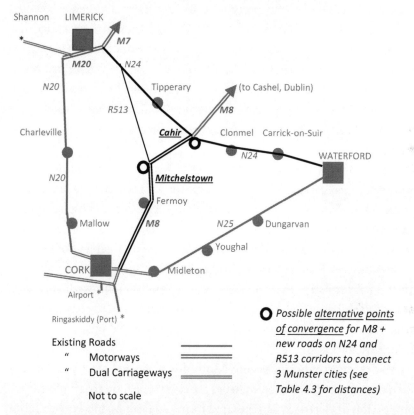

result in aggregate diversion from the most direct routes between them being less, and more evenly shared, as Table 4.3 shows:

TABLE 4.3

DISTANCES BETWEEN MUNSTER CITIES BY EXISTING AND POSSIBLE FUTURE ROUTES

Corridors:	Existing routes (km)	Via connection at Cahir		Via connection at Mitchelstown	
		Km	Extra distance	Km	Extra distance
Cork–Limerick	103	144	+41	110	+7
Limerick–Waterford	126	126	0	150	+24
Waterford–Cork	129	146	+17	146	+17
Total extra distance			+58		+48

Either version assumes substantial lengthening of journeys is acceptable in terms of increased energy use, and realistic in terms of driver behaviour. This is most likely to be the case for a Cork–Mitchelstown–Limerick route, as it involves the least extra distance. The extra mileage is greatest for a Cork–Limerick route via Cahir, and a Limerick–Waterford route via Mitchelstown, and these are also the routes where the diversion is concentrated at the Limerick end of the route, making it more likely that drivers will remain on existing, much more direct routes for that part of their journey.

Both versions also assume the three cities have to be connected by motorway, and that new inter-urban motorways will remain acceptable in the medium term. This cannot be taken for granted, as higher speeds on motorways lead to more energy use and generate extra traffic, relative to other types of road, and these negative effects may carry more weight in the future. A Dutch court decided to impose a speed limit of 90 km/hr on their motorways in 2019, in order to keep emissions within legal limits. If this happened in Ireland, trying to keep actual speeds on freshly built motorways well below their design speeds would be a self-inflicted enforcement nightmare.

The extra greenhouse gas emissions arising from use of a motorway should gradually fall as more vehicles are electrically powered and a higher proportion of electricity is generated from renewables. However, a lot of emissions are 'embodied' in new structures, particularly ones which rely heavily on energy-intensive materials such as steel and concrete. While there are difficulties in estimating the amount of embodied carbon in infrastructure projects, it is estimated to be 30–40% of the expected whole-life emissions of recent Irish buildings (Hegarty *et al*, 2022, p. 6, 10, 19, 30–32). Large, expensive infrastructure projects are likely to embody more carbon than more compact, lower cost ones, and these embodied emissions will mostly be upfront. It is worth trying to minimise them. In the period to 2030, Hegarty *et al* (2022, p. 36) consider that 'embodied emissions from proposed national development would overwhelm savings in operational emissions'.

(3) Metrolink/LUAS & the Queuing of Dublin Rail Projects

Dublin has quite a long history of rail schemes which have remained wholly or partly unimplemented due to the economic cycle. The Dublin Rapid Rail Transit Study (DRRTS, 1975) recommended an underground system connecting up the four existing rail lines which converge on central Dublin, but the recession of the 1980s meant the only part implemented was electrification of the existing coastal railway, renamed the DART. Adjusting to slower growth, the Dublin Transport Initiative (DTI, 1993) recommended three light rail lines, but growth then speeded up enough in the mid-1990s to create doubts about whether on-street sections of the LUAS system would have enough capacity. A mostly underground metro line was then proposed, instead of the LUAS connection through the city centre and on to Ballymun, Dublin Airport and Swords planned by the DTI. 'Metro North' received approval from An Bord Pleanála in 2011, but was immediately suspended due to the economic crisis. As the economy recovered, public participation on a revised version of this scheme (rechristened 'Metrolink') restarted in 2018.

The metro proposal re-emerged in the 'Fingal/North Dublin Transport Study (AECOM, 2014, 2015). Discussion of this study may seem somewhat academic at this stage, as the €2.3 – €3 billion estimates of the cost of a metro in it have been replaced by the €9.5 billion one cited in the Preliminary Business Case for Metrolink, published in July 2022.[34] However, this 2015 study was the point at which a metro proposal was readopted, and other light or heavy rail-based alternatives rejected, and subsequent development of the Metrolink project has developed from that recommendation.

The first stage of this study examined 25 possible schemes – heavy rail, light rail, and bus rapid transit – of which four survived for appraisal in the second stage. The cost of the option derived from Metro North, having initially been costed at €2.5–3 billion, was then 'optimised' by reducing capacity to 12,000 per hour in each direction, shortening platforms, and bringing a previously tunnelled section between DCU and Dublin Airport above ground.[35]

By contrast, its light and heavy rail competitors, initially costed at
€0.5–1.05 and €1.2–1.5 billion respectively, had become more expensive
in the second stage, at €2.24 and €1.83 billion, and similar to the optimised metro (€2.33bn). Their cost advantage having largely been
removed, cost benefit analysis showed they had negative net benefits,
while the optimised metro one had strongly positive ones (AECOM,
2015, pp. 49, 51, 55, 124, 134, 157, 164).

The light rail option ('LR3') followed much the same route as the
metro north of the city centre, before connecting into the recently
extended LUAS Green Line in Cabra. Its cost doubled between stages one
and two of the study, mainly because it was decided that a 2.5 km section
would need to be in tunnel in the city centre. Leaving it on street would
limit trams to a three-minute maximum frequency, which would leave
no spare capacity by 2033 (AECOM, 2015, pp. 108–22). The changes to
the metro and light rail options between the first and the second stage of
the study are summarised in Figure 4.5.

However, a coverage-friendly option is as much in need of optimisation as the preferred one. As with the metro option, this can be done by
aligning economically achievable capacity more closely with demand. The
light rail option has barely adequate capacity in city centre sections, but
this could be coped with by several different forms of load sharing:

(a) A segregated, limited access route between Swords, the Airport and
the city centre already exists – the Port Access tunnel – and is already
well used by buses connecting them. It would not be difficult to balance use of this existing route with that on a LUAS one, by
periodically adjusting services and access controls on the tunnel.

(b) The reduction in the interval between trams from one every two minutes possible in largely segregated suburban sections to one every
three minutes in largely on-street city centre ones can be avoided by
splitting the line at the point where it enters the latter, with the
second line running a short distance into the centre. Many urban rail

Figure 4.5 Options from Fingal/North Dublin Transport Study (2014–15)

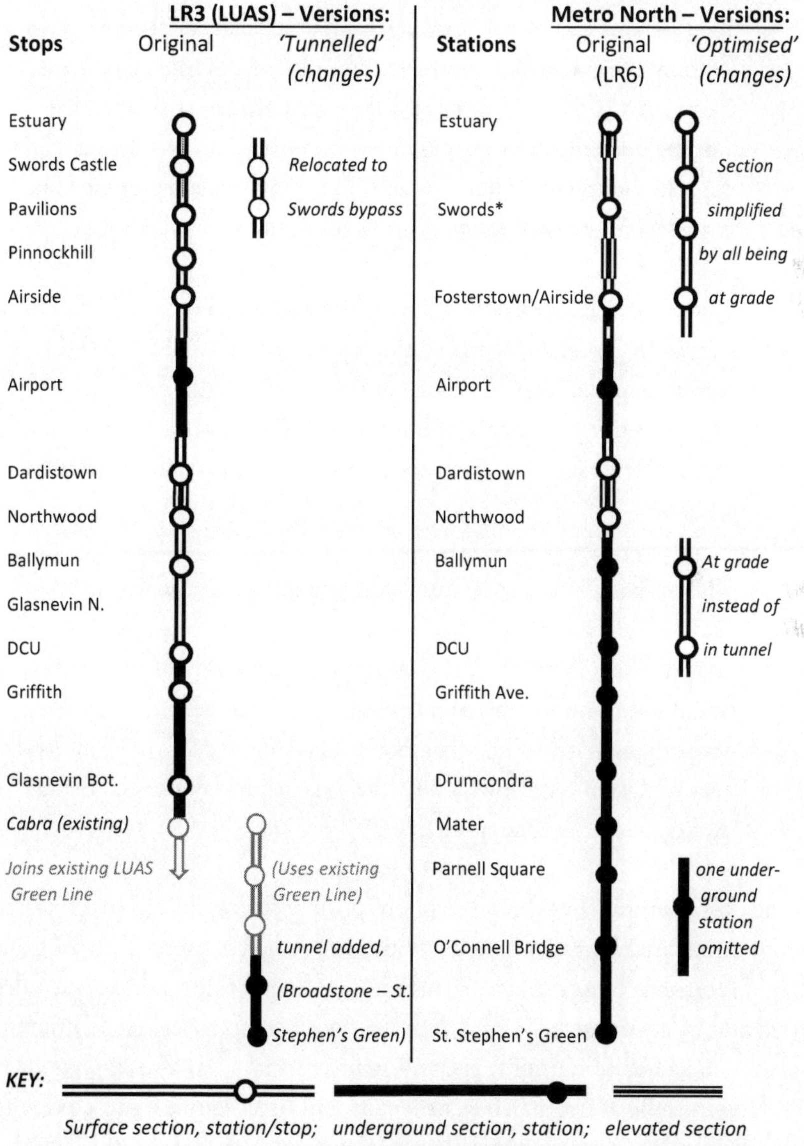

Stops	LR3 (LUAS) – Versions:		Stations	Metro North – Versions:	
	Original	*'Tunnelled'* *(changes)*		Original *(LR6)*	*'Optimised'* *(changes)*
Estuary			Estuary		
Swords Castle		*Relocated to*			*Section*
Pavilions		*Swords bypass*	Swords*		*simplified*
Pinnockhill					*by all being*
Airside			Fosterstown/Airside		*at grade*
Airport			Airport		
Dardistown			Dardistown		
Northwood			Northwood		
Ballymun			Ballymun		*At grade*
Glasnevin N.					*instead of*
DCU			DCU		*in tunnel*
Griffith			Griffith Ave.		
Glasnevin Bot.			Drumcondra		
Cabra (existing)			Mater		
Joins existing LUAS Green Line		*(Uses existing Green Line)*	Parnell Square		*one under-ground station*
		tunnel added,	O'Connell Bridge		*omitted*
		(Broadstone – St.			
		Stephen's Green)	St. Stephen's Green		

KEY: Surface section, station/stop;   underground section, station;   elevated section

* AECOM (2014, Fig. 3.7) shows Metro North with 3 stations N. of the Airport, but lists 4 (p. 51)

This simplified summary diagram is based on AECOM 'Fingal/North Dublin Transport Study' Appraisal Reports, Stage 1 (Nov. 2014), Figure 3.7, Stage 2 (June 2015), Figures 8.2, 8.12, 8.17.

services work on the terminus principle, with some passengers walking further to reach their final destination. Unlike a rail terminus, a light rail one need not take up any more space than a normal stop. In Dublin, the green line served such a terminus (at St Stephen's Green) from 2003 to 2017. While the difference between two- and three-minute frequencies may seem minor, it represents a 50% increase in capacity (30 trams per hour instead of 20). Splitting the proposed line could avoid the need to put it into a tunnel under the city centre.

(c)   Direct interchange between the light rail option and the rail lines to Connolly and Docklands could be provided for. AECOM's LR3 option requires a double change at Broombridge and Cabra (2015, p. 101), but few passengers would do this. More would do so with a direct interchange, diverting some passengers from trams in the city centre.

(d)   The proposed 3000-space park-and-ride garage on the M1 north of Swords is large enough to affect the balance between capacity and demand on a light rail line, and could be scaled back. Arguably this should be done anyway, as it will encourage 'rail heading' – making those living north of Dublin more inclined to drive down the motorway to the park-and-ride facility, and less inclined to use existing rail stations closer to their homes.

While the methods by which the metro option was reselected in 2015 may seem questionable, many people would nevertheless prefer it to a LUAS based alternative on capacity grounds.[36] Transport demand is not fully predictable, and a metro would definitely not become overloaded quickly, whereas a LUAS line might, even allowing for (a) – (d) above.

However, looking at the choice in isolation misses the coverage dimension. This can be viewed at different geographical levels. At the most local level, in the Swords–Airport–City centre corridor itself, the third LUAS line recommended by the DTI would have opened at the same time as the other two, around 2004, if a metro-based solution had not been preferred. If Metrolink opens in, say, 2034, there will have been a 30-year period in which the corridor's need for a rail-based form of public transport could have been covered, but wasn't. The risk of this situation continuing is greater with the metro option, as it is more vulnerable to a future cyclical downturn than a LUAS one would be.

If we look at transport coverage within the Dublin area as a whole, the Greater Dublin Transport Strategy (GDTS) 2022–2042 contains (NTA, 2022, pp. 150, 158–9, 161) an explicit queue, in the form of a post-2042 phase. Metrolink, as the largest pre-2042 component of the strategy, is a prime factor preventing coverage of the needs addressed by the post-2042 projects by the strategy proper. The queue includes eight additional LUAS lines, and also the DART+ Tunnel (previously known as the DART underground) connecting the northern half of the existing DART to Heuston station. This latter project has arguably been in a queue since 1975, when it was recommended by the DRRTS, and more definitely so since 2010, when it received planning consent.

The DART+ tunnel has been seen as competing with Metrolink, as they are both very large and expensive projects, and funding sufficient to allow both to proceed in parallel is unlikely. However, the DART+ tunnel and a LUAS line to Swords probably could both be accommodated within the funding implied by[37] the GDTS, allowing both to be operational for most of the middle third of the 21st century. Metrolink may thus limit coverage at this level as well.

This could have wider implications. The DART+ tunnel would overcome the main barriers to the fuller use of the Kildare and Maynooth lines, namely the position of Heuston station well outside Dublin's central business district, and the inability of the elevated line south of Connolly station to cope both with existing services on it, and a major increase in the frequency of trains from Maynooth. It would allow full realisation of the benefits of converting the Maynooth and Kildare lines to electrified DART operation under the DART+ component of the GDTS.

These corridors serve large developable areas, including SDZs at Adamstown, Clonburris and Hansfield, and are thus more strongly related to Dublin's housing capacity problem than Metrolink, which mainly serves areas which are already built up. Most development land west of Dublin is not seen as particularly upmarket, making land values there are more reasonable, but also reducing developers' interest in it. The DART+ programme and DART+ tunnel would convert the four radial rail lines converging on central Dublin into a completed system which facilitated movement to and through the city centre from all of them, and inclusion of the Kildare and Maynooth lines in this system could fully unlock underused potential in areas west of the city. When first introduced, the DART and LUAS greatly stimulated development in the areas they served.

In principle, the coverage effects of high-cost options on infrastructure provision should be viewed mainly at national level, but – as noted earlier – this has little political traction, due to the difficulty of identifying which infrastructure needs in which places at which times may be left unmet as a result. Coverage effects would be particularly serious, if the state became inextricably committed to a project as large as Metrolink immediately before a major economic downturn.

APPLYING COVERAGE-FRIENDLY OPTIONS

The common feature of the three examples cited above is that they involve option selection processes which neutralise the issue of cost, thereby facilitating a recommendation in favour of the most expensive one. The MCA process used for the N/M20 project achieved this simply by not including construction costs, while the Fingal/North Dublin Transport Study did this more elaborately by comparing a version of the metro with low-cost features (abandoned once that option had been readopted) with a high-cost version of the light rail option. The purpose of these examples is to show how conventional evaluation of options may prematurely exclude coverage-friendly options. Box 4.4 suggests ways in which this can be avoided.

Box 4.4 Parallel Development of Coverage-friendly Options

Projects usually start from a basic aim to be achieved, or problem to be solved. At this initial stage, the question 'What if funding for this project is substantially less than currently anticipated and/or the cost of the type of option most likely to be selected?' needs to be asked, to ensure that the initial long list of options includes lower-cost ones.

If subdivision of the project so that it addresses urgent needs first is possible, as in the Tipperary example, this can prompt an option which times its parts to match projected need.

Coverage-friendly options are likely to involve achieving the basic aim with a narrower range of secondary benefits, or less capacity, or a lower level of service than other options. If tested against higher-cost options on the basis of secondary benefits, as in the M20 MCA, they are likely to perform less well, and if modified to meet a specified capacity requirement, this may remove their cost advantage, as in the case of the North Dublin light rail option.

However, a coverage-friendly option needs to survive until the end of the selection process so that it can be compared with the preferred option, to see if it is worth paying the extra costs associated with the latter in order to obtain its extra benefits. If the coverage-friendly option or its cost advantage is eliminated at an earlier stage, this question never gets asked.

So, in addition to processing options in the normal way, a parallel work stream is suggested, to select an option which achieves the basic aim of the project at or close to minimum cost, and which achieves most in other respects, subject to that constraint. Both should take account of off-site works they make necessary or unnecessary, so that the process ends with a realistic comparison of preferred and cost-friendly packages.

The support given to high-cost projects by local interest groups and politicians might be less overwhelming if schemes of this type were not the only option realistically on offer, and if it was clearer that lower-cost alternatives might be implemented much sooner.

COVERAGE AND ECONOMIC WELFARE

At present, evaluation of options is designed to lead to selection of the most economically beneficial one, most usually measured via cost benefit analysis (CBA). CBA includes 'social' costs and benefits, which the operator of the facility does not charge for. CBA became widely used, particularly for transport projects, as it allowed reductions in travel time and road accidents, which were not reflected in revenues to the project operator, nevertheless to count as benefits which could outweigh construction and other costs. Early CBAs in the UK were carried out in the 1960s for the London–Birmingham motorway (the M1) and the Victoria Underground line. Social benefits in the latter case included reduced traffic congestion due to diversion of journeys from the road system to the Victoria line.

The aim of CBA is to maximise economic welfare (in this specialised sense), but this is not the same as maximising the coverage of infrastructure needs. Maximising the contribution to economic welfare makes no distinction between meeting primary needs, and securing secondary advantages in the way this is done. The contribution to economic welfare is measured by net benefits, and these will typically be greater for a high-cost, high-benefit project than for a lower-cost, lower-benefit one. By contrast, coverage is maximised by meeting primary needs – the basic objective of projects – at as low a financial cost as is reasonably practicable.

MCA also aims to maximise benefits – including social and environmental ones – but it measures them in a more qualitative manner, favouring options which provide a wide range of secondary advantages. This is also not the same as maximising coverage of infrastructure needs. There is a distributional choice, between aiming for the greatest benefits, one project at a time, thereby concentrating them around the limited number which can be afforded on that basis, or seeking more widely shared benefits via a larger number of lower-cost projects.

To increase general awareness of this choice, and to give a coverage-friendly option a high profile in each specific case, it and the preferred option could be summarised and compared at the end of the selection process. This comparison could be published, and included in the preliminary and final business cases submitted under the Department of Public Expenditure and Reform's public spending code (DPER, 2019, pp. 28–46), and in the Environmental Impact Assessment Report.[38] This prominence would make it less likely the coverage-friendly option would be weakly formulated, procedurally disabled, or offer only minimal savings than if it was buried deep within a long, iterative evaluation process, as is often the case at present. Its credibility would become important to the credibility of the selection process as a whole.

The comparison should show why the preferred option has higher net benefits, what these consist of in operational and other terms, and the extra cost involved. Financial and economic comparisons should include:

(i)   Capital cost: This is a crude basis for comparison, but is necessary information, and it should not be too misleading if it is supplemented by (ii)–(iv) below.[39]

(ii)   Financial Net Present Value (FNPV): Expenditure on and income from the project can be converted to present-day values, using a discount rate (e.g. 5%). Once expected future financial flows are put on a common basis in this way, their net present value can be calculated. FNPV is a more comprehensive guide to financial effects than (i) as it takes account of subsequent operating costs and revenues. It also facilitates comparison of alternatives which incur costs and become operational at different times.

(iii) Economic Net Present Value (ENPV): This measure is calculated in the same way as (ii), but includes benefits and costs which are not reflected in expenditure on the project or revenues to its operator. Public infrastructure projects which are not fully funded by user charges typically have a positive ENPV (economic benefits exceed economic costs) but a negative FNPV (financial costs exceed financial revenues).

(iv) Economic Benefit Cost Ratio (EBCR): This alternative to (iii) expresses aggregate benefits as a proportion of aggregate costs, whereas ENPV expresses net aggregate benefits (i.e. benefits minus costs) as an absolute amount. ENPV favours high-cost options, in situations where their benefits are a lower proportion of costs than for an alternative option, but their net benefits, in absolute terms, are higher.

The object of this comparison would be to identify cases in which coverage-friendly options performed well enough to represent a realistic alternative to preferred ones. Where they did, this would increase flexibility, which could be useful in circumstances where cost or timing issues were particularly important. This flexibility could be sought on a top-down basis, e.g. if a central government department or funding agency needed to make limited resources go further, or on a bottom-up one, e.g. if a local authority was willing to settle for a more modest scheme, if this allowed it to be brought forward and completed earlier.

COVERAGE AND CYCLICALITY

This flexibility could be useful in a variety of contexts. Where the policy context is changing, for instance due to the requirement that road schemes should not account for more than one third of state transport investment introduced after the 2020 election, it offers a way of meeting more road needs within a more limited capital envelope. In cyclical downturns, it would be a way of continuing to meet a reasonably wide range of infrastructure needs despite reduced resources, or, in conditions of economic uncertainty, if a stronger than normal guarantee that a particular project would actually go ahead was needed. It could also reduce the risk of an integrated local or sub-regional strategy being brought to a halt by the inability to fund an essential component, without which other components cannot operate effectively.

It may seem obvious that the state's capital and other expenditure is constrained for much of the economic cycle, and that committing to high-cost projects in these circumstances may delay them, or other more mundane but more necessary ones. However, awareness of this is anything but automatic, and does little to inhibit the flow of ambitious proposals. Actually funding and implementing them is more problematic, but the flow of announcements creates a climate in which governments are lambasted for delivering too little rather than for promising too much, and to which they sometimes respond by promising even more. Awareness of likely future costs in competing areas such as housing, health and pensions does little to dampen this tendency.

Greater openness to lower cost options, and greater willingness to move away from previously preferred ones to maintain coverage of infrastructure needs, may conflict with the 'need to increase certainty and visibility of the pipeline of projects' to provide the construction industry 'with confidence to invest and individuals with the opportunity to choose a career in the built environment' cited in the 2021–30 NDP (p. 175). However, increased certainty for consumers and businesses in other sectors (on whether and when their infrastructure needs will be met) may be more important than producer certainty (on how they will be met).

Keynesian arguments are sometimes advanced in favour of ambitious infrastructure programmes and high-cost projects. For instance, the review of the 2018–27 NDP was undertaken by the incoming coalition government in late 2020, on the basis that this was an ideal time to invest in 'a larger, more ambitious plan'.[40] In view of the reduction in demand due to the Covid-19 pandemic, this might indeed have been an ideal time from a Keynesian perspective to 'ramp up capital investment' and realise its multiplier effects, but this need is unlikely to apply to the entire decade to 2030. Even in the interval between those comments and the publication of the revised NDP a year later, the case for stimulus had been replaced by concerns that the NDP might be too pro-cyclical. It is not easy to match needs for economic stimulus which may be variable or relatively short term with ambitious long-term capital programmes, as later parts of these programmes may coincide with periods in which a Keynesian approach would point in the opposite direction.

This was the experience in the period when Keynesian ideas were dominant. Hillebrandt (1985, pp. 17–18) considered that:

> *One of the difficulties in the management of the economy is the problem of timing the action by government so that the effects ... occur at the correct time to achieve the desired objective. The lags in the construction process tend to be long and very variable ... Unless the government can foresee problems very far in advance, the effect will be slow to be useful at the beginning of the period and the major effect will come later, perhaps at a time when the contrary effect is required.*

In practice, public capital investment in Ireland rises when conditions allow, and falls when unfavourable conditions require this, without much real regard for Keynesian theory. The 2018–27 NDP proposed (p. 18) that public capital investment would average 4% of Gross National Income (GNI) for the 2022–7 period, but the revised 2021–30 one has increased (p. 43) this to 6%.[41] This mainly reflects the improvement in the current and expected state of the public finances, and, to a lesser extent, the urgency of the housing problem.

Creating a public investment fund, to ensure infrastructure projects could still proceed in a downturn, will not necessarily improve the balance between adopted projects and the funds to implement them. To some extent, it will reinforce belief in the practicability of high-cost options. It is unrealistic to expect public investment to operate on the ratchet principle and change in one direction only. When it does fall, the construction industry as well as the rest of society may benefit, if the response is increased reliance on lower-cost options, rather than planning on many projects being suspended completely.

156

Also, decisions on the economically appropriate level of capital expenditure in any particular period are only loosely related to decisions on the composition of such expenditure. The connection between ambitious programmes and ambitious projects involves associative reasoning, unless the desired volume of investment would be difficult to achieve without extensive reliance on the latter. Investment in ambitious projects can also be less effective as an economic stimulus if much of it is absorbed by property costs, or it is very capital intensive.

From the late 1950s, there has also been a belief that infrastructure investment should be concentrated in the areas with the greatest economic potential, even if this leads to project queuing elsewhere. However, policies reflecting this view have, in practice, led to extensive project queuing, even in the metropolitan areas where it would imply a need to meet needs promptly.

INTERDEPENDENCE OF PROJECTS

While the first part of this chapter emphasised the interdependence of different types of infrastructure at local level, as a means of making development possible, the second part was more concerned with how options are chosen for individual non-local projects. Circumstances in which non-local projects are closely interdependent do, however, arise quite frequently, and their coordination is – as at local level – complicated by the compartmentalisation of the Irish public sector. Possible responses to this are suggested in the discussion of regional policy in Chapter 6.

CHAPTER 5

CYCLICAL INTERVENTION IN THE OUTPUT MIX

Summary: Governments intervene in construction output most at two stages in the cycle. In troughs, they promote new construction products, as markets for the ones that dominated the previous cycle are saturated, and the methods used to promote them discredited. In late recovery or boom phases, such as the late 1970s, housing affordability becomes a problem, leading to interventions to slow price rises, and increase people's ability to pay. Social housing output also peaks at the end of a boom, and this led to oversupply and an output collapse in the 1980s. It could become less pro-cyclical if policy reacted more quickly to tightening and loosening in the housing market.

Urban renewal tax reliefs introduced in 1986 shaped the next cycle. By the late 1990s, incentives were overused, and the government had also lost control of house prices. It tried to regain it through the Bacon reports, but they were commissioned too late, and their demand-side measures reversed too early. More permanent measures, varied in line with the cycle, in ways announced in advance, might avoid this. A suggestion on promoting smaller units in Bacon II may be worth reviving, in a revised form, e.g. by varying taxes more, in line with the size and cost of units.

House building collapsed after 2008, leading to dependence on private rented housing in the most recent cycle. Governments encouraged international investment in it through tax concessions, relaxing controls on apartment size, quality and height, and by facilitating 'build to rent' and 'shared living' projects. From 2016 on, affordability was addressed by a help-to-buy scheme and rent controls in some areas. Incentives for the private rented sector could usefully be targeted more selectively, on lower rent, longer lasting tenancies. The social housing actually provided under the 2016–21 Rebuilding Ireland programme was mostly turnkey units bought from developers, and this will also apply to the more ambitious targets in Housing for All (2021–26), unless there is a major increase in local authority designed/ contractor-built units.*

This chapter continues the sequence illustrated in Figure 3.1, and deals with the construction and disposal of buildings, once a site for them has been acquired, and local infrastructure provided for them. Once these are in place, provision of new buildings depends on a conjunction of interested parties: developers to organise their construction, purchasers, investors or state agencies willing to pay for them, and users of the completed structures.

In Ireland, most new buildings are constructed by private sector developers. The resources needed, while summarised in the economist's standard list of factors of production – land, labour and capital – involve specific types of each: available, developable land; a range of construction skills and specialist contractors; and banks or other institutions to finance developments, and their purchase when completed. These factors are not necessarily freely available, and the loss of skilled labour, financial capacity and experienced developers after the crash of 2008 meant all were in short supply for a decade afterwards, and, to some extent, still are.

Private sector developers produce completed buildings for disposal through the property market. While the volume of development is largely determined by the level of demand in the national economy, the mix of construction industry products is shaped mainly by the ability, willingness and volume of different types of purchaser and user to pay for them, as the bids those producing them can make for the resources required are limited by what buildings can be sold or rented for.[1] If the capacity of the industry is limited by the scarcity of key inputs, this process determines which types of output are most affected.

A CYCLICALLY-PROMPTED PATTERN OF INTERVENTION

Governments intervene frequently to influence the mix or volume of construction output which results from market forces, and also to alter the pattern of publicly funded output they have inherited. These interventions include concerted initiatives prompted by problems characteristic of specific phases in the Irish construction cycle, which, to some extent, are repeated in successive cycles. Two recurring types of initiative have played a dominant role:

(a) Bottom of cycle/early recovery initiatives prompted by depressed conditions in the construction sector, and designed to kick-start a process of recovery (e.g. 1985–6, 2013–15). As the leading markets of the previous cycle are typically saturated, the methods used to promote them discredited, and the construction sector unusually open to product innovation at this stage (Lansley, 1991, p. 134; Hillebrandt et al., 1995, pp. 168–9), a new approach is needed. The formula underlying this new approach appears to be validated by the recovery, which reinforces government commitment to it, and ensures that the characteristic methods of intervention, and their land use and distributional consequences, persist for the rest of that particular cycle.

(b) Late recovery or boom phase initiatives, prompted by unusually acute capacity problems in the housing sector (to which the initiatives described in (a) may have contributed) and designed to restrain price rises and redirect output towards more affordable types of dwelling (1978–82, 1998–9, 2016+).

This chapter describes how such initiatives shaped the 1976–84 and 1985–2012 cycles, and are shaping the current (2013+) one. There is an element of repetition – in each cycle, a pragmatic and initially successful response to constraints at the bottom of the cycle runs into difficulties, partly because of a tendency to double down on the initial, apparently successful formula, but mainly because of the absence of any system for managing the cycle and anticipating demand surges in the housing market. Suggestions on the form such a system should take are included within the narrative account of the last 2½ cycles which follows.

These suggestions are not simply the wisdom of hindsight. We have to allow for the probability that the Irish economy will remain a highly cyclical one, and that characteristic problems associated with particular phases of the cycle will recur. Obviously, they will not recur in exactly the same form, so suggested solutions to the problems of previous cycles may smack of generals re-fighting the last war. However, the historical approach allows suggestions to be tested against real-world situations, albeit ones in the past.

It is also an antidote to the tendency to propose solutions to major problems in the current phase of the cycle, in isolation from previous and subsequent phases. This tendency is difficult to resist if the question is in the form 'What should we do now, in response to these current, very pressing problems?' as it almost always is. Some problems cannot be solved within a single phase of the cycle, and some attempts to do this have toxic after-effects in subsequent phases with quite different problems and characteristics.

A. GRANTS, DECENTRALISATION & SOCIAL HOUSING IN THE 1976–84 CYCLE

(i) **The 1975–6 trough**: Partly as a result of the 1973 oil crisis, there was a recession in the mid-1970s. The construction industry complained that the Fine Gael/Labour coalition government was dismissive of the adverse effects on the construction industry, discriminating against it and discouraging it by raising taxes, instead of promoting it through contra-cyclical measures.[2] The public capital programme was being cut,[3] new or increased taxes were being introduced, raising construction costs and damaging business confidence, while little was being done to stimulate construction demand.

While this trough was much milder than subsequent ones, it was sufficient to prompt proposals to promote recovery in the construction sector.

The prominent economist Brendan Walsh argued for this on Keynesian grounds:

> ... the response of those in charge of demand management to the externally caused recession of 1974/76 was to aggravate it by failing to expand the volume of output in the construction industry, the sector of the economy most sensitive to the level of government expenditure. The time is now opportune to ensure that this perverse type of demand management will not be repeated. (Walsh, 1977, p. 23)

This view was shared by the incoming Fianna Fail government (1977–81), in which another economics professor with Keynesian views (Martin O'Donoghue) was Minister for Economic Development and Planning. Walsh had drawn attention to demographic trends due to lead to large increases in the labour force in the 1980s. These also influenced O'Donoghue, who:

> diagnosed accurately enough the challenge facing the economy. His instinct that the cyclical recovery already under way would not provide a basis for the rate of development necessary to achieve full employment in the 1980s was correct. Not only could there be no going back to the slump of the mid-1970s. There could be no going back to the 'normalcy' of 1969–73 either, because that 'normalcy' was itself a variety of failure. (Lee, 1989, pp. 487–8)

Fianna Fail's 1977 election manifesto reflected this expansionist agenda in a politically effective form. It promised 'immediate abolition of [domestic] rates and of motor taxation as well as lump sum subsidies for first time house buyers' (Ibid., p. 483). Perhaps unintentionally, these three measures further stimulated the large-scale decentralisation of population already underway, encouraging movement out of inner-city areas and into new houses eligible for the £1,000 lump sum subsidy, in suburbs and commuter belts accessed by car. All three were also at the direct expense of the public finances, as they involved grants and tax reductions with immediate effect. These characteristics shaped the rest of the cycle, through the subsequent boom and downturn phases, until the start of the next cycle in the mid-1980s.

(ii) **Recovery and boom in the late 1970s:** As it happened, the stimulus to the construction sector in 1977 occurred at a point when the economy was already starting to recover from the recession for other reasons. As a result, the recovery phase was quickly replaced by a construction boom. One symptom of this was a housing market which was increasingly constrained by a shortage of mortgage finance. In August 1978, the government 'requested' the building societies to allocate 60% of their mortgage finance for mortgages of £13,000 or less, and a further 20% for mortgages of £13–16,000. They also asked building societies to insist on a Certificate of Reasonable Value (CRV) for all mortgages in both categories.[4]

The CIF argued that this intervention would do nothing to increase the supply of lower-priced houses and would create difficulties for builders with larger houses already under construction. Instead, it suggested a regulation requiring insurance companies and pension funds to invest 20% of their funds in the housing market (*Construction*, September 1978, p. 5). They later attributed a reduction in housing activity in the second half of 1978 partly to the uncertainty resulting from this intervention, which had upset the balance between first-time buyers and those trading up. They also saw the CRV system as counterproductive and as driving builders to the upper end of the market (*Construction*, June 1979, p. 4).

Despite this, the government's request to building societies was updated in August 1979, when they were asked to allocate 70% of funds to mortgages under £20,000, and 40% to first-time buyers.[5] In 1980, high interest rates led to a government subsidy to building societies, so they could offer competitive rates to depositors without raising mortgage rates.

Attempts at rationing were in parallel with the continued stimulation of housing and other construction markets, partly prompted by the pause in 1980–1, in which the market had no clear direction, leading to fears of a downturn. In response to this and to house price inflation, the £1,000 first-time buyers' grant was supplemented by a subsidy of up to £3,000 towards the first three years' mortgage repayments. The CIF also obtained government pledges to maintain the level of construction employment at December 1979 levels in 1980,[6] and to maintain the level of construction output in 1981, though by the end of that year they were questioning whether this would be honoured (*Construction*, December/January 1981/2, p. 5).

(iii) The Downturn in the early 1980s: The anticipated downturn took hold in 1982, and – as in the mid-1970s – led to recriminations between the construction industry and the government. The Public Capital Programme had reached an exceptionally high peak at over 14% of GNP in 1981–2, but fell steeply thereafter, to 12% in 1983, 9½ % in 1986, and 7% in 1988. The CIF accused the civil service of thinking the industry had previously reached an abnormal peak, and was now settling down to a more appropriate size,[7] and of creating '*an anti-investment climate*'.[8] The Minister for Finance responded to their criticisms of the 1983 budget by attacking them for 'sheer, naked self interest', saying that 'if I were a vindictive person, this would bias me against them'.

Initially, expenditure on social housing and other housing supports was unaffected by these cuts, and, in fact, increased. Output of new social housing units rose from c. 5,700 per annum in 1981 and 1982 to a peak of 7,000 in 1984. This was supplemented by a £5,000 'surrender grant' (available 1984–7) for local authority tenants who vacated a local authority house and bought a privately provided one instead. Around 7,700 households did this. These measures were partly in response to long waiting lists in the previous boom, and partly to help private house-builders dispose of unsold houses. The CIF acknowledged this, its president describing it as the only ray of light for a private housing sector facing complete collapse.[9]

These measures, in combination with resumption of large-scale emigration from 1984 on, produced a destabilising surplus of local authority housing. Despite reductions in output to around 5,500 new dwellings in 1986 and 3,000 in 1987, there was large-scale vacancy by then, with around 1,000 vacant local authority dwellings in Cork and Limerick cities. As a result, social housing was an obvious target for the policy of further public expenditure cuts pursued by the incoming Fianna Fáil government from 1987 on, and output fell to c. 1,500 units in 1988 and 750 in 1989. This was accompanied by extensive sales of existing local authority housing, through an exceptionally generous tenant purchase scheme introduced in 1988. As management and maintenance costs could exceed rental income, this could improve current balances, as well as providing a one-off capital sum. Over 30,000 local authority houses were bought by tenants between 1988 and 1991, 18,000 of these in 1989 alone.

The late 1980s have been seen as the point when 'the state walks away' from public housing (Ó Broin, 2019, pp. 47–52), by largely abolishing the 'property based welfare system which had slowly and incrementally been constructed over ... the preceding century' (Norris, 2016, p. 197), and shifting 'Irish housing policy towards commodification through financialisation and marketisation and the promotion of housing as a financialised asset' under the influence of neo-liberal ideas (Hearne, 2020, p. 120).

Cyclicality and Social Housing

While these are largely accurate descriptions of the longer-term consequences of the policy shift which occurred at the end of the 1980s, the social housing version of the economic cycle contributed to this shift. Figure 5.1(a) illustrates the cyclicality of social housing output, and Figure 5.1(b) expresses this as a percentage of the total number of households at the time.

The rise and fall of social housing in the 1980s were not isolated incidents, but part of a wider tendency for output to overreact to the economic cycle. Social housing had averaged 5,600 dwellings per annum between 1950 and 1958, but the economic crisis of the late 1950s led to a shift in general economic policy with the publication of 'Economic Development'. This diverted public investment away from social infrastructure, which was seen as having reached levels similar to those in comparable countries. Its author (T.K. Whitaker) had commented that housing was absorbing the same proportion of gross capital formation as agriculture, manufacturing and other construction put together (Norris, 2016, p. 145). In a departure from the high and sustained level of investment in social housing from the early 1930s, which had transformed housing conditions, output fell to a low point of 1,238 units in 1961.[10]

This led to a sense there was under-investment in social housing by the mid-1960s. The 1964 Housing White Paper considered there was an immediate need for an extra 50,000 houses, with a further 98,000 required by 1970, half of them social houses. In 1973, when social housing output was around 5,800, the incoming Minister for Local Government, James Tully, saw previous housing policy as half-hearted and inadequate and the housing situation as an emergency. As local authorities could not increase their output quickly, a parallel, supplementary construction programme was operated by the National Building Agency (NBA) (Ó Broin, 2019, pp. 36–7; Hearne, 2020, pp. 114–15). Output rose to a peak of 8,800 units in 1975, then fell gradually until 1981 before reaching a secondary peak of 7,000 in 1984.[11]

The reduction in output in the early 1960s reinforced a catch-up, crisis mentality on public housing from the mid-1960s onwards, which may have contributed to subsequent problems in the sector. New building technologies were seen as a way of increasing the rate of output quickly, sometimes with unfortunate results, as evidenced in the high-rise flats in Ballymun, and expensive-to-heat panel-clad construction instead of masonry walls in three NBA estates in Cork, which triggered a rent strike. The larger and more disastrous surge in high-rise social housing in Britain in the 1960s, prompted by a parallel desire to ramp up output,[12] damaged the image of public housing internationally. Many of the large Irish local authority housing estates which came to be seen as suffering from poor facilities and ghettoisation were built in the 1970s.[13]

While the dismantling of the social housing programme at the end of the 1980s may have been influenced by those ideologically opposed to it, and shaped by pragmatists who had limited belief in it and saw reducing the state's high level of debt as vital, the combination of oversupply in that decade, and accumulating problems on local authority estates built in the late 1960s and 1970s, nevertheless presented both with an open goal.

Over-reaction in the downward direction kept social housing output depressed until the 2002–8 period, when it recovered to the long-run average output of c. 0.4% of households. It collapsed again in 2010–16, and undersupply then helped produce an acute housing crisis, which has led to widespread calls for very large increases in social housing output.

Commenting on the pro-cyclical nature of investment in Irish public housing, Norris and Hayden (2018, pp. 6, 38, 55, 74, 94) pointed out that it concentrated new construction at times when costs were highest, and dispersed design teams when output collapsed in recessions. The latter point remains highly relevant. Although there is now widespread agreement on the need for a major increase in public housing output, it not clear that an essential preliminary – rebuilding of local authority design teams – is in fact occurring on the scale necessary. The obvious alternative – a further increase in purchases of new houses from private sector developers on a turnkey basis – is likely to lead to more crowding out of first-time buyers.

Norris and Hayden (2018, p. 88) also felt the risk that numerically ambitious housing targets will lead to mistakes has not gone away, quoting a Limerick Council official saying that when 'under pressure politically from your elected members to deliver housing numbers ... That's when rationality almost goes out the window. It's about delivering and being seen to deliver ...' They pose (p. 5) the question: 'Can a better way ... of funding council housing be identified which ensures that the

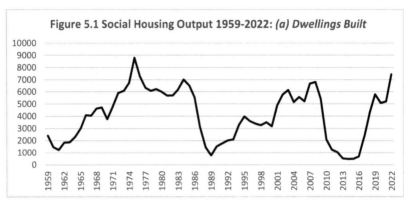

Figure 5.1 Social Housing Output 1959-2022: *(a) Dwellings Built*

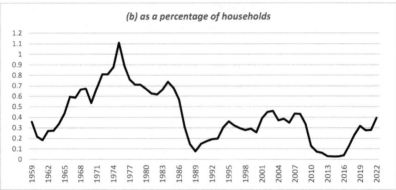

(b) as a percentage of households

Sources: Housing Agency, Historical Data series to 2010; Housing Agency/Department of Housing Social Housing Delivery series 2005–22, Census Housing Volumes and 2022 Preliminary Results

sector can deliver housing in a consistent fashion which avoids sharp peaks and troughs in supply?'

This question can be split into the desirability of more consistent output, and the need for a form of funding which would promote this, and would be accepted as 'off balance sheet' by Eurostat. Recent interest in cost rental housing[14] is partly based on the hope that it could be structured so as to meet the latter requirement.

On the first issue, the social housing programme is necessarily pro-cyclical, because of the cycle's effect on demography and household formation, but it is mistimed. Figure 5.2 shows the strong demographic

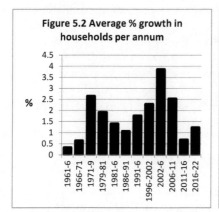

Figure 5.2 Average % growth in households per annum

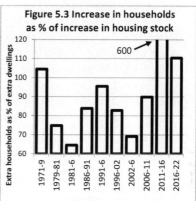

Figure 5.3 Increase in households as % of increase in housing stock

Sources: Fitzgerald (2005), Table 4, Census Housing Volumes, Preliminary Results of 2022 Census

basis for the output fluctuations in Figure 5.1, but in combination they show there is a time lag. Social housing output peaked a half decade or so after household growth, both in the 1977–88 cycle and in the and the 1989–2012 one, and it may do so again in the current one. This reflects the tendency for public sector construction to peak late in the cycle, noted in Chapter 2. The result is too little social housing when it is most needed, and too much after the need for it has subsided. The latter leads to a temporary surplus, which paves the way for almost complete closure of the social housing programme in trough periods. Rebuilding it takes time, making it more likely that the same pattern will be repeated in the next cycle.

Box 5.1 suggests ways in which fluctuations in social housing output could become more moderate, and better timed.

Box 5.1 Less Pro-cyclical Construction of Social Housing

Possible methods of reducing the cyclicality of social housing output include:

1. Recognising turning points earlier: Figure 5.3 shows the increase in households has been close to – or over – 100% of the increase in housing in some inter-censal periods, and 20 or 30% below it in others. Shifts from tight to loose markets, or vice versa, are a fairly reliable signal to increase or reduce output. For instance, the shift from

a tight market in 1971–9 to a looser one in 1979–81 implied that increasing rather than reducing social housing output in 1983–4 was high risk. The shift from a loose market in the 1980s to a tight one in the early 1990s implied low social output in the mid-late 1990s was also high risk. Taking more account of market tightness or looseness would reduce such risks, and even out construction rates. To do this in the future, we will need reliable estimates of increases in households and housing units between censi.

2. Moving away from supply stimulus in loosening markets: Demand which would normally be met by social housing was used to reduce over-supply in the private housing market in the 1980s and after 2008. This facilitated collapses in social output. In loosening markets, trying to moderate house prices by stimulating supply is high risk, and not in the medium-term interests of public or private housing sectors.

3. Avoiding disproportionate cut backs in social housing: In economic crises, such as those of the 1980s or after 2008, capital expenditure was halved, but investment in social housing was discontinued almost completely. This happens because the adverse effects of social housing cuts then are not immediate, but experience over the last decade has shown they are all too real in the medium term. It may be unrealistic to expect social housing to be cut less than other forms of public invest-ment in a severe recession, but cutting more in such conditions is unwise.

4. Using tenure flexibility to help stabilise social housing output: The needs of many households could be met by several forms of tenure, and this flexibility could be used to limit variations in social housing output, but, in practice, it has been used more to facilitate them. The obvious example is undue use of social tenancies in the private rented sector, which facilitated under-provision of social housing in the 1990s and after 2008. However, neglect of the private rented sector (including unrealistic rent controls) reinforced demographic pressures to over-provide public housing in the 1970s, contributing to scale-related problems in some of the housing built then.

5. Using flexibility between sub-tenures: The same principle applies to different forms of tenure within the social housing sector. Demand and demography move in unpredictable ways, and a social housing pro-gramme which can distribute output between different social tenures can be more responsive and robust. This is an additional argument in favour of cost rental housing, for households with incomes too low to be owner-occupiers, but not low enough to qualify for conventional

social housing. Meeting the needs of low-income groups should have priority, but a substantial social housing programme is more likely to be maintained if there is confidence there will be no hiatus in demand for it, and that it will not contribute to renewed polarisation between public and private housing.

B. RECENTRALISATION AND TAX INCENTIVES IN THE 1989–2010 CYCLE

(i) A change of direction in the trough of the mid 1980s: The main initiative undertaken at the bottom of this trough involved a reaction against the main characteristics of the previous cycle. This was partly because the suburban property markets on which development in the previous cycle had mostly relied were saturated, and the state no longer had the resources for generous grants and expansive capital programmes, and partly because of concern at rapid deterioration of inner-city areas.

It therefore aimed to revive the construction sector, in ways which checked unduly decentralist trends and consequent inner-city decay, and avoided adding to government debt. It promoted urban renewal in inner-city areas, incentivised by tax reliefs which would be drawn down in the ten years after construction projects had been completed. Tax reliefs were available in those areas for most development types, including private sector housing – something conspicuous by its absence there in the 1970s and early 1980s. This latter type of development minimised 'deadweight' – tax lost to incentivise projects which would have happened anyway. The reliefs covered rehabilitation as well as new construction.[15]

The urban renewal tax reliefs had a genuinely transformative effect. The shift in tone from previously scathing critics such as Frank McDonald is one indication of this. In a 1996 review, he quotes the views he expressed on Dublin in the mid-1980s as 'probably the shabbiest, most derelict city in Europe, chaotic and disorderly like the capital of some Third World country'; but then went on to say, 'That was certainly the way I saw it in 1985; it is not my view today. Despite its traffic congestion,

171

crime and drug abuse, the city has improved immeasurably over the past decade or so.'[16]

While much of the development benefitting from urban renewal tax reliefs was normal commercial development, albeit in previously run-down parts of city centres, the incentives for private housing in Dublin and other cities achieved a more dramatic result, by reversing the rapid population loss previously characteristic of their inner areas (as shown in Table 5.1).

TABLE 5.1

PERCENTAGE CHANGES, INNER-CITY POPULATION, 1971–96

	1971–81	1981–6	1986–91	1991–6
Dublin*	-26	-14	-8	+ 14
Cork	-21	-16	-6	+ 16
Limerick	-21	-14	-9	+ 8

Source: Censi of Population, 1971–96. * Area within the canals

Re-introduction of new private housing into inner-city areas was a crucial step, because it used much more land than intensive uses like offices, and was thus more effective in reducing the amount of vacant inner-city property.

(ii) **Tax reliefs in the recovery and boom phases** continued to shape the character of this cycle. Further inner-city areas, and parts of 30 large towns, were designated for tax reliefs between 1988 and 1995 (KPMG, 1996, p. 7), and the period in which tax reliefs were available was also extended. When they eventually expired, this prompted discussion on what form a new round of urban renewal tax reliefs should take. A largely positive 1996 review by KPMG had pointed out that 'the market will inevitably favour the least risk option'. Within designated areas, undue dominance of particular project types and-sub-areas could be prevented, by using area plans to control the development mix through more precise use of objectives than normal in a development plan. Incentives should be available only for uses and in locations essential to the objectives of the plan, whose development would be unlikely without them. The plans should look at the overall area needs in an integrated way, and not just its current physical condition (KPMG, 1996, pp. 153–6, 160).

The CIF disagreed with the view that designation should mean more than just cranes on the skyline, arguing that it had been initiated in 1986 on that basis. It had had simple aims – attracting private sector investment and tackling physical dereliction – and it favoured staying with this winning formula. Complex regulations would deter developers. Designated areas should be large enough and the range of developments assisted flexible enough to provide choice and avoid inflation of site prices (*Construction*, April 1997, pp. 8–9). The CIF's priority was that the new designated areas achieve 'critical mass' (*Construction*, November 1997, p. 19); the volume of development should have priority over its nature and effects.

Interestingly, this argument was about the form a new round of urban renewal tax incentives should take, not about whether further incentives were needed at all by 1997, when broadly-based urban renewal was well-established, and a construction boom underway. Initial designations in the 1980s had occurred in a deep recession, and stimulus from the extra investment preceded the cost of tax reliefs to the Exchequer, as many of them were spread out over the decade after construction, when the economy and government finances had started to recover. In a rough and ready way, the incentives were contra-cyclical.

By contrast, new construction industry tax incentives announced from the mid-1990s on were launched in strong recovery or boom conditions. They were numerous and diverse: the success of the urban renewal incentives encouraged a plethora of other tax relief schemes. The follow-on urban renewal schemes did, in fact, involve more targeted tax reliefs along the lines suggested by KPMG, but were applied widely, to 38 large and 100 small towns. In addition, there were also area-based incentive schemes for seaside resorts, airports and business parks adjoining them, and a rural renewal scheme covering all or part of seven north western counties. Less area-specific incentives became available for third-level educational institutions, student accommodation, nursing homes, convalescent homes, private hospitals, sports injury facilities, and child-care facilities. Reliefs for hotels also became much more generous.

While the merits of some individual post-1995 tax reliefs may be open to argument, collectively they represented gross overuse of this form of incentive, in conditions where they were pro-cyclical. An assessment of post-1999 area-based schemes estimated their cost to the Exchequer by mid-2006 at €1.9 billion, and then commented that their main impact was yet to come, as claims under them would continue for a considerable period after they were closed to new entrants (Goodbody, 2005, p. 145). This meant the state had committed itself to sacrificing future tax revenues – some, as it turned out, foregone when it was close to bankruptcy – in order to stimulate further construction activity at the height of a boom.

The incentive for hotels was an extreme example. A 2009 report on 'Overcapacity in the Irish Hotel Industry' recommended the 'orderly elimination' of 15,000 surplus hotel rooms – more than half the 26,800 constructed since 1999. Due to the incentives, insolvent hotels were being kept open, as closing them would prevent investors claiming capital allowances in the future and make them subject to clawback on ones already claimed, at a total cost to them of €1.5 billion.[17] As well as contributing to the shortfall in state revenues, these investments were mostly funded by bank debt, which had become a threat to the solvency of the state. Of the €5.2 billion invested in hotels, €4.1 billion was loan finance, which the banks could not write down or foreclose on without further damaging their own solvency (Bacon, 2009, pp. ii–v).

Both the lessons of the successful initial round of urban renewal incentives introduced in the mid-1980s, and those arising from overuse of tax reliefs from the mid-1990s on were, if anything, too well learnt. The first led to this method of influencing the construction output mix being applied too widely and uncritically, and the second to it being generally discredited.

(iii) **Tax disincentives to contain housing market overheating?** As memories of difficulties in maintaining access to the market for first-time buyers in the late 1970s were still fresh in 1990, the issue was revisited promptly as the market recovered. As early as May 1989, the CIF attributed calls for cutbacks in mortgage lending to misplaced hysteria generated by some recent Dublin house prices, and argued that this would undermine the recovery. In the 1990 budget, larger new houses with floorspace of over 125 square metres became subject to 6% stamp duty. This was criticised by the CIF, who argued that it would add £5,000 to new house prices, and discriminate against larger rural families who would become liable for stamp duty on the site as well as the house. By the end of 1990, the CIF considered that the imposition of stamp duty on larger houses could not have come at a worse time for the industry, while the Irish House Builders' Association (IHBA) felt it had destabilised the market and slashed demand for trading up (*Construction*, November, 1990, p. 23; December 1990, p. 13).

When the **recovery resumed in the mid-1990s**, after a pause in 1991–3, the CIF seems to have consciously decided to head off any repetition of the 1990 intervention, by a public relations offensive to counteract discussion of a rise in interest rates by commentators concerned at inflationary pressures in the housing market:

> ... the Federation's strategy would be to 'move the focus' from housing, to see no change or a minimal alteration in overdraft and mortgages, and to respond rapidly to any references to housing or construction ... the CIF had managed to prompt a 'rethink' by a number of media and sectoral interests ... the rate changes to date had been minimal. (*Construction*, September 1996, p. 10)

This is the nearest thing to a smoking gun, as regards the construction industry's role in the ultimately disastrous loss of control over the housing market. It was lost in late 1996 and early 1997, when price rises of 15% per annum became established. Prompt action might have re-established control, but it became more difficult to use traditional interest rate measures as European monetary union came closer.

Alternative methods of controlling house prices were possible, but even more vulnerable to opposition from the construction industry. In the following spring, for instance, the ESRI suggested a surcharge on new mortgages as a means of limiting housing prices. The IHBA denounced this as a tax on home ownership, and pointed out that they had been pressing government and local authorities for supply-side improvements for some time: 'The Government must stop tinkering with this problem and address instead the fundamental issue of the supply of suitably zoned and serviced land' (*Construction*, May 1997, p. 15).

The IHBA thus saw supply and demand-side measures as alternatives, and wanted the state's managerial role in booms confined to the former. The difficulty with responding to surges in demand through supply-side measures only is that they take longer than, say, a rise in interest rates to have an effect. For instance, a decision to extend water supply and sewerage systems at a faster rate involves time lags, while the extra schemes are designed and constructed, and houses are then built on the newly serviced land. Excess demand will continue to affect prices during this interval. This is a problem for governments, but an opportunity for developers. Since building costs, such as labour and materials, rise only gradually in response to demand pressures,[18] much of the increase in prices will feed into developers' profits and land values.

(iv) Boom conditions from 1997 on meant that the CIF's public relations efforts were only temporarily effective, and prompted belated government attempts to regain control through the Bacon reports. When the first of these was published in April 1998, the CIF supported its supply-side proposals, but attacked the main demand-side one – making interest payments on houses bought for letting purposes not tax-deductible. The IHBA described publication of the report as 'a black day' for house-builders, reflecting the failure of government to recognise land supply, rather than investors, as the source of the problem (*Construction*, May 1998, p. 7).

The first Bacon report's terms of reference asked it to identify the factors influencing the rise in house prices since 1994, particularly in Dublin, and assess how they were likely to influence prices and affordability in the future. The report attributed accelerating price rises in 1996–7 to a surge in demand, due to rising incomes and substantial net in-migration. As it is difficult to increase the rate of housing output quickly in response to changes in demand, the short-term effect was a large increase in prices. In the longer term, higher prices should stimulate increased supply, and cause prices to stabilise or fall (Bacon, 1998, pp. 1–4, 32).

However, there were two potential difficulties. Firstly, econometric analysis suggested that supply was less elastic in Dublin than in the rest of the country. A 1% increase in current real house prices stimulated a 0.92% increase in housing output in the state, but a 0.35% one in Dublin. This seemed to be due mainly to the more restricted availability of development land in the Dublin area. Secondly, in markets where asset value is a consideration, price rises do not necessarily reduce demand, and may, in fact, make house purchases for investment reasons more attractive. A positive feedback loop can become established by which price rises make the asset more attractive to investors, and increased investor demand causes prices to rise further. If unchecked, this can lead to a speculative bubble. The existence of various tax incentives to invest in rental housing, inherited from periods of slack demand, increased the risk of this pattern emerging. Investors were already an important component of demand, and were estimated to account for around 25% of mortgages (Bacon, 1998, pp. 28–9, 38–51, 85).

The report aimed to improve the balance between supply and demand in the short term, so as to moderate price increases and affordability problems, and restore equilibrium more quickly. Proposals to speed up a supply response included higher housing densities, extra funding for infrastructure servicing development land, a temporary reduction in CGT to encourage owners of development land to sell, and lower stamp duties on second-hand homes for first-time buyers (to improve their access to the market). On the demand side, removal of three inherited incentives – section 23 tax reliefs on the capital cost of new rental property, exemption from stamp duties for investors buying new houses, and tax deductibility of mortgage interest on rental properties – was recommended. Investors in, say, shares could not set the interest they paid on loans to acquire them against tax, and allowing investors in housing to do this distorted choice between types of investment (Bacon, 1998, pp. 84, 88–95).

(v) **The second Bacon report** (1999, p. 11) was commissioned partly to assess the effect of measures proposed in the first. Bacon I underestimated housing market momentum, but price growth had slowed from autumn 1998 on. A benchmark projection in Bacon I, which allowed for the effects of the proposed supply measures, had suggested that private house completions for 1998 would rise to c. 38,000, and prices by 10–12% (Bacon, 1998, pp. 75–8). A year later, actual private output for 1998 was estimated at 39,000, but 1998 prices were 20–25% above 1997 levels for new houses, and c. 30% above for second-hand ones (Bacon, 1999, pp. 15, 24).

Bacon II contained further recommendations to improve the effectiveness of the Bacon I supply-side measures. As the reduction in CGT on development land to 20% was having limited effect, because land had to have outline planning permission to qualify for it, removal of this requirement was recommended. The Bacon I recommendation on higher densities was being applied unevenly, so a formal ministerial directive was suggested. Temporary sewerage facilities in advance of the Dublin North Fringe Interceptor Sewer were also recommended, as they seemed technically feasible, and capable of providing for up to 15,000 houses (Bacon, 1999, pp. 62–5). Development of existing towns in the outer counties adjoining Dublin, improved public transport access to them, and the overall distribution of economic activity nationally, all required urgent review, preferably in the context of regional and national spatial strategies (Bacon, 1999, pp. 55–6).

VARIANTS ON BACON II

However, by 1999, it was widely felt that restoration of housing market equilibrium would take some time. The IHBA, for instance, felt that demand would remain high for ten years (*Construction*, July/August 1999, pp. 2–4). This raised the question of whether more drastic interventions to promote affordability under existing (unbalanced) market conditions were needed. The focus of debate shifted from the Bacon measures, designed to correct for market failures, to ones which selectively replaced market mechanisms with administered ones.

A short but interesting section of Bacon II can be read as a commentary on affordability measures being canvassed in early 1999. These included some variant on the Kenny report:

> *Some believe that an appropriate solution ... is to engineer ... an across the board reduction in new house prices from their current levels. Most usually, it is argued that a reduction in land prices ... should be ... the means used.* (Bacon, 1999, p. 58)

Bacon's response was that a general reduction in house prices, sufficient to restore affordability to households who had lost it, could lead to a negative equity problem for recent purchasers. Falling prices, like rising ones, are liable to positive feedback: they encourage house buyers to postpone purchases, which promotes a further decline in prices (*Ibid.*).

Bacon's counter-suggestion involved adapting housing mix requirements already found in some development plans to encourage, or even require, a given proportion of each housing site to be reserved for dwelling types aimed at the lower end of the market. For instance, they could require two-bedroom terrace houses of, say, 750 square feet (70m²) built at 16–20 per acre (40–50 per hectare),[19] in place of the standard 1,100 square foot (100m²), three-bedroom semis at 10 per acre normally provided for the starter market. Construction and land savings might reduce the overall cost of producing each unit by 20–30% (Bacon, 1999, pp. 59–60).

This approach could be taken further. To guarantee such savings were passed on, the price might need to be specified, but there would then be an implied subsidy to purchasers, equal to any reduction in the margin between sales revenue and construction costs on that part of the site. Depending on circumstances, this might be at the expense of the builder, or the original landowner, or purchasers of other houses on the site. Bacon (1999, pp. 60–1) did not recommend going this far, as the subsidy would be arbitrary, and deciding what part of the site was reserved for this type of housing would be administratively cumbersome. However, he recommended full use of existing planning powers to match housing units to households.

Other options included the shared ownership principle – the prospective householder takes out a mortgage on part of the value of the property, and pays rent on the remainder – or liberalising rules on income to loan ratios. Bacon (1999, pp. 61–2) felt that while the market remained out of balance, both would increase demand but not supply, thereby raising prices.

There are similarities between the shared equity option discussed by Bacon, and a more complex variant, partly to be financed by builders, proposed by the IHBA shortly before publication of the Planning Bill in August 1999 (*Construction*, July/August 1999, p. 3). This may have been a last-ditch attempt to avoid what became Part V of the Bill, which they detested: the cover story on the October 1999 edition of *Construction* was 'New Planning Bill – Recipe for Disaster'.[20] The CIF argued Part V would do nothing to increase the supply of housing land, which was where the real problem lay, and would only produce uncertainty.

The suggestion which Bacon II did favour – measures to increase the proportion of smaller, lower-cost units in new housing output – may have continuing relevance, as the housing market has been almost as much out of equilibrium in the post-2013 recovery as in the late 1990s. Affordability quickly became an issue in this recovery, but there was little sign of a response in the form of volume output of lower cost units. A 2016 SCSI report, which compared the cost of building starter homes in Dublin with average incomes and borrowing capacity, took a 1200 square foot, three-bed semi as representing the average starter home. This was a realistic assumption, as much of the output then was of that general type, but reliance on it in a report arguing that new housing was unaffordable illustrates how marginalised lower-cost housing types such as the two-bed terrace units referred to by Bacon had become.

Box 5.2 suggests a variant on the smaller unit approach, incorporating tax measures.

Box 5.2 Extendible Starter Homes and Variable Taxation

Bacon II's suggestion of a planning requirement for some higher density two-bedroom terrace houses for the starter market came with a caveat. To ensure savings were passed on, prices could be specified, but this might imply a subsidy to buyers from others on that site.

To avoid this, the state might, for example, offer a selective tax rebate to first-time buyers of new homes under say 90m2 (970ft2). It could be at its most generous at a reference size and price, and become less so to the extent these were exceeded. A possible formula might be:

$$\text{Net rebate (paid to buyer)} = \left(\frac{\text{reference floor area (m}^2)}{\text{actual floor area}}\right) \times \left(\frac{\text{reference price}}{\text{actual price}}\right) \times \text{Gross rebate}$$

(subject to a maximum of 100% of gross rebate)

Builders would have an incentive to keep the net rebate to as high a percentage of the gross rebate as possible – this would be an obvious selling point – and so stay as close as possible to the reference price and floor area. Such 'tapering' rebates would allow price and floor area cut off points beyond which no rebate was available to be set relatively high – ensuring flexibility – while focusing support on smaller, lower-cost dwellings. A formula which includes price and floor space allows for higher prices in cities and larger houses elsewhere.

As Bacon pointed out, while the market is out of balance, measures which increase demand without a corresponding increase in supply raise prices. While it is difficult to increase overall supply if the industry is already operating close to capacity, it should be easier to increase it in a particular market segment, by redirecting capacity to it from other segments, such as upmarket housing. This could be achieved by a modest increase in stamp duty on new houses of, say, $120–150m^2$ ($1290–1615ft^2$), and a larger one for those over $150m^2$. Rebates and increases in stamp duty could be designed so their combined effect on overall demand was broadly neutral. This would increase the number of houses produced, as small homes use less construction resources (and land) than large ones.

There are precedents for most of these features. The percentage of mortgage interest on which relief has been available has been varied on numerous occasions. The 6% stamp duty rate on houses over 125 square metres in the

---

1990 budget aimed to prevent larger houses pre-empting too much construction capacity and affecting the affordability of smaller ones. More recently, Budget 2018 raised the stamp duty rate on commercial development from 2% to 6%, partly to achieve a better balance between commercial and residential development.

The gross rebate could be varied in line with the changing output of small units and whether the overall housing market was tightening or loosening (see Box 5.1 above). It would thus rise when numbers were low and markets tight, and fall as numbers fell and markets loosened.

Assuming the SCSI estimate of c. €370,000 as the price needed for a semi in Dublin in 2020 was correct, and, like Bacon II, that a small terrace house costs 20–30% less than a semi, this implied a gross price of €260,000–300,000. If full refund of the current 13.5% rate was seen as the maximum rebate possible, the net price would have fallen to €225,000–260,000.

The system would promote smaller terrace houses most, as they are normally the lowest cost way of providing a small dwelling, but would be flexible enough to promote other dwelling types where appropriate. As young families can rapidly outgrow town houses, the system could allow for higher reference prices for houses designed to be extendible.

Figure 5.4 suggests that, in the period for which information is readily available, terrace houses were a low percentage of all new homes in tight markets, at c. 4% or less in 1977–81 and 1996–2000 (the time of the Bacon reports). However, their rise coincided with loosening markets, in 1982–5[21] and in 2001–3. Like social housing, terrace housing output is low in periods when it would be of most use in addressing affordability problems, and high quite late in the cycle, when such units may contribute to oversupply, as they did in the 1980s.

Box 5.3 suggests how this timing issue might be addressed.

Box 5.3 Signalling Starter Home Measures in Advance

As the stamp duty and tax rebate measures suggested in Box 5.2 would take time to have an effect, they need to be in place as soon as a recovery is underway, and the intention to do this should be signalled before then. If builders know rebates and stamp duty will increase – and improve the relative economics of smaller homes – in a tight market, they can factor this into the projects they are planning, and will have less cause to complain of uncertainty and disruption of plans due to a change in incentives. To the extent that they expect a rising market, they are likely to increase the proportion of such homes in their developments, or at any rate position themselves to be able to respond rapidly to such a change. This should shorten the time lag before extra starter homes result.

As suggested in Box 5.2, rebates and stamp duties could be reduced once the number of units qualifying for the former had increased and markets had loosened, to minimise any risk of oversupply then. This phase-driven approach would require monitoring of planning applications for smaller houses, as a guide to volumes two–three years ahead.

In a falling market, houses become difficult to sell, partly because potential buyers may delay purchases to see if prices will fall further. If rebates were also reduced, but by an amount less than the fall in gross prices, this would slow the rate at which net prices fell, weaken the motive for deferring purchase of smaller homes, and reduce instability in that part of the market.

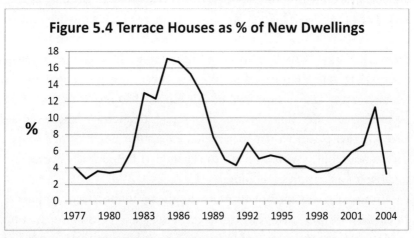

Figure 5.4 Terrace Houses as % of New Dwellings

Source: Department of the Environment Annual Bulletin of Housing Statistics series

SUPPLY AND DWELLING TYPE

The approach outlined in Boxes 5.2 and 5.3 may appear to run counter to the frequently repeated view on the overriding importance of supply, and the subtext to it, that the mix of new housing supplied is a secondary issue. Supply at the upper end of the market will result in existing houses being vacated and sold or rented to other households, who will, in turn, vacate other units and so on, allowing a 'trickle down' effect which should increase supply at the lower end.

One difficulty with this theory is that compact, low-cost new houses require less construction resources than large, expensive ones. If those resources are limited, a higher proportion of large houses is likely to lead to a lower total number of extra units built. Any amount of trickling down isn't going to change the resulting ratio between households and dwelling numbers. There will also be some leakage from the trickle-down process, for instance as a result of some wealthier purchasers of larger houses holding onto their previous dwelling as a second home.

A somewhat similar issue arises in relation to apartments, at least at present. The construction only cost per square metre in a semi was estimated at €1,569 (SCSI, 2020, p. 14), as compared with €1,950–€3,137 in an apartment (SCSI, 2021, p. 16). At these rates, €5 million would cover the construction costs of 40 two-bedroom terrace houses of 80m^2 each, or of 20–32 apartments of the same size, with higher-rise apartments schemes being at the lower end of this range. If supply is treated as an overriding consideration, this arguably implies that terrace houses should have a higher priority than apartments, except for units for one or two person households with no plans to expand, with floorspace below that suitable for a conventional house.[22]

Admittedly, strategies to promote supply do not necessarily prioritise an efficient output mix. They can involve the state focusing support on particular property types and locations on the basis of their current or expected momentum, and some of those who emphasise supply may have a strong quantitative market response to policy interventions primarily in mind. However, this latter line of thought has more relevance in situations where construction output is constrained by market sentiment rather than physical capacity.

(vi) Strengthening of demand-side measures in Bacon III: The third Bacon report could claim some progress had been made, as private house completions had risen to 43,000 in 1999 (as opposed to the 42,000 projected in Bacon I[23]), and prices were rising at around half the rate prevailing two years previously by the first quarter of 2000. However, housing demand was being fuelled by faster employment growth, and a decline in interest rates. Around 100,000 extra jobs were created in 1999 alone (Bacon, 2000, pp. 1, 13, 28). More worryingly, modelling recent trends suggested that:

> *... gathering momentum in demand, based on price expectations, appears to have become more important in the past few years ... this is consistent with the emergence of a significant speculative or transitory demand factor ... with, for example, demand being brought forward in the expectation of avoiding house price inflation as well as purchases for the purpose of speculation. (Bacon, 2000, p. 62)*

Before 1997, a 1% increase in disposable income was associated with a 1.2% increase in prices but the current price response to a 1% rise in incomes seemed to be c. 4%. As a result, the potential for instability and vulnerability to shocks was increasing. Sharp rises or falls in price would feed strongly into future prices, possibly leading to a pronounced correction in which price falls could 'overshoot'. The same logic which led investors to buy assets with rising values could lead them to sell if their value was falling (Bacon, 2000, pp. 65–7).

The additional demand-side measures to discourage investors proposed in the third Bacon report included an annual tax on dwellings acquired other than as the principal residence of the purchaser. An exemption from this tax for landlords who complied with relevant regulations and were willing to rent on a long-term basis was suggested. Rebalancing stamp duty rates, so they became more favourable for first-time buyers at the lower end of the market, and less favourable for non-owner occupiers, was also proposed. Stamp duties were seen as a suitable way of discouraging speculative or transitory demand, because they applied to all purchasers, whether they needed a mortgage or not (Bacon, 2000, pp. 10, 87).

(vii) **Premature retreat from the Bacon recommendations:** From late 2000 onwards, the demand-side measures recommended in the Bacon reports were progressively dismantled. This reflected the status of the reports and the interventions they recommended as temporary measures, adopted in response to an extreme situation. Once property market conditions moderated, it seems to have been assumed that they could be reversed. Perhaps on the last in, first out principle, the 9% stamp duty on house purchases not for owner occupation,[24] and the 2% anti-speculation tax on such properties for the first three years of ownership recommended by Bacon III and included in the 2000 Finance Act (No.2), were removed via government-sponsored amendments to the 2001 Finance Bill.

Documents obtained by *The Irish Times* under the Freedom of Information Act showed that these changes occurred after the Minister for Finance had been lobbied by seven cabinet ministers, including the Taoiseach and the Minister for the Environment, six junior ministers, and numerous backbenchers. There had also been substantial direct lobbying, particularly from developers of holiday home schemes. Officials in the Department of Finance had advised against reversal of the measures, partly on the grounds that it would undermine the credibility of government policy in this area.[25] The pause in growth during 2001 led to further dismantling of the Bacon controls, with deductibility of interest on the purchase of rental housing units being restored from the beginning of 2002.

Rapid house price growth resumed in 2003. It was not as rapid in percentage terms, averaging 11% per annum in real terms between 2002 and 2006, as against 18% between 1996 and 2000. However, it was similar in absolute terms – a rise of €70–80,000 in 2002 prices, in both cases – and the rise in 2003–6 was on top of the 1996–2000 one. This second surge did not lead to any attempt to reintroduce the Bacon controls. Instead, the government seems to have accepted without much reservation the construction industry view that supply-side measures by themselves were sufficient to bring the housing market into equilibrium. Continuing price rises between 2002 and 2006, despite a 60% increase in the output of houses, demonstrated its incorrectness fairly clearly, but this was ignored by government and almost everyone else. There was a widespread belief that a decade of rapid growth in house prices would be followed not by a period of rapid decline, but by a 'soft landing'.

The same principle – that demand-side interventions to restrain a boom are only appropriate in its extreme manifestations – was also responsible for their late introduction. As we have seen, the CIF lobbied against such interventions in 1996, and the political will to face them down only became available in early 1998, when the first Bacon report was published and acted on. Except in extreme parts of the boom, governments and the construction industry agreed to treat the supply-side measures favoured by the latter as adequate.

Realistically, construction industry lobbying is likely to result in measures to restrain demand being introduced too late, and being withdrawn too early. Desirable as it might have been to have such measures in place from 1995 to 2007 inclusive, the political will would not have been there. However, this obstacle might, to some extent, have been circumvented if the housing demand side measures had been treated as variable attachments to permanent features of the tax system, rather than as emergency measures.[26] This could be done, by applying to new or second-hand housing, which is not the principal residence of the owner, a similar strategy to that suggested for taxation of capital gains on development land in Chapter 3. This would involve extending the cyclically variable form of CGT for development land outlined in Boxes 3.5–6 (i.e. CVLVS) to housing in this category as well, so as to make acquisition for capital appreciation purposes in a rising market less attractive.

Box 5.4 outlines how this approach could work.

Box 5.4 Cyclical Restraint of Speculation in Dwellings

CVLVS, on the principles outlined in Boxes 3.5, 3.6 and Table 3.3, could be applied at cyclically variable rates to sales of residential properties, other than ones which had been the principal residence of the vendors. CVLVS rates would thus increase as output volumes and house prices rose, and reduce the net gain achievable by buying houses in a rising market and then selling them on. Obviously, worthwhile gains would still be possible, but the balance between risks and possible net gains would be less favourable.

This system could moderate cyclical swings in both directions. Investor purchases can help provide liquidity in a declining market, and provide a floor to prices. The system would go into reverse in those circumstances, with CVLVS rates falling in the downturn and trough phases. Providing this approach was public knowledge, investment purchases would become more attractive then. Rates would start to rise again once a recovery was under-way, but the rate on gains on houses bought in the trough phase and resold in early- or mid-recovery phase would not have risen high enough to be a major deterrent.

Knowing in advance that CVLVS rates would be designed to offset price rises and falls should in itself moderate cyclical swings in investor demand. Drastic measures can seem unavoidable where the aim is to slow market trends with a lot of momentum behind them, but are less necessary if less momentum is allowed develop in the first place.

If CVLVS applied only to development land, there would be a risk of it diverting investor demand from land to houses, further inflating the value of the latter. Applying it to existing investor-owned housing as well reduces this risk. Increases in the value of existing housing – whether due to rising site values, or changing tastes, or increases in building costs – are windfall gains not attributable to the actions of the owner, which the wider community can legitimately seek to share.

For taxation purposes, CVLVS would split capital gains investment funds made from disposals, from the profits from they made from renting, with tax concessions becoming confined to the latter. This could discourage short-term investment oriented towards the former, but not more socially useful, longer-term investment, oriented towards the latter.

CVLVS on existing investor-owned housing would also discourage the undesirable practice of holding new units vacant, widespread before the 2008 crash, and also evident currently (see article by Killian Woods in Sunday Business Post, 20/6/21, cited in Chapter 3). An RPT-type levy on such units (as suggested in Box 3.8) is needed, but cannot easily be set high enough to be effective by itself, without prompting numerous exemptions which would undermine it.

(viii) **In the 2008–10 downturn**, the construction industry complained at successive cutbacks in public capital investment,[27] which fell by 52% between 2009 and 2012. As private investment had collapsed, the CIF saw public investment as 'the key to averting an escalation of the construction crisis', but there had been 'an abject failure by the Government' to allow 'shovel ready work to go to tender', and the state's 'entire infrastructure development plan' was 'being wound down'. The reduced capital allocations were persistently underspent, so 'there was no relationship between announcement and actual commencement of public projects' (*Construction*, December 2009/January 2010, p. 5; February/March 2010, p. 30; April/May 2010, p. 31; June/July 2010, p. 27). Spending which did occur was often on items like rail rolling stock and hospital equipment, which did not create construction employment.[28]

The collapse in the market for private housing attracted less complaint. The government made some attempt to slow the crash late in 2008, by revising its housing loan scheme and increasing mortgage relief for first-time buyers. The IHBA accurately predicted a shortage of housing in Dublin, in the absence of further measures, as soon as confidence returned. Otherwise, awareness of the role of house-builders in the crash limited criticism of the government. The chairman of the IHBA admitted, 'we all got greedy. We lost sight of reality'.[29] The president of the Civil Engineering Contractors Association (CECA) distanced his members from them by saying that the vast majority of CIF members were not developers, and that a disproportionate amount of its energies were focused on NAMA.[30] The incoming president of the CIF accepted (*Construction*, Feb./March 2011, p. 12): 'There isn't much support or sympathy out there for people in construction, rightly or wrongly we are seen as part of the problem'.

C. INVESTMENT FUNDS AND CENTRALISED PLANNING IN THE 2011+ CYCLE

(i) **The trough of 2011–13:** While much more severe than the trough of the mid-1980s, this trough was similarly marked by a conscious departure from the characteristics of the previous cycle, involving a change both in aims and in means. The incoming Fine Gael–Labour coalition started to redefine both in a brief Housing Policy Statement (June 2011). While the need for social housing was high and rising, the financial situation ruled out a large capital-funded construction programme. This implied increased reliance on housing low-income households in the private rented sector.

On the positive side, the downturn and the associated decline in house prices had restored affordability to levels not seen since the early to mid-1990s, removing the need for the state to subsidise affordable housing, or to continue to require the affordable housing component in Part V transfers. In any case, the concept of affordable housing was now seen as more questionable, as it reinforced 'the high and often disproportionate value placed on owner occupation'. If a household was able to rent a high-quality home, it would not be necessary to use the resources of the state to support its move to owner occupation. This again implied increased reliance on the private rented sector.

The most pressing practical problem was to find sources of finance to support purchase of some of the accumulation of devalued property left over from the crash, so that the loans on it held by NAMA could at least be partly repaid, and also to finance new construction activity.

To promote the sale of devalued property overhanging the market, the 2012 and 2013 Finance Acts exempted property bought in 2013 and 2014 and held for at least seven years from CGT.[31] International investors willing to buy in a depressed market were thus offered the possibility of large tax-free gains. The attractions of this were increased by the actions of central banks, which depressed interest rates to very low levels to reduce pressure on debtor countries and financial institutions, and promote recovery.

The pre-2008 boom had been disproportionately based on owner-occupied, buy-to-let and buy-to-hold housing, and largely financed directly by Irish banks, though this, in turn, had been indirectly supported by extensive international borrowing, and also (as we have seen) by widespread tax reliefs. The markets for these product types were saturated, and the sources of finance for them had largely dried up. With the exception of some limited investment from NAMA[32] and ISIF,[33] there was little domestic financing of construction projects, and limited appetite for and confidence in property as an investment (Construction 2020, May 2014, p. 40). Overuse of tax reliefs had destroyed their credibility and made them a symbol of fiscal irresponsibility, and bank finances were too close to collapse for it to be likely that they would resume funding of the prospective beneficiaries of tax reliefs on a substantial scale. Small, rehabilitation-oriented tax relief schemes such as the Home Renovation Incentive and the Living City Initiative were introduced, but the maximum benefit under the former was €4,400, and the latter only applied to small parts of the five cities, plus Kilkenny.

As in the mid-1980s, new construction products, and new ways of promoting and financing them were therefore needed. Several tax concessions were introduced to make Irish construction projects more attractive to international investment funds. The best known version involved Real Estate Investment Trusts (REITs), which were provided for in the 2013 Budget. These could be used for development financed by shareholders, who would be protected by limits on gearing (REITs could not borrow more than 50% of the market value of their assets) and compulsory dividends (85% of property-related income had to be distributed to shareholders). For the individual investor, this allowed more liquid investment in property, on a smaller scale and with less risk than, say, buying a new house or apartment or commercial premises to let.

(ii) **The post-2014 recovery:** By 2014, it was becoming clear that demand was recovering, particularly in the Dublin housing market, and that a corresponding recovery in supply would be difficult to achieve quickly. House prices in Dublin rose by 14% in the year to March 2014, and rents by 8%, resulting in hardship for some tenants. The size of the private rented sector had almost doubled between 2006 and 2011, and pressures there were making employment creation and attraction of foreign direct investment (FDI) more difficult.[34]

The massive loss of capacity in the construction industry since 2008 limited any response. New housing output was estimated at 8,300 in the state and 1,360 in Dublin in 2013 – less than a tenth of 2006 levels, and far below the ESRI's estimate of need (25,000 houses a year). Two thirds or more of construction firms in each size category above 10 persons engaged had been lost, plasterers and bricklayers in employment had fallen by 71% and 82%, and construction apprentices in 2015 were 19% of the number in 2007.[35]

While it is normal for the building industry and government construction policies to be playing 'catch up' in the recovery phase of the cycle, the gap which needed to be bridged from 2014 on was exceptional. The government's May 2014 policy document report 'Construction 2020 – A Strategy for a Renewed Construction Sector' noted (pp. 6–8) that the sector had shrunk to 6.4% of (depressed) GNP in 2012, and international comparisons, demography and infrastructural deficits in Ireland suggested it needed to be around 12%. While the construction industry had been too big during the boom, it was now seriously underperforming, and, in order to have the housing and infrastructure needed, planning for them and building them had to start immediately.

Perhaps inevitably, the recovery led to an unusually wide range of government initiatives, designed to speed up the catch-up process, or at any rate reassure the public that a major effort to do this was being made. Even more than in previous cycles, the high cost and poor availability of housing created major political problems for the government. As a result, it had little choice but to implement most of the more obvious and widely canvassed generic measures available, though some were applied in ways which suggested limited belief in and commitment to them, and left the government open to accusations that they were being applied half-heartedly. The levy on vacant sites, discussed in Chapter 3 above, fell into this category.

REBUILDING IRELAND

The flagship document on housing for the incoming Fine Gael minority government was 'Rebuilding Ireland – An Action Plan for Housing and Homelessness' (July 2016). It involved 84 actions grouped under five 'pillars', and estimated (p. 27) the cumulative housing deficit in Dublin at 50,000 units. The rapid economic growth which was now occurring there and in other cities was resulting in price inflation, especially in the private rented sector, and this was resulting in significant homelessness, which was dealt with under Pillar 1 of the plan. It was to be addressed (pp. 34–5) by a 1,500-unit rapid build programme, increased Rent Supplement and Housing Assistance Payments (HAP), and a Housing Agency initiative to acquire 1,600 vacant dwellings. However, the rapid build programme fell behind schedule, the number of homeless households continued to rise, and the aim of limiting the use of hotel rooms to emergency accommodation only by mid-2017 was not fulfilled, then or in subsequent years.

Pillar 2 aimed to accelerate the provision of social housing. An earlier (2014) Social Housing Strategy had included a commitment to providing 35,600 new social units by 2020. Actual output by local authorities and housing associations in 2016 was 1,250, with another 1,400 being acquired by purchase. 'Rebuilding Ireland' (pp. 44–6) raised the target to 47,000 units by 2021, but less than half of these were actually to be built by local authorities or housing associations, and more than half were to be acquired through purchase or long-term leasing. As Hayden and Norris

(2018, p. 63) pointed out: 'Purchasing dwellings from the market means that local authorities are competing with other purchasers and thereby contributing to price inflation, whereas the construction of new dwellings would increase supply and ... dampen inflation.'

'Rebuilding Ireland' also qualified its support for local authority housing, by favouring (pp. 46, 50) smaller-scale and infill schemes, as a way of improving tenure mix, and larger schemes on state land developed on a mixed tenure, public-private partnership (PPP) basis. While the desire to avoid large, single-tenure estates was reasonable, there was little emphasis on ensuring that this did not seriously slow the output of social housing. The process by which the Department of Housing approved funding for local authority projects also remained slow and cumbersome. Despite a reduction in the number of stages at which approval is needed, from eight to four in recent years, all the local authorities interviewed by Hayden and Norris (2018, pp. 47, 96) criticised the micromanagement and delays involved in the system.

There was a striking contrast between this perceived tendency of the Department to delay construction of social housing – where it was directly involved – and its commitment to speeding up and simplifying the planning process, for which local authorities and An Bord Pleanála were responsible. Pillar 3 ('Build More Houses') included re-routing of planning applications for 100 dwellings or more, so that they bypassed local authorities, and instead went direct to An Bord Pleanála, on the basis that most would be appealed anyway. However, as 'Rebuilding Ireland' noted (p. 60), there were existing planning permissions for 27,000 new homes in Dublin at the time, of which only 4,800 were actually under construction, implying that the problem lay elsewhere.

Promotion of apartments

Other planning changes focused on reducing construction costs for apartments, and were set out in 2015 and 2018 revisions to the Departmental

Guidelines on Apartments. These allowed 40m² studio apartments, fewer dual aspect apartments,[36] and less parking. These amendments were expected to save at least €20,000 per apartment.[37] The 2018 version included (p. 4), 'Specific Planning Policy Requirements (SPPRs)' which local authorities had to comply with,[38] included allowing 50% of apartment developments to be studio or one-bedroom apartments. Ones with nine units or less would be unrestricted, except for a maximum of 50% studios.

The 2018 Apartment Guidelines contained new sections on 'Build to Rent' and 'Shared Accommodation' development. The first was defined (pp. 27–30) as long-term rental units, managed by an institutional landlord. They would not be subject to any restrictions on dwelling mix, and could be built more rapidly, as they were unconstrained by the rate at which units could be sold. The second – also known as co-living or shared living – were effectively bedsits, sharing common kitchens and other facilities (pp. 31–3).[39]

Student apartments also benefited from government support. 'Rebuilding Ireland' noted (pp. 75–6) that 3,750 units were under construction or in planning in 2016 but 'an even greater level of provision of student accommodation is required', as the Higher Education Authority estimated unmet need at 25,000 student bed spaces. Accordingly, student housing complexes would qualify for the fast-track planning process for developments of 100+ dwellings. Student accommodation was also an attractive investment, and often became the dominant form of new development near third-level educational institutions, creating concerns amongst existing residents of such areas that they would become student ghettos. Both student accommodation and new apartments built or bought by investment funds typically had high rents, and were aimed at the upper end of their respective markets.

Further planning guidelines on 'Urban Development and Building Heights' were issued in December 2018, requiring local authority Development Plans (pp. 5–11) to identify areas where higher buildings were not only desirable but 'a fundamental policy requirement', with increases in height and density 'not only ... facilitated but actively sought out and bought forward'. These requirements were presented mainly as ways of achieving the more compact and densely populated urban areas sought by the 2018 National Planning Framework, but applied to commercial as well as residential development, and to mixed-use development.

In practice, the main beneficiaries of government efforts to cut the cost of apartments were investment funds, acquiring new units for letting. While prospective owner occupiers could theoretically benefit from lower apartment costs, purchasers would need combined household incomes of €97,500–€135,000, if they were to conform to Central Bank rules, and to buy at prices which reflected costs. The SCSI's 2017 report on The Real Costs of New Apartment Delivery indicated (pp. 19–24) a viability gap of €80,000–€140,000 between the price at which medium-rise apartments could be sold, and the cost of constructing them. The government's measures were unlikely to reduce prices by anything like this amount, and some would make apartment living on a long-term basis less attractive. Higher buildings would not help, as construction costs per m² usually rise with increases in height, and reduced land requirements per unit do not necessarily compensate, as permitting higher densities may raise land values.

Investment funds could pay prices which fully covered costs, because low interest rates made quite modest yields attractive by comparison, particularly if supplemented by strong capital appreciation and favourable tax treatment. As a result, new apartment developments increasingly came to be sold to them en bloc. For developers, this had the added attraction of allowing them to avoid the costs and uncertainties involved in selling unit by unit.

The government was presumably aware that apartment construction for owner occupiers remained marginally viable or uneconomic in Ireland, but viable and attractive for investment funds, and that reliance on apartments would promote dependence on the upper end of the private rented sector. It is possible it saw this as temporary phenomenon. In any event, the 2018

Guidelines cited the NPF's estimate that 550,000 new homes will be needed by 2040 and its aim of providing at least half of these within existing 'urban envelopes'. Declining household size, increasing numbers of elderly people, and greater labour mobility all point to a need for apartments 'to become more and more the norm' in urban areas. It is 'critical' they become 'increasingly attractive and desirable' and that 'economic and regulatory conditions are such that apartment development attracts both the investment and the seeking out of this crucial form of housing by households.'

PRIVATE RENTED HOUSING IN THE RECOVERY PHASE

Government support for the private rented housing and investment funds partly reflected the limited options available. At the upper end of the market, such funds were a new source of otherwise scarce finance for new residential construction, built at higher densities, in line with compact urban development policies. At the lower end, supplementing the rental payments of lower-income households in private rented accommodation had largely replaced provision of new social housing. This policy had been adopted almost by accident in the 1990s, as a by-product of low social housing construction, but became increasingly important during the boom, and even more so after the crash of 2008.

Post-2011 governments were thus making a virtue of necessity, but they also believed an increased role for the private rented sector was desirable anyway. They saw the past emphasis on facilitating owner occupation as excessive, and an increase in private rented housing as actively desirable. Pillar 4 of 'Rebuilding Ireland' ('Improve the Rental Sector') criticised (pp. 27, 71–2) the tendency to see it as a residual sector, and as a stage on the way to owner occupation or social housing. It saw rental housing as flexible and able to respond to changing needs, and more of it was needed if Ireland was to develop an affordable, sustainable and stable housing sector. Private rented housing had doubled since the mid-

1990s, and now housed almost a fifth of the population. There was a need to change

> *attitudes such that the advantages of rental as a form of tenure are more widely recognised. A strong rental sector should support a mobile labour force that is better able to adapt to new job opportunities and changing household circumstances. The rental sector must also cater for a diverse range of households, including students, low-income households and mobile professionals.*

Support for the private rented sector was complicated by the split between a small if rapidly expanding stock held by institutional landlords, and a far larger stock held by individual ones. In September 2018, 80% of the 172,820 registered landlords owned only one rental property (Ó Broin, 2019, p .182). This individually owned stock was the focus of multiple problems. 'Rebuilding Ireland' recognised (2016, pp. 72–3) that, despite increased acceptance:

> *a viable and sustainable rental sector is a key building block in a modern economy ... the rental sector in Ireland is not yet ... truly viable or sustainable .... Severe supply pressures, rising rents, ... encumbered buy to let properties, examples of poor accommodation standards and a shortage of professional institutional ... or other landlords with long term investment plans all act as impediments to delivering a strong and modern rental sector.*

In response, it promised action in four key areas: security of tenure, supply, standards and reform of Residential Tenancies Board services. This latter reform should include accelerated dispute resolution – where possible on a non-adversarial basis –streamlined eviction of problem tenants, and increasing awareness of the rights and responsibilities of landlords and tenants.

As an afterthought to 'Rebuilding Ireland', the government introduced rent pressure zones (RPZs) late in 2016, initially in Dublin and Cork, followed by another 16 RPZs in 2017, and 27 more in 2019. Rent increases were limited to 4% per annum in RPZs, an earlier attempt by the previous Minister (Alan Kelly) to limit rent increases to (the then very low) rises in the consumer price index having been vetoed by the Minister for Finance (Michael Noonan), as likely to discourage future investment in rental housing (Ó Broin, 2019, p. 92).

However, new units were not covered by the 4% limit, so the rent charged in a sequence of new developments by 'modern' institutional landlords could rise steeply. This feature presumably underlay the comment of the former CEO of IRES REIT: 'We've never seen rental increases like this in any jurisdiction that we're aware of'.[40] At a time of rising rents, this feature could also create an unintended incentive to delay first lettings, so as to raise the base on which subsequent 4% increases were calculated.

TARGETING SUPPLY INCENTIVES

Supply incentives in the private rented sector include the exemption from Corporation tax and CGT for REITs in the 2013 Finance Act, though shareholders are subject to a 20% withholding tax on dividends. The consequent stimulus to supply might indirectly benefit lower income households through a trickle-down effect, but REITs are not designed to do this directly. On the contrary, the higher the rents a REIT succeeds in charging, the more it benefits from its exemption from Corporation Tax, and from the relatively low tax shareholders pay on dividends.

The treatment of individual landlords is less generous, as in most cases they pay income tax at the higher rate, and may thus pay around 50% on net rental income (Ó Broin, 2019, p. 184), but the proportion of mortgage interest payments eligible for MITR has been increased in steps from 75% in 2016 to 100% in 2019, again without reference to rent levels in the properties on which the loans have been taken out.

Established tax concessions have sometimes been changed or removed, in order to redirect output to a different market segment. As we have seen, a number of established incentives for investors in new rental housing were removed in 1998 in line with recommendations in the first Bacon report, and the third Bacon report included proposals for an annual tax on dwellings acquired other than as the principal residence of the purchaser, with an exemption for landlords willing to rent on a long-term basis. These measures aimed at a reduction in investor demand, an easing of the upward pressure they exerted on prices, and redirection of some output from them to owner occupiers.

DKM (2014a, p. iv) commented on the absence of measures to help lower income families which were in employment, not in receipt of state support, and in need of rental accommodation. This group is at particular risk of being squeezed between subsidised renters and mid- to high-income ones in Dublin.

It might be possible for private rented sector incentives to redirect resources towards lower income households – and landlords who have been letting to them on moderate terms – by varying incentives to take account of rent levels and length of tenure, as outlined in Box 5.5.

Box 5.5 Rebalancing Incentives in the Private Rented Sector

Instead of a REIT or landlord having an absolute right to a tax concession, regardless of the rent charged or the duration of tenancies, the right to such concessions could be made proportional to these. For instance, the percentage of a tax concession such as MITR or exemption from Corporation Tax which could actually be claimed could be calculated as:

$$\left[\left(\frac{\textit{Reference rent per } m^2}{\text{Actual rent per } m^2} \right) - \left(\frac{\text{Reference period}}{\text{Average length of tenancy}} \right) \right] \times 100$$

(subject to a maximum of 100%)

The reference period could be quite short (e.g. one year), so the longer the average tenancy, the less the subtraction from gross eligibility. If, say, the reference rent in a particular area was €15 per m2 per month, a landlord who charged €25 per m2 would qualify for relief on 60% of eligible profits under the relevant tax concession. If the actual average length of tenancy was five years and the reference period one year, this would reduce eligibility by a further 20%. However, a landlord charging the reference rent and with an average tenancy of ten years could claim 90% of the gross tax concession.

Under such a system, high rents and/or short tenancies would thus reduce or eliminate eligibility for tax relief, but more moderate rents and longer tenancies would allow the bulk of the gross relief to be claimed.

Incentives inversely related to rents would be less likely to have distributionally perverse consequences for tenants, or for the type of accommodation landlords offer. Incentives related to length of tenancy should make it more in their interests to offer well maintained units of reasonable quality and space than to maximise rents in temporary shortages. Landlords would have a continuing motive for retaining long-established tenants.

Housing for All envisaged (2021, p. 44) new properties continuing to be let at market rents, to ensure continuity of supply. While qualifying existing incentives probably would affect supply, the levels at which reference rents and periods were set could be used to strike a balance between supply and distributional effects. A gradual, predictable increase in the weight given to the latter could promote a shift in the mix of planned projects, without unduly disrupting ones on which construction was about to start.

Incentives of this type are not a substitute for stronger regulation of the sector, but would make it easier to enforce, and less dependent on frequent, adversarial assertion of tenant and landlord rights. Ó Broin criticised (2019, p. 186) the 2016 Strategy for the Private Rental Sector as lacking a vision on how to turn it into 'a sector where people would willingly choose to live for long periods of time'. This is a key criterion, but the sector also needs to become one where landlords would willingly choose to let a given property for a long period. This type of incentive could promote both, particularly if combined with the measures outlined in Box 5.4 to reduce the influence of asset values in the sector.

The effectiveness of this approach would depend on the proportion of landlord income and expenditure it could be applied to. For example, the Residential Landlords Association of Ireland has lobbied for Residential Property Tax (RPT) to be treated as a tax-deductible expense of letting (Sirr, 2019, p. 260). If this view was accepted, and RPT as well as mortgage interest became deductable, subject to the formula outlined above, the formula's influence on behaviour would be increased.

Rebuilding Ireland referred briefly (p. 12) to discussions with the Central Bank on introduction of a Help to Buy scheme, and this was provided for a few months later, in Budget 2017. The scheme allowed a tax rebate of 5% of the price of a house, up to a maximum of €20,000, for houses costing up to €500,000, to help first-time buyers raise the 10% deposit needed for a mortgage under Central Bank rules. The upper limits to rebates were raised to 10% and €30,000 in 2020 (NESC, 2020, p. 20).

The scheme was discussed in 2019 and 2022 Parliamentary Budget Office (PBO) reports.[41] They noted that 21% of pre-2019 purchases benefiting from it were for properties costing more than €375,000, and this had risen to 29% by 2021. Loan to value ratios indicated that 41% of pre-2019 beneficiaries and a third of 2021 ones already had the 10% deposit required by the Central Bank, and thus did not need assistance from the Help to Buy scheme to satisfy this criterion (PBO, 2019, pp.1–3, 2022, pp. 7–8). The PBO recommended (2019, p. 9) that

> *future housing schemes should take distributional impacts into account and potentially direct resources towards lower income households in the rental and social housing sector.*

One way in which the Help to Buy scheme could be more tightly targeted would be to modify the current eligibility limit, whereby houses costing up to €500,000 qualify. This was justified on the basis that it would be undesirable to have a 'cliff', which disadvantaged new housing selling at slightly above a lower maximum price. However, a cliff could also be avoided using a 'slope', with the amount of assistance decreasing as the price of the house increased. The formula in Box 5.2 above would have this effect.

OUTPUT UNDER 'REBUILDING IRELAND' (2016–21)

In aggregate numerical terms, new construction under the Rebuilding Ireland programme did not fall too far short of its objectives. Housing output increased by around 10,000 units every three years, from *c.* 10,000 in 2016 to over 20,000 in 2019 and almost 30,000 in 2022[42]. It did not achieve its target of 25,000 by 2020 or earlier, having stalled at 20,000 in 2020 and 2021, but probably would have done if Covid-19 had not intervened. Overall output thus grew quite rapidly, albeit from a very low base.

However, supply did not keep pace with growth in household numbers (see Figures 5.2 and 5.3), let alone make inroads into the unmet demand which had accumulated in the 2010–15 period, when very little new building occurred. Rebuilding Ireland cited (pp.22–23) a 2014 ESRI report as the source of its 25,000 per annum target. It acknowledged caveats in that report outlining circumstances in which it would need to be considerably higher, but argued that

> *The housing challenge is not simply about providing more homes, it is also about moving away from cycles of volatility in supply and affordability. Ireland needs to move towards a more stable, cost effective, affordable housing provision model.*

On the arguments put forward in this and previous chapters, by 2016 it was too late for any plan, whatever its content, to have any chance of realising this aspiration. Ireland was back in a steeper than usual recovery phase of another cycle, in which, unavoidably, the 'policy response was to chase a fast moving target'.[43] The prospect was for more instability, not less.

Some of this instability was the result of reforms to the planning system under Rebuilding Ireland, to facilitate faster processing of applications and to prevent it becoming a barrier to some types of development, such as smaller apartments in higher buildings. As we have seen, planning applications for more than 100 housing units could be made direct to An Bord Pleanála from 2016 to 2021 under the Strategic Housing Development (SHD) system, and guidelines requiring local authorities to permit smaller apartments and promote higher buildings were enforced via SPPRs.

The commitment to facilitate investors made sense early in the recovery phase, as few other ways of funding new residential construction were available at that stage. It similarly made sense to facilitate apartment development, as that was what investment funds were mostly interested in buying, and was also the dominant type of development in Dublin, where housing shortages were first to emerge. As the shortages started to become acute, the government came under sustained pressure to be seen to be taking effective action, which led to them doubling down on this commitment.

The destabilising consequences of this approach included a surge in the number of judicial review applications. By 2021, more than half of SHD applications were subject to judicial review (Mitchell, 2022, p.13). An Bord Pleanála became overloaded by the need to respond in judicial review cases, as well as by the SHD applications themselves, and the processing of other applications was slowed down by this overload. For this reason, it is difficult to be sure that the net effect of these measures on output was positive.

As the SHD process was unpopular as well as dubiously effective, the 2020 Programme for Government included (p.58) a commitment to terminate it, which took effect in 2022. It was replaced by a formalised pre-planning process for large-scale residential developments (LSRDs), accompanied by a reduction in the ability of planning authorities and An Bord Pleanála to seek further information (Housing for All, p.84). In a section headed 'Improve the Functioning of the Planning Process', Housing for All also indicated (pp.85–86) that a review of the planning system by the Attorney General would be completed by the end of 2022. This led to the publication of a draft Planning and Development Bill early in 2023, which included new restrictions on the right to seek judicial review.

There was in any case an obvious difficulty in attributing low housing output to planning delays and restrictions. In each of the years from 2004 to 2007, over 75,000 units were built, under a planning system which had not benefited from any of the reforms referred to or introduced under Rebuilding Ireland, so it is far from clear why that system should now struggle to process output of 20,000 or 30,000 units a year.

The SHD episode illustrated a certain lack of realism in its supporters, in that they presumably did not expect preventing objectors from seeking a second opinion within the planning system would lead them to transfer the dispute to a legal arena on such a large scale.[44] It also suggested that efforts to prevent some types of legal challenge in future could lead to an arms race between objectors and the government, with each manoeuvre being answered by a counter manoeuvre. Legal restrictions can also be outflanked by political change, particularly in view of widespread public scepticism on the effectiveness of some of the more contentious types of development – such as high rent apartments in high rise buildings – in addressing the wider housing shortage.

Lennon and Waldron suggest (2019, p. 1608) construction and property interests used the housing shortage to advance their own agenda, in circumstances where neither they nor the government were inclined to make fine distinctions between increasing output and increasing profitability. As a result of the 2008 crash

> *housing supply has been severely curtailed for a decade, despite the fact that demand has soared following the recession, particularly in Dublin… However, the development sector has opportunistically utilised this crisis to position the planning system as a key barrier to housing supply and has consistently sought planning reforms that are ever-more facilitative of development interests.*

This charge is plausible, given the tendency within the sector to demand 'certainty' on the outcome and timing of decisions on planning applications, and to ignore the large number of unimplemented planning permissions, on which certainty is available. The sector probably was being opportunistic, but it is in the nature of the cycle to create such opportunities.

If the main aim of both the sector and government was to expand apartment construction for investment funds, it was to some extent achieved, though government support for this was quite slow to have an effect, with its full impact only becoming apparent in 2020. Nevertheless, this housing type grew fastest under Rebuilding Ireland (+ 2,900, 2018–20), as Figure 5.5 shows. Permissions for apartments expanded even more rapidly, being double the conventional estate houses permitted in 2020, and treble in 2021. However, apartment permissions were less likely to be implemented, as there were three to six times as many permitted but uncommenced apartment units as houses in each year from 2019 to 2022 (Mitchel, 2022, pp. 11, 19).

The other main outcome of Rebuilding Ireland was a steep rise in turnkey social housing (+ 2,700, 2017–19), but not in social housing built directly by local authorities and approved housing bodies (AHBs). [45] Rebuilding Ireland intended (pp. 44, 46) that the majority of the 8,000 new social units per annum it envisaged would be built by local authorities or AHBs, with the remainder acquired on a 'turnkey' basis. In reality, there was a large shortfall in output from the first source, but only a modest shortfall from the second, with the result that turnkey purchases accounted for around two-thirds of social output from 2019 onwards.

HOUSING FOR ALL

The plan period for Rebuilding Ireland came to an end in 2021. Its successor was a €20 billion housing package for the next five-year period (2021–26), called Housing for All and published in September 2021. Its unprecedented cost implied that the shortcomings of its predecessor were due to inadequate financial support by the state. There were however numerous precedents for most of its individual components, and they mostly involved expansion, continuation or revival of previous schemes.

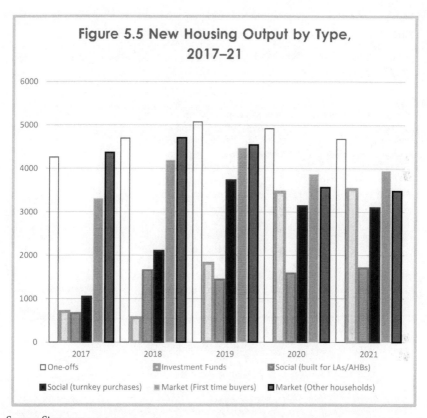

Figure 5.5 New Housing Output by Type, 2017–21

Source: Sirr, 2022, pp.5, 24

They approached housing from a wide variety of angles. Table 5.2 classifies them according to how loosely or tightly targeted they are, and whether they are supply or demand side.

The main new demand-side ones were loosely targeted, and involved continuation of the Help to Buy scheme in place since 2016, and shared equity schemes, on similar principles to the ones under which a total of 16,500 loans were provided between 1990 and 2011. The owner occupier guarantee, while confined to conventional houses in new estates, is an attempt to escape from the unintended consequences of tax concessions to REITs and investment funds, and is

TABLE 5.2

FUNDING/MARKET INTERVENTIONS IN HOUSING FOR ALL

Targeting by market segment	Supply side interventions	Demand side interventions
General (not targeted by type of user demand)	– Project Tosaigh (LDA help for stalled projects – 1,000 units p.a.) – Croí Cónnaithe Fund: Cities (to make apartments for owner occupation viable) – Croí Cónnaithe Fund: Towns & villages (serviced sites, refurbish vacant properties)	
Loosely targeted	– Local authority provided units for affordable purchase – Cost Rental scheme (middle income, 2,000 units p.a.)	– L.A. Affordable Purchase (L.A takes shared equity stake) – 1st Home Scheme (State equity +bank loan) [2 sch. = 4,000 p.a.] – Help to Buy scheme continued
Tightly targeted	– Social Housing (output at 10,000 p.a.) – Housing 1st (homelessness – 240 p.a.) – Fresh Start (after separation/divorce)	
Redirection of output		– Owner occupier guarantee (LAs can specify % to be owner occupied in estate)

reminiscent of the Bacon report measures to discourage investors in the housing market.

These measures were designed to facilitate owner occupation, and this aim is less obviously qualified by arguments on the merits of the private rented sector as a long-term option than it was in Rebuilding Ireland. However, large-scale demand-side support for tenants in the private rented sector continues through schemes such as HAP, accompanied by some regulatory changes to protect tenants.

On the supply side, the Housing for All target of 10,000 social houses per annum is higher than the previous target of *c.* 8,000 in Rebuilding Ireland, and is also higher than previous peaks in units actually produced, at least in absolute terms. In proportional terms, the target is *c.* 0.5% of total households, which is above the long-run average of 0.4%, but well below the pre-1987 percentage (see Figure 5.1 above). Affordable housing to be provided by local authorities reinstated the rather similar Affordable Housing Scheme which existed from 1999 to 2011, under which local authorities provided land on which houses were built for sale at discounted prices to eligible purchasers (Sirr, 2019, pp. 7, 117–8, 27–9).

Increasing cost rental output to 2,000 units per annum is more innovative, in the sense that this would move this type of housing from an experimental form of tenure into the mainstream. There has been growing interest in it in recent years, as an alternative to the private rented sector. It works on the principle that rents reflect the historical cost of provision, rather than current market rents, and thus fall below the latter as the relevant stock ages. It operates successfully and on a large scale in Vienna. Tenants are mixed income, in contrast to conventional social housing in Ireland, which is allocated on the basis of greatest need and is primarily occupied by those on social welfare and other low-income households. Cost rental would also be closer to self-funding, so state support for it is more likely to be treated as 'off-balance sheet' by Eurostat, and thus less constrained by EU limits on government deficits.

Project Tosaigh and Croí Cónnaithe (cities) are entirely new supply-side measures. Both involve direct state financing or subsidising of private sector development and are designed to address the large number of unimplemented planning permissions, presumably on the basis that construction could start quickly if their financial problems could be resolved.

Croí Cónnaithe (cities) aims to address the 'viability challenge' for owner occupied apartments. It will apply

> *to developments over a certain height/density threshold and, through a competitive bid process, will ensure that these developments can be built at lower*

cost for sale to owner occupiers. The level of Exchequer investment per home will be a maximum of 20% of the total cost of the eligible unit of residential accommodation... Effectively, the home will be delivered to purchasers at a lower cost with the reduction broadly equivalent to the level of VAT and development levies (Housing for All, pp.91–92).

The approach is not too different from that suggested in Box 5.2 above, except that the subsidy or tax rebate is directed at the most expensive type of home (high density apartments) instead of the cheapest (terrace houses). This focus on high-cost units is reflected in a maximum subsidy of €144,000, and will result in fewer homes for a given level of support. The competitive element in the scheme might however concentrate minds on finding ways of reducing the high cost of apartment construction in Ireland, by methods other than reducing standards in ways likely to make them less attractive to owner occupiers.

Project Tosaigh addresses unimplemented planning permissions which are stalled for various reasons, with inadequate development finance likely to be the principal difficulty in most cases. This needs to be put in context:

Up to 2008, high levels of debt were possible to finance development, with loan to value (LTV) financing available for more than 90% of construction costs. Fiscal policies aimed at de-risking development lending to the building sector have restricted lending to a maximum of 60% LTV, but this is has led to a funding shortfall for many locations. It is now common for LTV levels of 50–60% to be imposed by mainstream lenders to reduce their exposure to market price falls. Slightly higher levels of financing can be obtained from non-regulated lenders ... but these are typically complex, bespoke arrangements, subject to special conditions ... (Reynolds 2021, p.66).

It is not clear how far the gap left by the reduction in bank lending after 2008 still restricts private sector housebuilding,[46] given increased availability of funding from international and other investment funds, private equity firms, state bodies and (for larger companies quoted on the stock exchange) equity finance from shareholders. Project Tosaigh implies that the gap is still there, but it is a relatively small one, as the 1,000 units per annum it is expected to affect are a small fraction of the 70,000–80,000 which Housing for All (2021, pp. 17, 91) estimates are in developments which are permitted but not commenced.

Alternatively, Project Tosaigh may have been approached with caution, in view of possible claims of moral hazard or distortion of competition. This raises the question of whether there are alternative methods of easing development finance problems, which would be less exposed to such claims. Box 5.6 outlines one possibility.

Box 5.6   Part V as a Source of Development Finance for Housing?

Availability of development finance for lower cost private sector housing could be increased by local authorities paying some of the amount due for housing units or land transferred to them under Part V, in the form of advances. In a development of conventional houses, an initial advance could be made when development commences, secured on the land allocated for the Part V units, and a second one when construction of those specific units was under way. This option could be available to builders, once the price of the property to be transferred had been agreed.

The range of housing projects to which this approach could be applied would initially be limited, due to the reduction of the maximum transfer under Part V from 20% to 10% in 2015. While the 20% maximum was restored by Housing for All (p. 41), the 10% one will continue to apply to planning permissions which had already been granted by 2021, and (until 2026) also to land bought by the developer between 2015 and 2021.

However, the problem is unlikely to go away, and this particular solution could be widely applied in the medium term. There would also be advantages in giving Part V a more central role in the development of housing, and (perhaps in combination with the suggestion in Box 3.3) moving beyond the rather half-hearted commitment to it which has prevailed until now.

The need to bridge the development finance gap for housing projects could also be reduced, by buying or leasing fewer social housing units[47] from developers, as suggested in Box 5.7.

Box 5.7 A Shift towards Contractor-built Social Housing?

Around two thirds of the new social housing units provided in 2019–21 were acquired from developers on a turnkey basis, rather than being designed by local authorities and AHBs, put out to tender by them, and built by contractors under their supervision. If this pattern remains in place, the doubling of social housing output planned by Housing for All will result in doubling of turnkey purchases.

The assumption behind Project Tosaigh is that the post-2008 financing gap continues to limit the output of spec-built housing by private developers, and this is a widely shared view. Development finance should be less of a constraint on the provision of social housing by contractors, as they are taking fewer risks than speculative developers, and the financial terms available to them should reflect this. If there are cases where contractors still have difficulties in arranging sufficient finance, adjustments to the timing of payment for work done may resolve these.

Providing the size of the pool of relevant construction skills shared between developers and contractors is not an overriding constraint on their combined output, expanding construction by contractors should increase overall supply, as more of the units built on a speculative basis can be sold to households, without limiting the expansion of social housing. The two tenures can expand in parallel, with the ability to finance speculative building less of a constraint on the overall volume of housing produced.

To reach the Housing for All social housing target of 9,500 new homes per annum without increasing turnkey purchases, the number of units designed by local authorities and AHBs and built by contractors will need to almost quadruple, from 1,700 in 2021 to 6,400.

Institutions do not adapt rapidly, and the causes of over-reliance on turnkey purchases are quite deeply embedded. Lengthy and elaborate procurement processes deter smaller contractors, and similarly lengthy Department of Housing approval procedures have encouraged local authorities to move away from housing schemes designed and supervised by their own architects and technical staff, towards a culture of managers and property professionals doing deals. Change will only occur if there is a strong commitment to making it happen over a substantial period.

SCALE AND AMELIORATION

Despite the scale of public investment proposed, Housing for All is often seen as inadequate. The housing spokesman of the main opposition party, Eoin Ó Broin, proposed (2019, pp. 168–171) even greater increases in output of social housing (14,000 units a year instead of the 10,000 a year in Housing for All) and affordable housing (9,000 instead of 6,000). This would not necessarily involve greater economic resources, as in Ó Broin's view (p.12)

> *the key features of our current housing system are an under-provision of public non-market housing and an over-reliance on the private market to meet housing need. This involves massive subsidies to landowners, developers, landlords and investment funds.*

There is an intermediate possibility, less generous to the latter groups, but not involving such a large increase in public housing. On the supply side, the terms on which the state interacts with landowners and investment funds could become more stringent, especially in the upper part of the cycle, and on the demand side, supports could be more tightly targeted, redirecting them in ways which will meet the most pressing needs more effectively.

With some exceptions, successive Irish governments have tended to believe that full cooperation from private sector suppliers, and worthwhile improvements for a substantial proportion of households, can only be reliably achieved by interacting with both on a generous and loosely defined basis. While there is probably some truth in this, we have arguably got to a point where we cannot afford to proceed on that basis, without setting ourselves up for another round of cyclically driven punishment to follow the current one.

Ó Broin asks (p. 3)

are we really consigned to the Hobson's choice of an inadequate amelioration or an impossible revolution?

Realistically, amelioration is never going to be fully adequate, because Ireland is an unusually open part of a constantly changing international economy. The recent tendency for mobile capital to be funnelled into housing markets was not peculiar to Dublin, but applied to many other capital cities, including Berlin and London. Ó Broin attributed this (p .146) to the €11 trillion of safe assets bought from investors as quantitative easing after the 2008 crash and replaced with new money at 0% interest rates, leading to the money displaced searching for safe assets with worthwhile yields, and finding them in residential property in large cities.

International investment flows may move in different directions at different times, but even the most approximate match between investor priorities and otherwise unmet housing needs in different parts of Ireland will only happen for some of the time. The concentration of economic growth in sectors which prefer to locate in central parts of medium to large metropolitan areas concentrates property investor interest there as well, and also boosts demand for housing from users. Ireland is unusually exposed to this problem, because it has only one such metropolitan area, which contains nearly half the population of the state.

As a consequence, housing problems in the Dublin area arise in a more than usually acute form there, and disproportionately dominate discussion of housing issues in Ireland. They also tend to spread outwards to other parts of the state after a time lag, through the effect on property market expectations, longer distance commuting, and (during the Covid pandemic) the relocation made possible by remote working.

There is a long-established line of thought, which sees the problems faced by the Dublin area more as failures of regional policy than housing policy, and as likely to be more manageable if more were done to redirect growth from Dublin to other parts of the state. This argument can also be made in relation to construction cyclicality. Certainly, recoveries and booms start in the Dublin area, they are more intense there, and house and property prices peak at much higher levels there.

The question of whether Irish housing crises and construction sector cyclicality could be more adequately ameliorated through a more effective regional policy, is worth pursuing further, and is discussed in the next chapter.

CHAPTER 6

A REGIONAL ALTERNATIVE?

Summary: *The property market would be less cyclical if growth was less concentrated in Dublin. A variety of regional policies have aimed for this, some based on achieving greater economies of scale for growth centres outside Dublin, like the 1968 Buchanan report, others emphasising improvements to their development capacity, or – like the current National Planning Framework – relying on some combination of the two. Both in the mid-1990s and from 2015 onwards, employment in Dublin grew much faster than its housing stock. During recessions, reports should be prepared on regionally based contingency measures, to cope with possible imbalances of this type in a future recovery.*

Population in metropolitan areas has grown at fairly consistent long-run average rates from the 1960s on, and these incorporate the spatial effects of state policies. Since Dublin and its commuting hinterland have more than double the combined population of the other metropolitan areas, its dominance will continue to increase, unless it grows much more slowly in future, and the other cities grow much faster. The NPF aims for this outcome, but does not include convincing causal mechanisms for realising it.

While regional policies are oversold, abandoning them could increase Dublin's share of growth further. The dominance of functionally defined central government agencies does not help regional balance, but a greater role for cross-compartment ones could offset this.

Construction cycles start in Dublin. The post-2014 recovery was initially almost confined to Dublin, and remained largely concentrated there, as did the associated housing problems. Early in the previous cycle, the CIF attacked references to a so-called property boom, saying it was, in fact, confined to a small area of Dublin 4.[1] When the boom phase of that cycle was about to take off in earnest, in the mid-

216

1990s, rapidly escalating house prices in Dublin were the most obvious early symptom, which took some time to spread to other parts of the state.

This raises the question of how far the cyclical issues this book deals with are, in reality, regional policy issues. To put it another way, if economic growth early in the cycle is heavily concentrated in Dublin, and the Dublin area either cannot or does not mobilise the property market, construction and transport capacity necessary to accommodate it satisfactorily, boom and bust, long-distance commuting and gridlock are natural consequences, and through spread effects and influence on expectations, may come to affect much of the rest of the country. Arguably, more balanced distribution of growth early in the cycle would make more use of spare capacity elsewhere in the state, property prices and congestion costs would peak at lower levels, and subsequent downturns would also be more moderate.

Ireland has had a variety of regional policies, some explicit, others more implicit, and both have emerged with increasing frequency from the 1960s onwards. Broadly speaking, their success has been inversely related to their explicitness in terms of the desired distribution of growth between Dublin and other urban areas, leading to some cynicism. However, some regional policies could perhaps be rescheduled and reshaped to work with the cycle, rather than ignoring it or working against it, and the main purpose of this chapter is to review Irish regional policies from the 1960s, from that particular angle.

Crudely, the policies in question can be grouped historically by their characteristic aims:

(a) Raising regional economies of scale closer to European norms (from the 1960s on)
(b) Increasing regions' capacity for development, and removing bottlenecks (from the 1980s on)
(c) Combinations of (a) and (b) (from the 1990s on).

The following sections deal with these in turn, as proposed and/or implemented.

A. REGIONAL ECONOMIES OF SCALE

In the second half of the twentieth century, Irish policy makers were understandably concerned that the small-scale and dispersed character of economic activity in Ireland, relative to most other European countries, would make it uncompetitive, particularly outside Dublin. However, their attention shifted between the three main types of scale economy, as summarised in a contemporary textbook (Glasson, 1974, pp. 149–50), and successively adopted in Ireland, in the early 1970s, 1980s, and 1990s respectively:

(i)   Those resulting from concentration of economic activity in general in large urban areas, where businesses can support, and benefit from, access to a wider variety of higher quality infrastructure, skills and services, and so be more competitive than businesses in small towns or rural areas ('urbanisation economies')

(ii) Those which occur when large individual firms have lower unit costs and other size-related advantages over smaller competitors (firm-size economies)

(iii) Those arising where spatial clustering of firms in the same industry (or closely related ones) results in better availability of the specialised skills, services and sub-suppliers they need, and more favourable conditions for innovation ('localisation economies')

Of these, (i) can form the basis for a regional policy, (ii) for an industrial one, and (iii) for an industrial policy with a regional dimension. This section deals mainly with (i), which was an important strand in Irish public policy up to the mid-1970s, and from the late 1990s on.

Initially, bringing in new manufacturing firms was seen as the main way of achieving regional objectives. The 1952 Undeveloped Areas Act started the process of grant-aiding new industry, and applied it to counties on the west coast, where emigration was highest and the rate of development lowest. The 1956 Industrial Grants Act extended grants to the rest of the country, but at a less generous rate than in the west. When Irish economic policy was reoriented away from protectionism in the late 1950s, this grant differential was questioned:

> *in our present circumstance, with virtually the whole country undeveloped, it seems wasteful to subsidise remote areas specially by providing more extensive grants ... this ... entails additional burdens on the community as a whole and retards progress in the more suitable areas where concentrated effort could give better results ...* (Department of Finance, 1958, p. 160)

The conclusion was 'if we are to have any hope of success ... we must site our industries at, or convenient to, the larger centres of population' (*Ibid.*). In other words, industrial policy should promote urbanisation economies, rather than try to compensate for their absence. The case for and against reorienting industrial policy towards such economies was vigorously debated for the next decade and a half (NESC, 1975, pp. 45–9).

GROWTH POLES AND GROWTH CENTRES

This practical debate within Ireland had a theoretical international counterpart in the theory of growth poles. This was based on the observation that economic growth occurs unevenly, propelled by innovatory industrial firms or sectors, and with a strong tendency for other businesses and sectors to cluster or 'polarise' around them. Initially, this process might be at the expense of less dynamic areas, but, in the medium term, it would start to benefit adjoining areas through 'spread effects'. French economists were the prime contributors to the development of this theory (Glasson, 1974, p. 146), especially Perroux and Boudeville.

Perroux saw polarisation as occurring in economic space where proximity was measured by the level of interaction between economic actors, rather than in 'banal' geographic space:

> *Perroux's economic space, in which spread effects are felt, is global. He argues, for instance that Latin America's true growth poles still lie in Europe and ... the United States. Such a concept is useless for regional planning which is confined to a single country. As a consequence, economists who found themselves involved in practical regional planning simply discarded the pure theory of Perroux. They converted it into a totally different theory which treated growth poles as urban centres, and spread effects as being generated in ... the region adjacent to the urban centre ...* (Higgins, 1988, pp. 43–4)

Perroux's ideas were thus adapted in a way which emphasised localisation economies:

> *The concept of a growth pole is associated with the notion of propulsive industry. Since we are examining the regional setting and not the national space, it would be preferable to describe poles as a geographic agglomeration of activities rather than as a complex system of sectors different from the national matrix. In short, growth poles will appear as towns possessing a complex of propulsive industries.* (Boudeville, 1966, p. 112)

Propulsive industries could be identified by their dominance, oligopolistic position, and price leadership, and also by their high regional linkages and multiplier effects. They generated or attracted other businesses through their demand for inputs, and for onward processing of their products. By attracting labour, they stimulated population growth, and investment in housing and social overhead capital in the area concerned. The resulting external economies benefited the propulsive industries, and reinforced their dominance (Boudeville, 1966, pp. 112–17).

To convert this into a regional policy, existing or potential clusters of related industries with growth potential in particular regions would need to be identified, and assistance selectively focused on them. This might involve inserting new, hopefully propulsive industrial projects into regional economies, or surveying these economies to identify potential leading industries and industrial clusters. Both approaches were applied in continental European countries in the 1960s and 1970s (Boudeville, 1966, p. 107; Buttler, 1975, pp. 31–2, 62, Ch. 7).

The growth pole approach involved some theoretical problems, and some practical attempts to apply it were notably unsuccessful. This encouraged its redefinition in a way that further emphasised the role of town size, and de-emphasised industrial clustering around a leading sector (Buttler, 1975, pp. 31–6). The term 'growth centres' was applied to this variant:

> a pole policy necessitates the development of a selected industrial focus composed of propulsive firms from leading industries, the intention being to foster local-isation economies. In contrast, the centre policy does not involve the selection of related industries, but rather the concentration of investment in a chosen location of those facilities which will create urbanisation economies that are attractive to industry ... a growth pole policy will inevitably result in a growth centre and the resultant urbanisation economies. However this is not necessarily true in reverse for a growth centre policy may not lead to the development of a growth pole of linked industries. (Glasson, 1974, p. 156)

Confusingly, the Irish regional policy debate in the 1960s and 1970s related to growth centres, but the term 'growth poles' was widely used. A series of official reports in the mid-1960s argued for concentration of new industry in a few regional centres, where better ancillary services and infrastructure, and specially built industrial estates would be available, making it easier to attract firms, and more likely that they would grow (Walsh, 1976, pp. 27–9).

URBANISATION ECONOMIES AND THE 1968 BUCHANAN REPORT

This debate culminated in the 1968 Buchanan report, which recommended focusing industrial growth in the main provincial centres, so as to realise urbanisation economies. Growth targets were expressed in population terms, and involved doubling the size of Cork and trebling that of Limerick/Shannon between 1966 and 1986. Dublin, Cork and Limerick would become national growth centres, and serve as the main centres for industry. Second-tier regional growth centres were envisaged, with Waterford, Dundalk and Drogheda as centres for regional expansion, Sligo and Athlone as regional service centres, and Galway combining both roles with a tourism one (see Figure 6.1). A third, local tier, to act as a focus for services in remoter areas, was suggested (Buchanan, 1968, pp. 107, 122–3).

Lower tiers in this hierarchy may have been included partly to deflect anticipated criticism from areas at a distance from the proposed industrial centres. If so, the precaution was ineffective. The government, in its reaction to the report in press statements, in May 1969 and May 1972, supported both the growth centre policy, and one of building up medium and small towns.[2] A clearer indication of their intentions was given by the omission of practical steps necessary to the Buchanan strategy. For instance, Cork and Limerick were not included in the Designated Areas eligible for higher grant level,[3] nor was an organisation similar to the Shannon Free Airport Development Company (SFADCo) created for the Cork area, which were the methods proposed by Buchanan (1968, pp. 190–1) for boosting and managing industrial growth in those cities.

By contrast, practical steps were taken in relation to dispersal. The area covered by the IDA's small industry programme was extended, and a pro-

FIGURE 6.1 GROWTH CENTRE PROPOSALS IN THE BUCHANAN REPORT

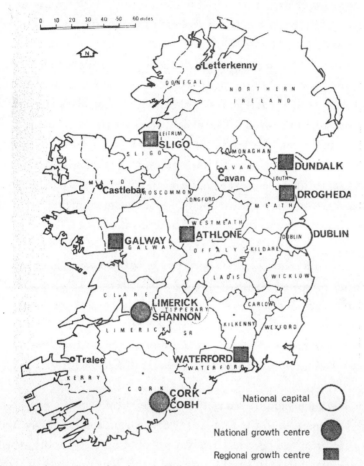

Source: Buchanan, Regional Studies in Ireland, Map 37

gramme of 54 IDA advance factories, mostly in medium and small towns, was initiated in 1971 (Walsh, 1976, pp. 33–4). The IDA Regional Industrial Plans for 1973–7 provided job targets for 47 town clusters, which included 177 individual towns,[4] and this was explicitly endorsed by the 1972 government statement as being consistent with the longer-term regional strategy they had outlined.[5]

The government's ambiguous approach is understandable in political terms, as growth centres proved highly contentious: 'Few development issues have generated so much controversy and emotion as the concept of spatially polarised growth' (O'Farrell, 1974, p. 499).

A common theme running through all the government press statements on the issue, including the (pre-Buchanan) one in 1965, was the determination to retain and actively develop an industrialisation policy for small and medium-sized towns which were not growth centres, and for remoter rural areas.[6] The established industrial policy in the 1960s was one of dispersal. Local public opinion, and more particularly, local business interests from these areas were never likely to accept passively its replacement by a growth-centre policy. These pressures may have been balanced, to some extent, by city-based business interests:

> spatially dispersed pattern of foreign investment in Ireland is clearly associated with the correspondingly decentralised petty business interests which control the Irish state ... Indeed, it may be that the attempt to have a growth-centre policy implemented in the 1960s reflected an attempt on the part of city-based business interests to replace business lost under the new economic policy (with city-based theorists providing the required 'ideological' input) ... (Breathnach, 1982, p. 53)

However, any such support was not obvious or vocal.

Even if opposition to the Buchanan report from smaller towns and remoter rural areas had been less, the way the public sector was organised would have made its implementation unlikely. Bannon (1989, p. 145) pointed out that the report could not easily have been carried out by a central government composed of loosely-coupled sectoral departments. It raised:

> serious questions about the divisions of power within Cabinet with respect to forward planning and resource allocation. The national strategy proposed by Buchanan ... was in effect a framework within which all public sector decisions would be made ... implementation of such a programme would have required

an inter-departmental approach to planning, with ultimate policy vested in a Cabinet sub-committee. It was unrealistic to believe that the Department of Local Government ... or indeed the proposed super-ministry of Regional Planning, would ever have received the freedom to implement such a programme.

The attitude of the IDA, which would have had a key role in applying the Buchanan strategy if it had been adopted, presented more immediate problems. The IDA did not accept that most incoming industry would prefer to locate in one of the main urban areas. It argued the situation was changing, and that new industry was now more willing to set up in small towns, pointing to the increasing proportion of job approvals in rural regions in the late 1960s (IDA, 1972, p. 15). During the 1970s, they were able to prove this, and channelled so much industry into the least industrialised regions, that by 1980, they were converging with more developed ones, in terms of the proportion of the work force in industry (Mansergh, 2001, p. 223).

Factors other than the higher level of grants available in designated areas were seen as making locations outside larger urban areas acceptable or even attractive to industrialists. Industrial relations difficulties – a feature of the 1970s – were less likely away from the larger urban areas. Also, tendencies towards 'deskilling' meant absence of an industrial tradition amongst rural workers was viewed more positively. The branch plant nature of much inward investment meant more of their needs were met from within the same multi-national company, making local suppliers and services less relevant (Breathnach, 1982, pp. 45–50).

The IDA had established a successful marketing operation on behalf of small town and rural Ireland, and argued that this could continue in parallel with efforts to build up growth centres:

in practice, development or growth centres can co-exist in Ireland with industry in the smaller centres. The importance of development centres in stimulating ... competitive and self-generating industrial growth is also recognised, but many smaller urban centres are suitable for a wide range of smaller and less technologically complex industries. (IDA, 1972, p. 15)

The IDA was not going to abandon an industrial segment, which promised large numbers of projects in the short term, to concentrate on one which might provide a smaller number of projects in the longer term. It would have made no sense for it as an organisation to damage its own short-term performance, and sacrifice much of its support base, in deference to a theoretically based strategy of uncertain effectiveness under Irish conditions.

FIRM SIZE AND THE 1982 TELESIS REPORT

The inconclusive controversy over Buchanan left Ireland without a policy on economies of scale. However, the 1982 Telesis report[7] proposed seeking these via firm size, arguing that (1982, pp. 3, 151, 247) industrial policy in the 1960s and 1970 had widened the gap between average incomes in Ireland and those in most industrialised countries, as the multinational companies attracted did not employ many skilled workers, or buy internationally traded inputs from Irish companies. Irish-owned firms in traded sectors were still low wage, reliant on the UK as their export market, and subject to numerous closures and contractions (Telesis, 1982, pp. 89–90). Growing Irish firms were mostly in non-traded areas such as packaging, cement, and metal fabrication, where growth in foreign firms had expanded demand, and they were protected from imports by low value to bulk ratios. Some had grown to the point where they were expanding through purchase of similar plants abroad (Telesis, 1982, pp. 88, 112–6). To raise incomes as well as employment, Telesis argued industrial policy should be redirected to build up strong indigenous, export-oriented companies, and skilled sub-supply firms, as:

No country has successfully achieved high incomes without a strong base of indigenously owned resource or manufacturing companies in traded businesses. Home based companies inevitably bring managerial and high-skilled technical employment, a requirement for high levels of services, and direct income to the home country. When the going is rough, they tend to make decisions in line with the national interest of the country in which they live. (Telesis, 1982, p. 185)

The IDA was as sceptical about this aim as it had been about growth centres. Due to the shortage of indigenous entrepreneurs, it argued for a two-stage policy, aiming firstly at increasing their number, and then at identifying and supporting stronger companies. It also questioned proposed cuts to grants to foreign firms, as existing incentives reflected international competition, and were based on detailed experience, and experiments could damage Ireland's reputation for consistency (NESC, in preface to Telesis, 1982, paras 8–10). A Company Development Programme was set up, in line with the central Telesis recommendation of building up large, internationally competitive, Irish-owned industries, but by 1992, early hopes for it 'seem to have evaporated' (Culliton, 1992, p. 63).

LOCALISATION ECONOMIES AND THE 1992 CULLITON REPORT

Spatial clustering played a key role in the next major report on industrial policy, the 1992 Culliton report. Like Telesis, it reflected dissatisfaction with the results of the established one. Its recommendations dealt partly with the broad context for industrial policy, including taxation, infrastructure, education and training, partly with its management, including reform of institutional structures and incentives, and partly with its actual content.

On the last of these, Culliton aimed to develop the competitive advantages of Irish industry. This aim reflected a concern that much overseas investment was being attracted to Ireland on a quite different basis: that of tax concessions and relatively low labour costs – 'factors that can easily be replicated by competing countries or regions' (Culliton, 1992, p. 66). Similarly, the focus on attracting companies from rapidly expanding high technology and pharmaceutical sectors was questioned, on the basis that Ireland had no special competitive advantage in these areas. A greater contribution from Irish companies 'with deeper roots in the economy' was needed, but foreign companies which were well integrated into the economy and had their core functions here could be equally valuable (Culliton, 1992, pp. 22, 74).

One of the principal methods by which competitive advantage could be increased was through the development of clusters. Clustering, like polarisation in the 1960s, was seen by a temporarily dominant school of thought on economic development as a process which occurred naturally in many countries, and was central to economic growth:

> ... first one industry emerges from the environment: soon supplier industries develop to serve it. Investment in education, training, R&D and infrastructure reinforce the process. As expertise further develops, it is spread to other industries that require similar skills, technologies and infrastructure. This process continues and spreads to other related industries. The growth and success of individual firms spills over to others.
>
> This approach is endorsed by international evidence on the process of industrial expansion, and by new insights on how economic growth comes about. (Culliton, 1992, p. 74)

The insights referred to were derived from the work of Michael Porter and his colleagues. Porter (1990, Ch. 3) saw the competitive advantage of countries as specific to particular industries – no country was good at everything – which could be developed where four conditions applied. Briefly, these were:

- Availability of factor advantages, advanced and specialised knowledge and skills
- Home markets with sophisticated consumers of the relevant product, which anticipated global demand trends
- The presence of related and supporting industries
- Rivalry between firms committed to the relevant product in the long term.

Porter saw these four sources of competitive advantage as being mutually reinforcing, particularly if they were geographically concentrated in a particular region or city, which, in his view, was frequently or even normally the case. The group of firms benefiting from this dynamic interaction, and linked to each other by supplier-buyer relations, or by having common customers and a common technology, were described by Porter as a 'cluster'.

The Culliton report (1992, pp. 74, 82) saw these ideas being applied by focusing support on market segments and niches where sources of competitive advantage already existed within Ireland to some extent. Geographical proximity to supporting educational and research programmes would be important, and would encourage clustering in particular regions. A favourable institutional climate for this approach could be created by combining functions relevant to the development of competitive advantage and support for indigenous industry in a new agency, which operated through regional boards. The advisory and consultancy role of this new agency would be distinct from marketing Ireland for inward investment, and this difference should be reflected in institutional separation of the two functions.

Like the Buchanan and Telesis reports, the Culliton recommendations on clustering were neither wholeheartedly implemented nor explicitly rejected. The institutional reforms proposed by Culliton were largely implemented, though paradoxically this may have distracted attention from the clustering objectives these reforms were intended to promote:

The section on cluster formation was perhaps the most original and innovative section of the Culliton Report ...: Despite this, it vanished without trace in the subsequent media coverage of the report, which focused instead on the more politically 'juicy' elements such as tax reform and reorganisation of the state agencies. (Breathnach, 1995, p. 9)

Breathnach (1995, p. 11) thought official commitment to clustering unlikely, partly because of the tension between established industrial policies and the cluster approach, which was critical of those policies. Also, the proposed new agency (Forbairt) did not in fact operate through regional boards. It was given a structure similar to the IDA, with a strong central organisation with sectoral policy units and plans, complemented by regional offices. This was an important omission, as Porter saw local or regional governments as more aware of local strengths, and of how they might be developed into regional clusters. Central institutions often lacked detailed local knowledge, and were inclined to rely on generalised incentives which promote sameness between regions, rather than build on regional differences. This argument has wider application, not confined to industrial policy.

However, a NESC research project on clustering did suggest continuing official interest. It (Clancy et al., 1998, pp. 29–32) drew up a short list of eleven relatively successful indigenous industries, and commissioned studies of three: dairy products, software, and music. The most promising was dairying, which benefited from specialist educational, research and marketing institutions, rivalry between co-ops (at any rate over milk supply), and geographical concentration in South Munster. However, it had few related and supporting businesses within Ireland, other than milk suppliers (O'Connell et al., 1997, pp. 69–79). The conclusion drawn was that clusters were scarce and underdeveloped. This raised the question of why indigenous industry had been doing so well in the previous decade in their absence:

To a considerable extent, this growth has occurred in small or medium sized enterprises, spread quite widely across a range of sectors which were quite weak to begin with and are still not particularly strong. In addition, part of the growth of indigenous industry has occurred in a limited number of larger more prominent companies, in sectors which themselves look rather insubstantial. Thus, the growth has not occurred in a concentrated manner within a limited number of sectors, so as to produce strong sectors or clusters of related sectors.
(Clancy *et al.*, 1998, pp. 37–9)

By implication, progress was possible without clusters, and Porter's theory failed 'to capture the dynamics of the Irish economy' (O'Donnell, 1998, p. 58), perhaps being more applicable to large mature economies, as critics argued. O'Donnell suggested (1998, p. 65) Culliton was partly designed to reassure trade unions that the 1987 Programme for National Recovery was not a first step towards a low-wage, low-skill economy. If so, large-scale inward investment in high-skill sub-sectors in the mid-1990s removed the need for this. Promoting localisation economies seemed unnecessary, so long as Ireland enjoyed rapid growth owing little to them.

ECONOMIES OF SCALE AND AGENCY OPERATIONAL AGENDAS

The failure of attempts to enhance economies of scale to gain IDA support illustrates a wider point. Government agencies usually have their own operational agenda. Telesis accepted that the core role of the IDA was marketing, and its exceptional expertise in that area: 'The IDA has developed a marketing organisation which is unquestionably the most dynamic, most active, most efficient and most effective of its kind in the world' (Telesis, 1982, p. 172).

The coverage of IDA sales offices, the quality of their industrial intelligence, well-targeted identification of prospects, ability to respond and make decisions, and the dedication and esprit de corps of IDA staff all contributed to this. In the early 1990s, an IDA director explained their approach:

The underlying tactic was to seek out new business areas before our competitors, develop a marketing strategy to convince potential investors of the relevance of Ireland, evolve a pricing policy that was relevant to the sectors, and then seek to achieve a dominant market share in that business area. (Flinter, 1991, p. 194)

This pinpoints the divergence between the IDA's approach and that of the three reports. Flinter is describing a market-led rather than a policy-led approach. A medium-term industrial or regional policy which defined which types of firm from which industrial sectors the IDA should try to attract, to which locations, would be in constant danger of seeking projects which were not available at the time, while neglecting opportunities to attract those that were. To avoid this, the IDA naturally seeks as far as possible to formulate operational policy/marketing strategy itself, using fairly short-term planning horizons, and keeping open the option of changing policy quickly and informally if circumstances so required. Operational autonomy is a necessary feature of a marketing-based approach.

Much of the IDA's opposition to attempts to apply international theories on economies of scale to manufacturing in Ireland seems to have been well founded, in the conditions prevailing at the relevant times. However, if Ireland's mainstream policy of attracting foreign direct investment were to run into major difficulties, interest in such theories would probably revive.

B. REGIONAL DEVELOPMENT CAPACITY

From the mid-1970s on, government interest shifted from regional policies within Ireland to European regional policy. The European Regional

Development Fund (ERDF) originated in negotiations on enlargement of the EEC to include Ireland, the UK, and Denmark in 1972. The Community budget was dominated by the Common Agricultural Policy (CAP), which meant the UK would be a net contributor. However, the UK had serious regional problems, and would be a net beneficiary from an ERDF, so Heath, the British Prime Minister, made creation of a regional fund a priority. Germany, as the principal prospective contributor to a regional fund, supported UK accession, partly to put itself in a better position to grasp opportunities created by the decline of the British capital goods industries. Germany also recognised that Italy and Ireland, as well as Britain, would be unlikely to agree to the first steps towards economic and monetary union (EMU) in the absence of a regional fund (George, 1991, pp. 192–4).

These factors had weakened by 1974, as the first oil crisis had made short-term progress towards EMU unlikely, and the incoming Labour government was seeking renegotiation of British membership. A threat by the other main prospective beneficiaries of a regional fund – Italy and Ireland[8] – to boycott the December 1974 European summit in Paris was necessary in order to secure even a much-reduced Regional Fund (George, 1991, p. 195).

The formative period of European regional policy, in the 1970s and early 1980s, coincided with the displacement of Keynesian ideas on regional policy by supply-side ones, prompted by the economic crisis of the late 1970s. The Keynesian view was that disadvantaged regions suffered from insufficient aggregate demand, which could be remedied by diverting some of the industrial expansion in the more prosperous areas of each country to such regions.[9] At a practical level, this approach became more difficult to apply, as industrial contraction started to predominate over expansion, and mobile industrial projects became scarcer.

Public awareness of the supply-side approach at this time was influenced by its role in the rhetoric of the Thatcher and Reagan governments, but this created a misleading impression:

To emphasise money supply and taxation is to emphasise the doctrinaire aspects of what is loosely known as monetarism. In fact, supply side issues run much wider ... The fundamental stance is ... that governments should use monetary means to establish a predictable environment in which individuals and firms can make sensible judgements about the future ... This in turn places the focus on the markets for the factors of production for land, labour and capital. The question to be asked is: Where are there bottlenecks in supply, and how might they be eased or removed? (Chisholm, 1990, p. 55)

Commission interest in a supply-side approach was signalled by their appointment of a study group on the contribution of infrastructure to regional development in 1979. This group, which reported initially in 1982, and more fully in 1986, took an explicitly supply-side view:

regional disparities are ... a long term type of problem, and not the result of short term fluctuations. As a consequence, the emphasis must be on the supply or capacity side and not on the demand side of the regional economy. (Biehl, 1986, p. 62)

A supply-side approach was complemented by increased emphasis on using indigenous resources. This was prompted partly by reduced mobile investment, partly by disillusionment with capital intensive industrial projects which had little relationship to the economies of the areas where they were located,[10], and partly by increased interest in small businesses, which were seen as better able to exploit local resources (CEC, 1985, pp. 402).

For European Regional Policy, growing theoretical distrust of isolated projects 'parachuted' into a regional economy was reinforced by a second perspective. In the late 1970s and early 1980s, the ERDF had very limited resources, applied mostly to support small-scale projects which were largely unrelated to each other (Nevin, 1990, p. 296; Williams, 1996, p. 71). This criticism was cited by, and perhaps to some extent originated within, the Commission itself: 'The stage of development in a particular region will never be improved by handing out a few grants here and a few grants there' (CEC, 1985, p. 7).

To some extent, this view reflected tensions between national governments and the Commission over control of the regional fund. In some regions, the projects may well have formed part of a coherent strategy but, if they did, it was a national or regional strategy rather than a European one. However, national policies were losing their momentum at this stage: 'By the time the ERDF was placed on the Community agenda, most member states were engaged in consolidating existing regional development measures – there was little political support for any new measures' (Hart, 1985, p. 210).

Also, whatever the merits of established arrangements, they were demonstrably not delivering convergence at the European level. The economic downturn following the oil crisis of 1973 had certainly halted, and arguably reversed, the previous tendency towards gradual convergence between the richer and poorer regions of the Community (Nevin, 1990, p. 296).

Both the theoretical shift to a supply-side approach, and the practical criticism of the early ERDF as unduly small scale and diffusely applied, implied a need for a critical mass of investment in selected locations, a strategic focus on how it was applied, and synergy between individual projects. The Commission-sponsored report on the contribution of infrastructure to regional development outlined a theoretical basis for this (Biehl, 1986).[11] This was based on the idea that a number of different factors need to be present for a region to be able to develop, and that identification and improvement of deficient factors – 'bottlenecks' – was the way to allow it to do so. Biehl (1986, pp. 62–3) defined a number of broad types of 'potentiality factor', such as natural resources, population, location, settlement structure, sectoral mix, and infrastructure. While factors like location and resources are given by nature and not alterable, other factors, including infrastructure in particular, are.

Infrastructure was used in a broad sense to include research institutes, social and educational facilities and so on. It needed disaggregating, as satisfactory aggregate infrastructure indicators could conceal inadequacies in particular categories (Biehl, 1986, pp. 21, 95). Regional policy needed to identify absent or deficient potentiality factors in a region, and bring them up to standard. Conversely, resources did not need to be spent on potentiality factors which were already present and had adequate spare capacity (Biehl, 1986, pp. 71–2).

The report differentiated (Biehl, 1986, pp. 10, 16, 302) between fast-growing, dense, centrally located regions, which tended to have overused infrastructure and capacity bottlenecks, and slow-growing, lower-density peripheral regions, which often had spare capacity, but had more difficulty in attracting mobile factors, such as entrepreneurs and skilled labour. This implied a policy of subsidising infrastructure in the regions where it is overused, and attracting entrepreneurs and skills to those where it is underused. However, in seriously underdeveloped regions, many potentiality factors may be deficient, and a full range of instruments, including infrastructure investment and training subsidies, may be needed.[12] Given the high costs involved, funding for this approach needs very careful control (Biehl, 1986, p. 75).

In under-developed, sparsely populated regions, it might be uneconomic to try to assemble a full range of potentiality factors, but trying to achieve synergy between projects and agencies through an integrated development approach would still make sense. In more developed regions, with more factors already in place, a more comprehensive attempt to identify and remedy the deficient ones would be more realistic.

THE STRUCTURAL FUNDS

The generic shift from a Keynesian to a supply-side agenda was a necessary precondition for the major increase in structural funds in the 1990s. The prospect of a reformed EU regional policy which would provide effective supply-side funding for poorer member states was needed, because it offered prospective recipients a credible case for a large increase in funding, and donors the possibility that relatively modest contributions over a limited period would increase the prosperity of the recipients, to the point where further significant funding was unnecessary. These perceptions shaped the lead up to the first major increase in structural funds in 1989:

> *From the start ... the clear aim was to encourage self sustaining growth in the less developed countries and regions rather than to provide demand stimulus or income maintenance on a continuing basis. From a purely economic point of view the Delors-I and II initiatives were seen by the net donor states as a means of providing the poorer peripheral members with a window of opportunity to rectify economic problems ... The implicit assumption among net donor countries financing the CSF aid was, presumably, that the funding, if successful, could eventually be wound down or redirected elsewhere ...* (Bradley et al., 1995, p. 2)

While recipient countries may have been less worried than donors by the risk of funding continuing indefinitely, they could not be certain it would not gradually diminish. Also, aid dependency is not a comfortable long-term position. Dependence on transfers may actually contribute to underdevelopment, as has been argued in relation to Italy's Mezzogiorno.

The practical consequences of the reform proposals generated during the formative period of EU regional policy for the structural funds were:

(i)   Concentration of resources on the least favoured areas

(ii)   Approval of finance through multi-annual programmes, rather than on a project-by-project basis

(iii)   Agreement on the priorities to be reflected in these programmes between the Commission and national governments

(iv)   Coordination of the various community funds, and also national and local policies, so that these programmes were 'integrated'

The first three were straightforward and unambiguous, and were implemented. Resources were greatly increased, and more concentrated on

'Objective 1' regions, including Ireland. Funding was overwhelmingly on the basis of agreed programmes from 1989 onwards.

The fourth presented more difficulties, particularly in relation to coordinating the actions of sectoral and functional agencies at regional level. In Ireland, the capacity to formulate, fund and implement operational programmes rested with these agencies, and was only minimally balanced by cross-sectoral inputs from regional advisory committees. Regional Development Organisations had been abolished as an economy measure in 1987, and were not restored (in the form of Regional Authorities) until 1994, so there were no regional level institutions in place during formulation of the 1989–93 and 1994–9 National Development Plans (NDPs).

The Commission envisaged the integrated approach they sought as applying to regions, but was 'open to the possibility of' sectorally-based integrated actions (CEC, 1986, pp. 2–4). The latter type of operational programmes, organised on a sectoral or functional basis, dominated Irish NDPs. These were integrated in the sense that they usually involved more than one structural fund, and several Irish agencies, but a 'lead department' was normally designated. There were some integrated local initiatives for disadvantaged urban and rural areas.

Sectoral and functional programmes allowed for synergy through a systematic approach to individual spending categories, but not via integration of a range of disparate activities. There was little evidence of interaction between the operational programmes. For the committees which submitted inputs from individual Irish regions to the National Development Plans, the scope for complex, mutual adaption between the agencies involved was minimised by the short periods within which they had to report to the Department of Finance, and the extent to which decisions were, in practice, being taken at national level anyway.

The Department of Finance coordinated bids at national level. This promoted coordination, in the sense of ensuring that Departmental bids for structural funds added up to the overall funds likely to be available. This was necessary, but unrelated to any quest for synergy.

Coordination at regional level remained weak after Regional Authorities were re-established in 1994. They were given a general function of co-ordinating public services in their region.[13] The difficulty of fulfilling such an abstract and unfocused role was illustrated by regional reports produced in the mid-1990s. The South East Regional Authority one (1996, p. 89) showed a matrix based on 38 organisations or types of organisation multiplied by 16 fields of activity (agriculture, rural development etc). Around 15% of the 608 cells contained a symbol, indicating around 90 points at which organisations needed to coordinate their actions with others. The South West Regional Authority (1996, p. 65) had a similar but larger 3,000 cell matrix, with symbols indicating the need for coordination filling around 600.

EMPLOYMENT SURGES IN DUBLIN

Weak coordination at regional level had practical effects, in terms of the slow response to the capacity problems generated by the surge in employment in the Dublin region in the mid-1990s. At that time, Dublin suddenly became a textbook example of a centrally located region with overused infrastructure. The potentiality factors Dublin had in abundance were labour, skills and third-level education – specifically, a large number of young and often well-educated workers. Birth rates had been high in the 1970s in Ireland, and those born then were now coming onto the labour market. Depressed conditions in the 1980s had resulted in high unemployment, numerous emigrants who would come home if prospects improved, and a low female participation rate. There was also a strong tradition of migration by young people to the Dublin region from the rest of Ireland. High unemployment and EU funding had combined to support an extensive training system.

Expansion of US foreign direct investment created a strong market for this labour supply, the IDA did the necessary marketing, and individual US multinationals who saw competitors successfully established in Dublin followed suit. Employment in manufacturing and international services, in slight decline in the early 1990s, and growing at 2–3% per annum in 1993–4, suddenly grew by around 10% per annum in 1995, and this continued until 2001.

However, there was more spare capacity in the labour market than for other potentiality factors, so employment grew at a rate other factors could not match. Figure 6.2 illustrates this, using housing as an easily measured capacity bottleneck. The housing stock in the Dublin and Mid-East regions had been increasing at around 2% per annum in the early 1990s, rising to nearly 3% per annum by 1996, compared with 9% in manufacturing employment, and 7% in services. As the neck of the housing supply 'bottle' could not be enlarged easily or quickly, the price of housing in Dublin went out of control in 1997.

FIGURE 6.2
EMPLOYMENT AND HOUSING TRENDS IN THE DUBLIN AND MID-EAST REGIONS, 1991–7

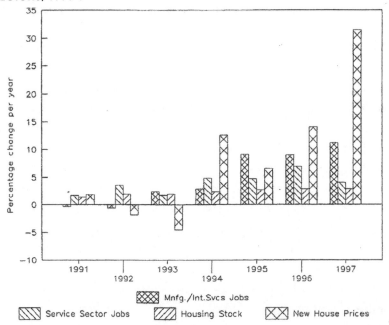

Source: Mansergh, 2001, p. 191, citing Forfás Employment Surveys, CSO Labour Force Surveys, DoELG Housing Statistics Bulletin, Censi

The IDA normally agrees industrial projects well in advance of extra employment actually coming on stream, and the scale of what was happening must have been clear to them by 1994. This may have led them to redirect some of the growth to Cork, Limerick, and Galway, as their regions all started to experience growth of around 10% per annum from 1997 as well. Within the Dublin region, however, this was happening rapidly and unexpectedly. There was no tradition of contingency planning which might have led the 1994–9 NDP to formulate possible responses to greater than expected growth in Dublin,[14] and the mechanisms for any coordinated regional response were largely absent.

The 1994–9 NDP gave the Regional Authorities, re-established in 1994, responsibility for 'reviewing and advising' on its implementation (NDP, 1993, p. 151). In theory, the Dublin and Mid-East Regional Authorities, each in practice a group of committees served by a minimal secretariat, should have jointly identified what was happening, and persuaded the large number of bodies represented on their committees to agree on a response as a matter of urgency. The more important of those bodies should then have gone back to their parent agencies at national level, and secured their agreement to immediate changes to their spending plans.

This was not a realistic prospect in the 1990s.[15] An appendix in the 1994–9 NDP described the sub regional review committee for the Dublin region as aiming to 'provide and maintain the number and types of sustainable jobs needed by the people of Dublin through creating an environment in which industry, services and tourism can flourish...'. Infrastructure was (understandably) seen as a means of attracting jobs, not as a way of keeping pace with an unmanageable influx.

As Figure 6.3 shows, a large gap between the rate of growth in employment and in the housing stock in Dublin re-emerged in the post-2014 recovery. By 2015, the former was back up at 8%, while the latter was at 0.5%.

While the state had learnt from previous experience, it was more effective in suppressing symptoms than in addressing causes. The principal symptom of concern was house prices. Growth in Dublin house prices

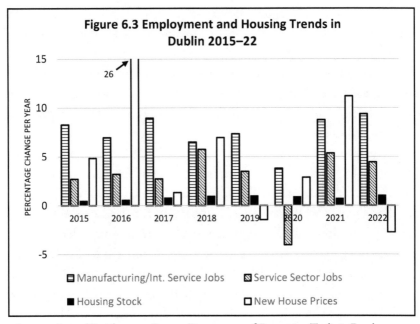

Figure 6.3 Employment and Housing Trends in Dublin 2015–22

Sources: Annual Employment Survey, Department of Enterprise, Trade & Employment, 2022, p. 19, CSO Labour Force Survey Series, CSO Residential Dwelling Property Transaction Series, 2022 Census Preliminary Results, Table 4.2.

may initially have been welcomed as a way of reducing negative equity on houses bought during the previous boom, but in 2016 they reached 95% of peak 2007 values, and prices rose by 26%. In response, the Central Bank set maximum loan to income and loan to value ratios for housing mortgages. This was reasonably effective in controlling increases in the price of housing from 2017 onwards.

The other main symptom addressed was sprawl. As we have seen, planning guidelines required higher densities, which in practice involved increasing the proportion of apartments. The requirement for realistic core strategies in line with national and regional planning targets in county development plans also reduced the amount of zoned land in the commuter belt. In numerical terms, growth in Dublin's housing stock in the 2016–22 intercensal period was not too far below that in 1996–2002, but was much lower in the Mid-East region, as Table 6.1 shows:

TABLE 6.1

INCREASES IN THE HOUSING STOCK IN THE DUBLIN AND MID-EAST REGIONS

	Average Housing gain per annum			Average Housing gain per annum (%)		
	1996–2002	2002–6	2016–22	1996–2002	2002–6	2016–22
Dublin	6819	26976	6214	1.8	6.6	1.1
Mid-East	5450	18027	3869	4.5	13.8	1.8
Dublin & Mid-East	12269	45003	10083	2.4	8.3	1.3

Sources: Housing volumes, Censi, 1996–2022

In percentage terms, the housing stock was growing much more slowly in 2016-22 than in 1996-2002. It is not clear how far this difference was due to the traumatised and barely functioning condition of the house-building and banking sectors at the start of the more recent recovery, and how far to weaker incentives. Central bank controls prevented the lavish increases in profit margins seen in the late 1990s, and insistence on increased apartment content in developments also affected margins, by raising costs more than prices. The 2002–6 period showed that the gap between growth in employment and in the housing stock could close, even in Dublin, but only in the latter part of the cycle, after almost a decade of sustained growth.

In both recovery periods, the cause of the problem was obviously the inability of the housing system and other forms of development capacity to respond to a strong recovery in employment quickly enough. This issue has been discussed at national level in previous chapters, but it arises earlier and in a more concentrated form in Dublin.

Box 6.1 outlines a possible regional response.

Box 6.1 Contingency Planning for Surges in Employment Growth

In Box 4.1, a Coordinated Local Infrastructure Investment Fund (CLIIF) section was suggested, to monitor and maintain a 'floor' level of infrastructure investment. This CLIIF section could have a role in contingency planning for unexpectedly rapid employment growth in metropolitan areas. This might involve:

(a)   Formulating in advance scenarios involving such growth

(b)   Identifying the sub-sectors in which this growth seemed most likely

(c)   Identifying the probable locational preferences of incoming businesses in those sub-sectors, between and within metropolitan areas

(d)   Assessing how far their employees (and those in services whose growth they stimulate) would be recruited locally, and how far they would in-migrate

(e)   Assessing the ability of relevant housing and transport markets and the infrastructure supporting them to cope with this growth

(f)   Identifying actions which could be carried out quickly, to avoid undue transport congestion, housing shortages and price rises anticipated under (e)

(g)   Frequent monitoring of inward investment prospects, planning applications etc, so as to give early warning if one of the scenarios under (a) was being realised

This type of assessment would need to be regularly updated, so as to take account of the latest information on inward investment and other market shifts, and of new infrastructure coming on stream. This implies a need for an in-house team – including property market expertise – to provide continuity.

The CLIIF section may not always be able to identify sufficient actions under (f) to avoid acute difficulties under (e), in areas identified under (c). If so, it could assess alternative, marketable locations which had or could easily be provided with spare capacity. This could help the IDA advise incoming firms on prospective capacity problems, and (if it is clear Dublin is likely to come under pressure), provide it with a basis for encouraging them to locate in other suitable areas.

Arguably, some of the housing measures described in the last chapter, such as shared living complexes, and smaller, build-to-let apartments accommodated in higher buildings, were attempts to respond quickly to a more modest recent surge in employment in internet firms in central Dublin, and were targeted at those working in them, many of them being young, mobile, relatively well paid, and with a preference for urban living. This might be taken as an indication that the lessons of the 1990s have been learnt, and that there is no need for the approach outlined in Box 6.1.

This would be a misconception. Firstly, as in the late 1990s, recent measures are reactive ones, adopted at a point when employment growth in Dublin was already generating acute problems in its housing market. Secondly, they involve overriding the normal planning system, to a much greater extent than they did in the 1990s, through ostensibly national policies which are, in reality, mostly aimed at Dublin. How much damage this does will vary, but in principle, local planning policies are likely to take more account of the specific circumstances of particular areas and sites, and aim for accommodation which is flexible and sustainable in the medium term, rather than just addressing the immediate difficulty. Thirdly, recent measures are too narrowly focused on growth in internet firm employees, and do not allow for its multiplier effect, which stimulates employment in local services. The housing needs arising from this are much less likely to be met by small, overpriced new apartments.

Box 6.1 tries to create arrangements which would ensure that the question 'where is fast employment growth most likely to occur, and can we cope with it if it does?' is asked, even in the depths of recession, when it seems irrelevant and academic. The resources to take action then will be very limited, but this is a reason for focusing them where they are most needed, and – to the extent that they will unavoidably remain inadequate – for considering well in advance how some growth could be diverted from Dublin to places with more spare capacity.

C . POLYCENTRIC REGIONAL PLANS

The ESDP in the 1990s

In the 1990s, the EU's emerging European Spatial Development Perspective (ESDP) helped revive interest in regional policy within Ireland. The ESDP promoted a trans-national approach to spatial planning within the EU, linking regions with similar characteristics in different member states, and suggesting cross-boundary policy responses. Countries which already had countrywide spatial policies served, to some extent, as a model.[16] The ESDP paved the way for the Irish National Spatial Strategy (NSS), and the National Development Plan (NDP) for 2000–6 envisaged (p. 45) the NSS drawing on ESDP goals and ideas.

To stimulate development of an ESDP, the Commission sponsored preliminary, experimental studies of what it might involve. The study relevant to Ireland treated it as part of an 'Atlantic Arc', extending from Scotland to Andalucia (CEC, 1994a, p. 170). Through a 'trend scenario', it expressed concern that peripheral, small-medium-sized cities and rural areas in places like the western half of Ireland would have poor access, and be condemned to relative isolation, economic decline and rural desertification. By contrast, growth would become increasingly polarised around cities with the critical mass to develop as major technology centres and high-quality international transport, such as Dublin (CEC, 1994b, pp. 152, 202–9).

The 'active scenario' suggested in response showed the creation of three large areas for 'the intensification of industrial modernisation and diversification' (CEC, 1994b, p. 211), which respectively linked Limerick and Galway, Waterford and Rosslare, and Dublin and Dundalk. Growth in the Limerick–Galway block was to be promoted by science parks in both cities, and by transport links linking it to Belfast, Dublin and Rosslare, continuing as sea routes to Stranraer, Holyhead, and Fishguard. Industrial areas were also shown around Belfast and Derry, leaving Cork as the only city not part of an industrial block or corridor.[17]

The broad-brush character of this scenario was representative of a style of spatial planning used in north-central Europe, involving simplified presentation of a few key, macro-scale policies on small-scale maps. Dutch planning, for instance, developed over several decades around the core concepts of the Randstad and the 'green heart' – the idea that the agricultural area within the ring of cities in the western Netherlands should remain undeveloped (Faludi and van der Valk, 1994, pp. 21–3). Other national plans were organised around major transport corridors. A 1992 Danish plan aimed to use the new centrality of Denmark, due to the Oresund crossing to Sweden, to develop the Copenhagen area as the leading urban region in Nordic countries. A 1993 plan for the former East Germany saw it becoming a transport hub for central Europe, and aimed to avoid excess concentration of transport routes and development around Berlin (Williams, 1996, pp. 109–12).

The ESDP itself was more a set of principles, rather than mapped proposals. Its most obvious contribution to Irish regional policy was the 'gateway' concept, defined as (ESDP, 1997, p. 55): 'cities which give access to the Union's territory (major seaports, inter-continental airports, cities where fairs and exhibitions are held, cultural centres)'.

Gateways fitted in well with traditional Irish regional policy concerns. They were an attempt to move away from the hierarchical urban structures which prevailed in many EU member states, towards a more polycentric system of regional cities (van Egeerat et al., 2012, p. 92). In an Irish context, this addressed concerns on the dominance of Dublin. Gateways were also seen as one of several types of urban area seen as acting as 'motors of economic growth' for their regions. This formula emphasised their contribution to the growth of surrounding rural areas – an antidote to the view that they competed with those areas for public investment and growth.[18]

The ESDP also saw (*Ibid.*) some smaller towns as capable of providing 'a driving force for the revitalisation of declining rural areas'. The Irish 2000–6 NDP made gateways the centrepiece of its regional development chapter, defining the five cities as existing gateways. It also echoed the ESDP on the possible role of smaller towns, which:

> *may not yet have all the attributes of regional Gateways ... are, nevertheless, showing the potential to lift the levels of development in their respective counties/regions. These have a key role to play in more balanced regional development, in terms of ensuring a more even spread of economic growth ... and alleviating the pressures on the larger urban centres.* (NDP, 2000–6, p. 43)

THE 2002 NATIONAL SPATIAL STRATEGY

The starting point for the NSS was the prospect of further acceleration of the concentration of the population in Dublin (Table 6.2). On a trend basis, it expected 80% of the population growth in the state to be in the Greater Dublin Area (GDA)[19] in the 2002–20 period, for demographic reasons, as well as due to the high share of new jobs and investment going to Dublin.

TABLE 6.2

PROJECTED % OF STATE'S POPULATION IN GDA (DUBLIN AND MID-EAST REGIONS)

1971		1981	1991	2002	2020 (trend)	2020 (high growth)
35.7		37.5	37.7	39.2	43.3	43.9

Source: NSS, pp. 27–32

To stabilise Dublin's share of national population, 75% of industrial and international service jobs currently coming to Dublin would need to be diverted to other parts of the country. This was unrealistic. However, if nothing were done, there would be further concentration in Dublin. Concentration in the GDA could be slowed, with its 'percentage share rising into the low 40s and then starting to level off' (*Ibid.*, p. 30), if some 15–25% of new jobs coming to Dublin were diverted to other areas.

To achieve this, a 'critical mass of population', and a range of skills were needed in 'strong cities and towns', which were in a 'focal' position in transport networks, and within which a long list of specific facilities were to be assembled (Ibid., p. 35). Support for 'clusters of international excellence' in Irish city regions would strengthen them and increase their number. Transport corridors between the cities or gateways other than Dublin needed to be improved, so they developed complementarily, and to some extent, functioned as a collective counterweight to Dublin.

The methods by which the NSS hoped to achieve its aims were thus a composite mix, incorporating most of the regional planning approaches already discussed in this chapter, including urbanisation economies, supply-side provision of infrastructure and other potentiality factors, sectoral clustering, and the 1990s belief in development corridors.

Mindful of the fate of the Buchanan report, the NSS tried to show how the benefits of urbanisation economies could be transmitted to secondary centres, and to the country as a whole, via secondary centres or 'hubs' (see Figure 6.4). Some[20] were 20 miles or so from gateways, to 'support and be supported by the gateways', and extend their benefits to a regional hinterland *(Ibid.*, p. 38). Others, in remoter areas further away from gateways, were seen as lifting 'the levels of development in their respective counties'.[21] In other cases, two or three medium-sized urban areas were grouped, to function collectively as gateways.

The gateways and hubs proposed by the NSS were shown as lying within five different zones, which, in combination, covered the state. Most gateways were in a band running north-south, from Letterkenny to Cork, described as having a 'strengthening' role. To the east of this band, the NSS designated a 'reinforcing' zone – an arc 50–90 miles from Dublin – reinforced mainly by grouping Mullingar, Tullamore, and Athlone into a new gateway, astride radial corridors focused on Dublin and on a semi-circular route linking it to Dundalk and Rosslare.

The area within 50 miles of Dublin was treated as *'consolidating'*, with emphasis on servicing recent and expected growth more efficiently, partly through better and more integrated land-use and transport planning. West of the 'strengthening' zone, paired hubs in Co. Mayo and Co. Kerry were seen as the main means of 'revitalising' a western coastal zone. A final 'co-operating' band along the border with Northern Ireland would be supported by tourism and transport developments (NSS, 2002, pp. 56–62).

The attempt to cover the country comprehensively was pursued in more detail, with region-by-region proposals on developing county and other towns in ways 'that capitalise on local and regional roles and are also linked to the roles of the gateways and development hubs' (NSS, p. 44). Rural areas would benefit from 'enhanced local employment options' and

FIGURE 6.4
NATIONAL SPATIAL STRATEGY: TRANSPORT FRAMEWORK, GATEWAYS AND HUBS

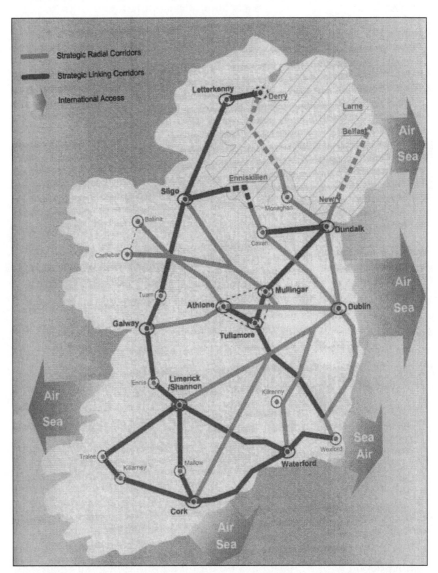

Source: Department of the Environment and Local Government, *National Spatial Strategy* 2002–22, p. 58 p. 61. Gateways are shown in black, hubs in grey.

'development of their resource potential' (Ibid.). This comprehensive approach reflected the NSS goal of 'balanced regional development', defined as 'developing the full potential of each area to contribute to the optimal performance of the State as a whole – economically, socially and environmentally' (NSS, p. 11). This aim justified efforts to realise this potential in each area, without implying that their growth rates would necessarily converge as a result.

The NSS commitment to corridors required a belief that economic interaction would, in future, occur more intensively over longer distances than in the past, partly as a result of upgraded transport corridors connecting the gateways and hubs, as shown in Figure 6.4. While this might indeed happen, the NSS based it less on economic evidence than on the need to avoid a backlash from smaller towns and rural areas, as with Buchanan. Without such long-distance interaction, there would be minimal urbanisation economies from pairing of economically complementary gateway and hub towns, or diffusion of employment growth to smaller towns and rural areas.

The decade after publication of the NSS revealed major differences in the economic performance of gateways. Despite the crash of 2008, Cork had 20% more jobs in manufacturing and international services in these sectors in 2011 than in 2001, and Galway 13% more, while employment in these sectors stayed the same in Dublin. Capacity to attract new foreign firms was concentrated in these cities. Conversely, all other gateways apart from Letterkenny lost employment, with Limerick,[22] Dundalk and the Midland gateway losing 20–25%, as compared with a 15% loss in the part of the state outside designated gateways and hubs (van Egeraat et al., 2012, pp. 103–6).

The credibility of the NSS was dented by the government office decentralisation programme announced in the 2004 budget, which relocated a large number of back-office functions to a wide variety of smaller towns. Bannon (2005, pp. 296–7) pointed out that only 24% of the jobs transferred were to go to NSS designated gateways and hubs, and saw the decentralisation proposals as the death knell for regional policy within Ireland for decades to come.

This episode had a high profile, being rather obviously designed to improve government performance in the 2004 local and European elections. Whatever its practical effects,[23] it symbolised the political expendability of the NSS. It also reflected disregard of the NSS by other state agencies. There was only a single token paragraph on the NSS in the report of the 2004 Enterprise Strategy Group, and no reference at all to it in the government's 2005 €34 billion transport plan (Breathnach, 2017, pp. 3–4).

This disregard reflected the tendency of agencies to follow their own agendas, and to continue doing so whether there is a cross-sectoral regional policy or not. For instance, the Department of Finance was following precedent in 2004, as an earlier round of decentralisation from 1987 onwards[24] had dispersed jobs in a fairly random manner, though without controversy, as there was no well-defined regional policy at that point.

THE 2018 NATIONAL PLANNING FRAMEWORK

The successor to the NSS – the 2018 National Planning Framework (NPF) – attributed its predecessor's limited success to the absence of statutory backing, its focus on gateways and hubs – creating a perception of winners and losers – and limited government adherence to it, symbolised by the 2004 decentralisation programme. While the NSS did influence the 2007–13 NDP, the crash of 2008 rendered the latter ineffective. The NPF argued it would avoid repeating these defects by aiming at a single inclusive vision, unlike past policies which had elevated one idea or area over another. Also, it would be on a statutory basis, monitored by an independent regulator, and tied into the 2018–27 NDP, which was structured around its aims.

The need to update the NSS increased as the recovery gathered pace from 2014 on, and turned out to be even more dominated by inward investment in Dublin than the previous cycle. The title of the strategy reflected its content accurately, as it did provide a general framework for planning, and not just a regional or spatial strategy. However, the latter aspects are the most relevant ones from the point of view of this chapter, and the description which follows focuses on those aspects.

The ESRI projected an extra 1,000,000 population, 660,000 jobs, and 550,000 households in the 2016–40 period. The NPF considered growth on this scale required a coherent plan, instead of the previous tendency to sprawl. In order to ensure urban centres of adequate scale, it included population targets for the five cities together with their suburbs. These growth targets involved a 20–25% increase in the population of Dublin City and suburbs, and a 50–60% increase in the size of the other four cities and their suburbs. The regional roles of Athlone and Sligo, and of two cross-border corridors – Letterkenny–Derry and Dublin–Belfast (including Drogheda, Dundalk and Newry) – were also emphasised. The belief in corridors was also reflected in re-endorsement of the Atlantic Corridor (or at any rate the section between Cork and Sligo), on the basis that connecting the regions to each other as well as to Dublin would be 'a major enabler for balanced regional development' and help them collectively form a counterweight to Dublin[25] (NPF, 2018, p. 41; NDP, 2018, p. 40).

The tools to make the projected levels of growth in the five cities happen included the building of skills pools, and attraction of technology firms, as well as place making with funding from a €2bn Urban Regeneration fund, so as to make them attractive to highly skilled workers. The compact growth sought by the NPF was seen as helping to attract skilled workers, by allowing them to live near their work, avoid long commutes, and use existing urban facilities. In the five cities and suburbs, 50% of new homes should be within the existing urban footprint.

This approach would also create locations for new enterprises which were people intensive and space intensive. Less intensive employment uses could be relocated to release well-located land for more efficient use. The necessary land management would be assisted by National Regeneration and Development Agency, which would use CPOs to acquire un-used and underused land, and ensure best use of public land. Overall planning within the five cities and their suburbs would be coordinated through Metropolitan Area Spatial Plans (MASPs).

The NPF covered the 2018–40 period, with the complementary NDP outlining the parallel investment programme to ensure its aims were realised up to 2027. In combination, they were comprehensive, and attempted to organise a wide variety of policies into an internally coherent whole. They can be regarded as an up-to-date version of the supply-side approach outlined by the EU Commission in the 1980s,[26] relying on infrastructure capacity and potentiality factors. The underlying 'build it and they will come' approach is optimistic in the highly cyclical Irish economy. The NPF and NDP programmes are themselves vulnerable to the cycle, being very ambitious, and without any apparent allowance for recessions and the drastic effect they have on capital spending.

D. THE PROSPECTS FOR CHANGING LONG-RUN URBAN GROWTH RATES

The city population targets in the NPF can be put into context by comparing them with long-run average population growth rates. Figure 6.5 shows these for each of the five cities, measuring them in several different ways. While NPF population targets are for the cities and their suburbs, this understates growth by omitting commuter areas. Also, suburb boundaries are periodically revised by the CSO, which may exaggerate growth at the time of revision (e.g. Cork, 1981). To avoid this, fixed boundaries for city hinterlands can be used, such as those of the sub-County Rural Districts (RDs) defined in 1898. These were centred on and named after urban areas, and the ones directly adjoining cities were named after those cities (e.g. Cork RD). Typically, they include quite a lot of the cities' commuting areas even today.

A third possibility is to use fixed boundaries with planning status. The Dublin region (i.e. Dublin city and counties), and the Mid-East region

Figure 6.5 Long-run Metropolitan Growth Rates, 1961–2022

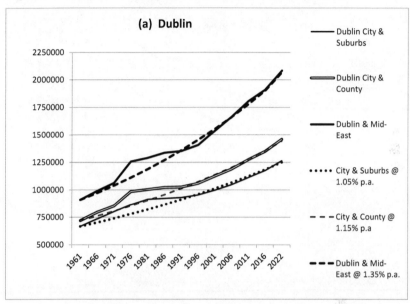

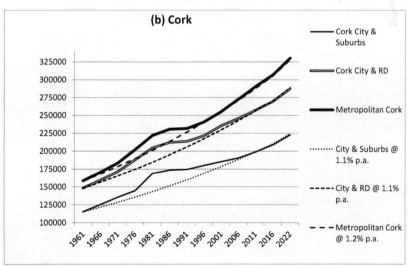

Source: Censi

Figure 6.5 [Cont.] Long-run Metropolitan Growth Rates, 1961-2022

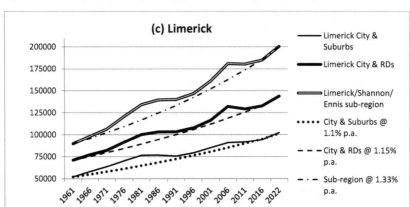

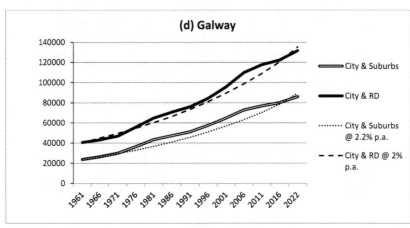

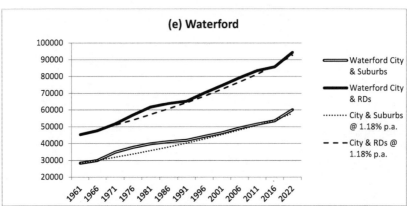

(the three counties adjoining Dublin)[27] are obvious examples. In Cork, the LUTS and CASP studies used a fixed area, albeit with a varying name (the City and Harbour area, the Greater Cork Area, Metropolitan Cork), for planning purposes, as it included all eight of the Cork satellite towns. The Buchanan report set population targets for – but did not define – the Limerick–Shannon–Ennis area, and Ennis RD and UD have been added to Limerick City and RDs to give population figures for this.

The main points which emerge from Figure 6.5 are:

(a) While growth rates for particular metropolitan areas vary a lot from one inter-censal period to another, reflecting the different phases of the cycle, they are fairly consistent for complete cycles. Most of the actual population figures for 1991 shown in Figure 6.5 lie close to the lines showing the average 1961–2016 growth rate for the relevant area. The 1991 census, like the 1961 and 2016 ones, recorded a demographic low point following a recession, so this closeness implies that average growth rates for the 1991–2016 cycle were similar to those for the 1961–91 one.

(b) This stability in long-run growth rates implies a stable relationship between rates for different cities. With the notable exception of Galway, all the City and Suburbs or City and RD units have been growing at roughly the same average long-run rate: 1.1–1.2% per annum. This is also true for Dublin City and County. All are growing faster than the state as a whole, which has a long-run growth rate (1961–2016) of 0.96%. For comparison, the NPF population targets imply annual growth rates of 0.75–0.95% for Dublin, and 1.7–2% for the other cities.

(c) If more extensive planning areas are used (Dublin and the Mid-East, and Limerick–Shannon–Ennis), the growth rate is over 1.3% per annum. Rural areas and towns in commuter belts often grow at a high percentage rate, while fully developed suburban areas typically lose

257

population as a result of the declining size of households, so loosely defined urban areas usually grow faster than more tightly defined ones.

(d) Whichever method for defining city populations is used, the aggregate population of the four smaller cities combined is only 30–40% of the population of Dublin.

(e) As a consequence, if the smaller cities grow at percentage rates similar to those in Dublin, the absolute increase in Dublin's population will be two to three times the aggregate increase in those cities. In those circumstances, it will be difficult to avoid persistent increases in the percentage of the population of the state living in Dublin.

At least on paper, the NPF resolves the mathematical difficulty at (d) and (e) above through targets which involve growth in Dublin slowing, and that in the other cities accelerating, to the point where Dublin grows at half the rate of the rest. This allows the NPF's regional level aim of equalising the amount of growth in the Eastern and Midland Regional Assembly (EMRA) area with that in the other two regions (all three shown on Figure 6.6) to be achieved.

The drastic change envisaged in growth patterns may be seen as politically necessary for an Irish regional policy. To mobilise support, it needs to offer regional balance – the promise that in the future, there will no longer be much more population growth in Dublin and its commuter belt than in the rest of the country. But credibility then becomes an issue. While Galway shows a provincial city can grow much faster than Dublin, the NPF requires all of them to do this, while Dublin grows much more slowly than at present. A more realistic promise – say that the rate of growth in the other metropolitan areas will be slightly faster than in Dublin and its commuter belt – would mean the latter would continue to grow as a proportion of the population of the state.

Prior to finalisation of the NPF, an ESRI research paper provided some basis for the proposed 50–50 split of population growth between

Figure 6.6 Regional Assembly Areas Used to Balance Growth in the NPF

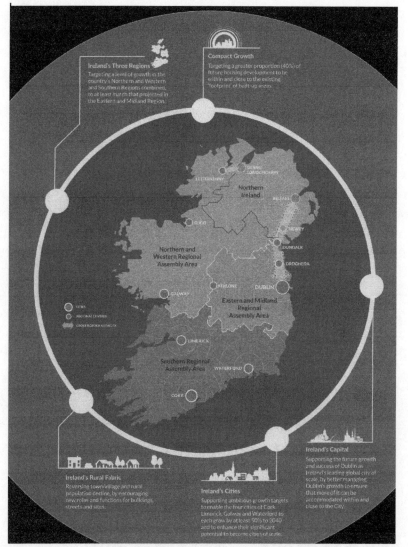

Source: *Department of Housing, Planning and Local Government, National Planning Framework* p.23

the EMRA area and the rest of the state, arguing that it was 'feasible', though in a rather specialised sense. An alternative split, with 68% of growth in the EMRA area, was seen as not feasible, because the level of growth in the number of households would push up house prices there, and this would discourage net migration into it (Morgenroth, 2018, pp. 65–70). The 50-50 split was seen as avoiding this problem in the EMRA area, apparently without transferring it to other cities which would grow faster under it.

However, an outcome can be feasible without being probable. An alternative response to high housing prices, due to rapid employment growth in particular areas or phases of the cycle, is decentralisation to commuting hinterlands. This is not merely feasible, it is what actually happened in and around Dublin in the last two cycles. As Figure 6.7 shows, growth was concentrated in Dublin City and County in recovery phases, shifted outwards to the Mid-East Region early in booms, and further out to the rest of Leinster later in them, before reverting to a more centralised pattern following recessions.

Even in the lower part of the cycle, the share of the state's population in Dublin and its commuting hinterland has continued to increase, but has not come anywhere close to the 43–44% projected for 2020 in the NSS trend and high growth scenarios (see Table 6.2). However, as Table

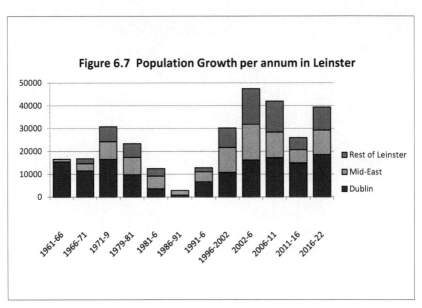

Figure 6.7 Population Growth per annum in Leinster

6.3 shows, there has been a steady though more gradual increase in the population of the EMRA area and Leinster in each successive inter-censal period, with the rest of the EMRA area (the outer commuting area) contributing most of this up to 2011, and the GDA subsequently, in accordance with the cyclical pattern evident in Figure 6.7.

TABLE 6.3

PERCENTAGE OF STATE'S POPULATION IN GDA, EMRA AREA, LEINSTER AND REST OF STATE

	2002	2006	2011	2016	2022
GDA (Dublin & Mid-East)	39.20	39.18	39.32	40.05	40.45
Rest of EMRA	8.35	8.54	8.83	8.84	8.89
EMRA (total)	47.55	47.72	48.15	48.90	49.33
Rest of State	52.45	52.38	51.85	51.10	50.67
State	100	100	100	100	100
of which:					
Leinster	53.75	54.08	54.59	55.32	55.74
Other 3 provinces	46.25	45.92	45.41	44.68	44.26

Source: Censi of Population

There will need to be strong positive reasons for the very large shift in regional growth patterns sought by the NPF, not just the mere absence of a particular type of obstacle. In their absence, the NPF may have unfortunate practical consequences. If the Dublin and Mid-East regions combined continue to grow at the observed long-run rate of 1.35% per annum, this will yield an extra 720,000 people by 2040. This would add around 200,000 to the NPF targets for the EMRA area for 2040.[28] Continuation of the trends in Figure 6.5 would also subtract 40–50% of the population growth the NPF envisaged in the three Munster cities.

The NPF projected national population growth to 2040 at around 1 million, as compared with the 1¼ million which results from projecting forwards the long-run growth for the state. If the NPF projection turns out to be correct, Dublin might not exceed the target by much, on a factored-down trend basis. However, the NPF targets for the Munster cities would be far ahead of trend, and – to the extent they have practical influence – would lead to unrealistic decisions.

The major unknown is how far pull-factor migration into Ireland, attracted by cyclically variable employment opportunities and wage levels in accordance with well established patterns, will be supplemented by migrants pushed out of their countries of origin by war and climate change. This seems likely to increase, but it is difficult to know by how much, or which parts of Ireland will be most affected.

BALANCED REGIONAL GROWTH THROUGH THE NDP?

The NPF relies heavily on the infrastructural proposals in the 2018–27 NDP. Like previous NDPs from 1989 on, the 2018–27 one brings together the parallel programmes of the various state agencies in an ostensibly integrated national plan. It is more closely linked to regional policy within Ireland than previous NDPs, but will not necessarily be any more likely than them to cause radical redistribution of population growth from the Dublin area to other cities.

NDPs are not produced in a year zero, in which policies with spatial effects are applied for the first time. They are the current version of a long-established mix of policies with different spatial effects, interacting with each other and with other economic factors. Each new NDP naturally includes some new features, but continuity normally outweighs innovation, and even the new features will not necessarily redistribute growth away from Dublin.

For instance, the 2018 NDP allocated (p. 21) €8.6 billion for 'sustainable mobility'. This included €3 billion for the Dublin Metro, €2.4 billion for Bus Connects, and €2 billion for the DART Expansion. The need for public transport is proportional to the size of an urban area, so Dublin's share of public transport investment should be greater than its share of the state's population. However, allocating 85% to Dublin takes no obvious account of the NPF aim that other cities should grow twice as fast as Dublin, especially in view of the crucial role that sustainable mobility has in increasing urban competitiveness.

As in many planning situations, the NPF may have accepted its inability to change the pattern of public investment much, and hoped that minor but well-chosen programmes backed by modest resources might have a disproportionate effect. In particular, the €3 billion allocated for the Urban and Rural Regeneration and Development Funds may have been included in the NDP with this hope in mind, and possibly also the €0.5 billion allocated for a 'Challenge-based Disruptive Innovation Fund'. However, the largest of these – the €2 billion Urban Regeneration fund – is open to Dublin as much as to other cities and towns, so the direction in which it will redistribute growth is unpredictable.

BALANCED REGIONAL GROWTH THROUGH PLANNING CONTROLS?

The NPF might be cited in support of the use of planning powers to control Dublin's growth rate, in the hope of diverting some of it to other parts of the state. While this may seem a poor alternative to using them to promote the growth of regional centres, planning powers in Ireland are primarily regulatory, as most development is carried out by the private sector. Such powers can be used to refuse permission for developments inconsistent with a development plan, but cannot make the private sector carry out ones consistent with it.

The NPF initially examined a 'regional dominance' option, involving the other regions growing twice as fast as the EMRA area, a regional parity one (growth in other regions at least equal to that in EMRA),, and a 'business as usual' one. It opted (p. 26) for the regional parity one, seeing the regional dominance alternative as not realistic or implementable, and likely to reduce overall national growth.

The Dublin Chamber of Commerce, in a submission on the NPF, treated this (undated, p. 11) as recognition that 'no constraint can be put on Dublin to achieve convergence in growth among the regions'. This carefully worded comment is correct, as the NPF does not aim for convergence. However, it does aim to avoid further divergence, which will occur if growth in the EMRA area continues to exceed growth in the other two regions. The issue of whether the growth of Dublin should be constrained to avoid divergence from the NPF may therefore arise, perhaps as a by-product of making the NPF legally enforceable.[29]

Planning powers could, in theory, be used to slow the rate of development of Dublin, for instance by restricting the amount of new office development. In the mid-1960s, the Wilson government tried to divert growth to regional centres through the short-lived 'Brown ban' on new offices in London. There are numerous possible variants on this type of policy, and some of them might attract worthwhile support within Dublin, if they primarily affected incoming, employment-intensive projects in the late recovery and boom periods, when they were most likely to put Dublin's housing and transport system under serious pressure.

There may be some theoretical support for this approach. Morgenroth (2012) points out that 'excess primacy' can reduce economic growth, and refers to the Williamson hypothesis, under which the costs of policies to reduce regional disparities are in the form of an inverted 'U', being relatively low in underdeveloped countries and highly developed ones, but higher for intermediate ones. Indeed, 'At high levels of development a positive relationship between aggregate efficiency and spatial equity is expected.'

Measures to divert growth from Dublin to other parts of the state might thus have a neutral or positive effect on national growth. However, it is not likely this could be demonstrated convincingly enough to persuade those whose interests lay in not accepting it. The obvious counterargument is that, by international standards, Dublin is not a particularly large city, and will be the only medium-sized one in Ireland for the foreseeable future.

The practical effectiveness of a control-based policy would depend on incoming businesses and the IDA being convinced of the government's determination, and factoring it into their locational advice to clients. This would only happen if it was clear the government was willing to allow some high-profile projects to be lost, and live with the political consequences. There is little evidence of this sort of determination on regional policy issues to date.

Unexpected shifts in the distribution of growth within countries do sometimes occur. This seems most likely to happen when changes in the international economy redistribute competitive advantage towards the same sort of places as those being promoted by public policy. Up till now, there is not much evidence of the distribution of population growth within Ireland being significantly changed, either by regional policies or by changes in the international economy. Shifts from dispersed, branch plant-led growth in the 1970s, to edge-of-city electronics industries in the 1990s, and city-centre internet companies recently, have had limited effect on Dublin's growth rate. Also, while the unexpected sometimes happens, the planned review of the NPF in 2024 (2021–30 NDP, p. 16) gives it little time in which to do so. A review after the 2026 census might give a better indication.

SEGMENTATION OF THE PUBLIC SECTOR AS AN OBSTACLE TO BALANCED REGIONAL GROWTH

The current centralised, segmented structure of the Irish public sector, and the attitudes that go with this, are seen as obstacles to implementation of regional strategies such as the NSS and the NPF, due to 'the culture of non cooperation between government departments which prevails in Ireland's central civil service. A review of the Irish public service published by the OECD in 2008 identified this as the single greatest problem constraining the service's performance' (Breathnach, 2017, pp. 4–5).

Breathnach cites several sources in support of his view that this leads to a silo mentality, and agencies prioritising defence of their functional autonomy. A 2006 Forfas report on NSS implementation referred to:

* Problems of cooperation between local authorities, and between them and central government agencies;

* Centralisation and compartmentalisation of government;

* Lack of regional leadership.

A 2010 Forfas report considered existing structures did not facilitate a coherent, strategic approach to regional development. The National Competitiveness Council saw governance as the key issue for managing urban growth, and highlighted the importance of a coordinated approach for city regions.

The conventional solution is devolution to sub-national units, involving less division of public sector activities by function and sector, and more by geographical area. Devolution has often been advocated, and has, from time to time, been given rhetorical support by governments, but experience strongly suggests it is not going to happen.

If meaningful devolution is unlikely, cross-compartment coordination could be promoted at cabinet level. As noted earlier, Bannon, in his comments on implementation of the Buchanan report, would have required 'an inter-departmental approach to planning' led by a Cabinet sub-committee, as no single department 'would ever have received the freedom to implement such a programme'. Breathnach, commenting (2017, p.8) on the NPF, argued that such a sub-committee would have required the support

> of a powerful national office capable of knocking heads together in the central civil service ... capable of forcing recalcitrant ministers to act in accordance with the NPF ... It is impossible, given Ireland's politico-institutional configuration, to imagine such an office ever being established, never mind acting effectively ...

Breathnach also dismisses other mechanisms to ensure implementation of the NPF. Putting it on a statutory basis may not help, as Ireland has a long history of poorly implemented legislation. It is unclear what action the Planning Regulator can take, if monitoring its implementation reveals non-compliance. Regional Assemblies have 'few functions, no powers, and little relevance to the city focused planning which is the main component of the NPF'.

Lewis (2010, pp. 127–8) considered that as radical revision of the role of local government in Ireland was unlikely, there was a need to 'move interest in centre-periphery relations away from a debate about delegation or devolution to examination of the links between central and local government'.

One possible line of thought would be to make use of one of the limited opportunities for improved coordination which periodically arise within existing institutional arrangements, or may arise in future. At local level, Box 4.1 suggested reviving and extending the Serviced Land Initiative (SLI) which operated between 1997 and 2009. Coordinating the actions of sectoral agencies at sub-regional or regional levels may be more difficult, but there are some starting points or precedents which might be developed, such as:

(a) **Metropolitan level strategic plans:** Local authorities are multi-purpose bodies, and can provide bottom-up coordination. From the mid-1960s on, groups of local authorities have been involved in non-statutory planning strategies for metropolitan areas, with government support, and the involvement of the relevant state agencies. Encouragingly, the 2018 NPF proposed (pp. 12, 45–7) putting Metropolitan Area Strategic Plans (MASPs) for the five cities and their metropolitan areas on a statutory basis.[30] Higher profile plans might have more influence over the way central government agencies exercise their control over funding.

(b) **Top-down project coordination:** High priority projects are sometimes led by a government department with a cross-compartment remit. For example, local initiatives in severely deprived areas, undertaken under the Programme for National Recovery in the 1990s, were sponsored by the Department of the Taoiseach. This had freedom of manoeuvre within 'a public administration divided into traditional functional departments forced to compete for dwindling resources' (Sabel 1996, p. 42),[31] and the necessary motivation, due to the importance of social partnership at national level.[32] This approach would be easier to apply to a key cross-compartment project than to an overall strategy like the NPF.

This approach could help coordinate implementation of specific projects at different levels of government. For example, Morgenroth[33] suggested the existing rail network would serve us better if we put more services on it, instead of tolerating overfull trains and poor frequencies. This applies particularly around cities, as this is where the congestion is. However, 'the really big issue is that we tend to separate various policy areas when they are actually connected'. For historical reasons, rail networks in Irish cities connect to the dockland side of their city centres, which are currently a focus for new inner-city office-based employment. There is obvious potential to connect these foci to new as well as existing residential development by rail. But this requires coordination between land use, transport and other forms of infrastructure, and between local and central government agencies, not just in principle, but also as regards timing. If the actions needed were treated as an integrated project, supported by top-down coordination, they would be more likely to happen, and to be effective.

(c) Redefinition of ministries by incoming governments: Each time a new government is formed, some ministerial responsibilities are regrouped, so the remits of some incoming cabinet ministers differ from those of their predecessors. This flexibility could be used to combine transport with responsibilities traditionally grouped under an 'Environment' department, including other infrastructure, housing and planning. In the UK, which has a fairly similar system of cabinet government, a Department of the Environment, Transport and the Regions was established when the Blair government first took office in 1997. The minister responsible was also deputy prime minister – usually a low profile post in the UK, but not in Ireland, where every government contains a Tánaiste, who is also a departmental minister and (usually) leader of the second party in the coalition.

If this was seen as involving undue concentration of power and responsibilities in one department, these functions could be split regionally, with a minister responsible for each of the three Regional Assembly areas. This form of devolution applied to Scotland and Wales, until they acquired their own parliament/assembly in the late 1990s.

While these are not ideal options, they reconcile difficult to change 'politico-institutional' dominance of central government departments, with cross-compartment remits. Regional departments would reduce the tendency to apply inappropriately uniform solutions to issues sensitive to urban size,[34] in a country whose capital is 5–20 times the size of the other cities. It would also allow differentiation of development roles, as the southern area would contain the three cities which need to grow much faster to achieve the NPF targets; the north western one, a city already growing at the target rate, plus a high proportion of remoter rural areas with weak urban structure; and the eastern one, Dublin and its hinterland, broadly defined.

Some ad hoc combination of (a) and (b), organised around specific projects rather than any general attempt to improve coordination, might conflict least with the grain of the Irish public sector, though it would also be the one least likely to secure long-term institutional reform. A cultural shift at government level, which made it less acceptable for central agencies to assume their sectoral or functional priorities should take precedence over metropolitan or other area-based strategies, would have some value.

CONCLUSION

There is an underlying dilemma. If efforts to achieve more balanced regional growth are abandoned, we may lose such limited opportunities as might realistically be available to moderate the concentration of growth in the Dublin area. Also, while the state's investment policies may stimulate the growth of Dublin more than other parts of the country already, they might do this even more strongly in the absence of any explicit regional policy. Further metro-scale projects which increase the qualitative gap between Dublin and other cities could emerge. Experience in a similarly dominant capital, from the late 1980s on, illustrates this risk:

> *All attempts to decentralise economic activity out of London were in abeyance. Every new government proposal – high speed trains from the north, new runways at Heathrow, subsidies for home ownership – aided the capital* (Jenkins, 2020, p. 307).

On the other hand, policies aiming at more balanced regional development in Ireland only seem to have political traction if oversold, or that at least seems to have been the prevailing assumption up until now.

The degree to which the increase in the percentage of the state's population in and around Dublin can be moderated is probably quite modest, but it is still worth doing. Ways of doing this might include:

- Requiring a more realistic and joined-up approach from state agencies in relation to each of the three Munster cities
- Greater use of the opportunities for locating new industries close to physically extensive renewable energy complexes in more rural areas – particularly in the west of the country – with the advantage that this would minimise transmission difficulties

The answer to the question at the beginning of this chapter – could more balanced regional development make more use of spare capacity in places other than Dublin and limit the effect of employment surges on congestion costs and property values? – seems to be that this is possible, but probably not on anything like the scale current or past regional policies have envisaged. The suggested system of contingency planning outlined in Box 6.1 to increase the ability of the various metropolitan areas to cope with employment surges might be more effective in increasing spare capacity in the smaller cities than in Dublin, as the steps it required would be fewer and simpler in those cities.

Otherwise, re-configuration of policies affecting development land, infrastructure and the housing market, as discussed in Chapters 3–5, seem to be the principal ways in which Dublin could cope with the cycle more effectively, though regional policy could play a helpful if relatively minor role. In so far as policy or economic conditions redistribute growth to other metropolitan areas, this acceleration is more likely to be sustained there, if the measures proposed in those chapters are used to prevent it being choked off by housing prices and shortages.

Unfortunately, it is easier to formulate more ambitious regional policy aims than to provide a convincing causal account of how they are to be realised. Given the dominance of the private sector, the ability of the Irish state to change the established pattern of growth is limited, and political and institutional factors make effective use of the influence it does have more difficult. It is reasonable to plan for radically different, policy-induced changes in the pattern of development if there are effective ways of bringing these about, but not otherwise.

CHAPTER 7

ESCAPE ROUTES
AND TIMING

Summary: Measures designed to reduce the vulnerability of each stage in the construction process to cyclical disruption could form part of a wider policy reset prompted by a downturn, similar to those prompted by the recession of the 1980s and the 2008 crash. Alternatively, it might be implemented more gradually, as a subsidiary part of a programme adopted in response to a housing crisis in the upper part of the cycle, of which the recent Housing for All programme is an example. If adopted at other stages of the cycle, there would be a risk that it would be disrupted by one or other of these major revisions in policy.

There may be more willingness to revise ways of evaluating infrastructure projects to improve coverage of needs, at times when the imbalance between ambitious projects and limited resources or capacity seems more likely than usual to lead to lengthy queuing of projects.

There is wide recognition that housing supply – and perhaps the overall construction process – are systemically defective. This may prompt structural reforms, but these will only stay implemented if the capacity to cope with the disruptive effects of the cycle is designed into them.

This book has argued that the state's construction-related policies need to be redesigned to cope with the sector's exceptional cyclicality, and has put forward suggestions on how this might be done. If the need for such redesign – whether by the methods suggested or by other ones – is accepted, how and in what circumstances could it actually happen?

RESETS

Recent history suggests durable policy change is most likely to occur as part of a periodic reset of construction policy, prompted by a downturn in output. As noted in Chapter 5, governments undertake initiatives to kick-start a recovery at the bottom of the cycle – e.g. in 1985–7, and 2013–15. This involves replacing saturated markets and increasingly unavailable methods of supplying them, characteristic of the previous cycle, with new markets and methods. These seem validated by the recovery, reinforcing government commitment to them for the rest of the new cycle. Policies adopted at that stage stand an above-average chance of staying implemented.

Resets occur when the policies which dominated the previous cycle are discredited, and require new policies, which include an explanation of where the ones associated with the previous cycle went wrong, and how this will be avoided in future. Policies to reduce the exceptional cyclicality of the Irish construction sector are inherently more plausible after a downturn, and the continuous impact of cyclically-generated housing problems from the mid-1990s onwards should reinforce this perception.

Most of the suggestions in this book are well suited to introduction in the trough phase, as their initial effect on the financial viability of development projects would be low and, in some cases, positive. Their aim would be to influence developers' expectations and their planning of future projects, as the recovery gains momentum.[1] There would be a good match between the recovery of the construction sector from an initially depressed base, and the phasing in of tax measures as it did so.

Most of the suggestions also involve low initial public cost, though there are several exceptions – specifically, the aim of maintaining a 'floor' level of local infrastructure investment[2] and social housing's share of public capital investment,[3] advance transfer of land under Part V, and acquisition of land for new towns.[4] However, these exceptions could be fairly tightly targeted on the areas most likely to recover first, and widened once the recovery was underway.

Such downturns – and the resets which follow them – will presumably occur in the future, as in the past, but it is not possible to predict their timing and intensity.

Also, by definition, public and private funding are in short supply in the trough phase, and the policies around which the reset occurs will be ones which can mobilise the limited resources which are still available in those conditions, on terms which those who control those resources will accept. A future reset programme will be built around such resources, as in the past. Their nature is unknowable at this stage, but they will be selected on the basis of their likely effectiveness in getting the construction sector moving again relatively quickly. The reset programme will not be built around more gradual, longer-term policies to reduce cyclicality.

At the same time, such policies stand some chance of being included as secondary elements or a minor theme in such a programme. While the problems which arise in the upper part of the cycle seem very remote in a trough, the sense that the construction sector has been a prisoner of the cycle is quite strong then. There should be some openness towards ideas on controlling cyclicality at that point.

To mobilise resources and motivate those who control them, governments in trough conditions offer generous terms. Offering first movers such terms, while making it clear that these terms will become more demanding for those who move later, when a recovery is well established, may be quite an effective approach from a tactical point of view, as well as reducing the risk of getting locked into terms which become unduly generous and pro-cyclical later on.

To avoid the latter, it is essential that future steps which will make these terms less generous or more demanding are outlined from the start, and that the timing of these steps is related to the market conditions or output volumes which will trigger them, not to some arbitrarily selected future date which is at least as likely to under- or over-estimate the speed of the recovery as to anticipate it correctly.

SUPERIMPOSITION OF REACTIVE POLICIES

However, at the time of writing (mid-2023) we are nearer the opposite end of the cycle, and hopefully at some considerable distance from a downturn. Policy changes are also concentrated at the upper end of the cycle, prompted by acute housing affordability and/or availability problems which emerge late in recoveries or early in booms, such as in the late 1970s, the late 1990s, and from 2015 onwards. These changes are dominated by reactive and often temporary measures, which are superimposed on the policies put in place in the previous reset, rather than substituted for them. They are superimposed, because the reset policies support market processes which are still very active, so there is quite a lot to be lost by walking away from them. The political parties which introduced them also remain largely committed to them and, to some extent, react to their limitations by intensifying them.

This is the situation in which Housing for All was published in September 2021. We have been in this situation from an unusually early point in the current cycle – 2015 – because the completeness of the collapse in new residential construction after 2008, the limits on loan to income ratios imposed by the Central Bank, and the geographical concentration of demand in Dublin, combined to bring forward the point at which affordability and availability problems in the housing market became acute. While a wide range of reactive measures were taken from 2015 on, the negative verdict on them implied by the results of the 2020 election reinforced pressure for a further package – the 2021 Housing for All programme.

Housing for All is an unusually unified and comprehensive example of the type of policy response prompted by the problems characteristic of this stage of the cycle. However, it is being put forward in less favourable circumstances than the main initiatives in the corresponding phase of the previous cycle – the Bacon reports and Part V. These were published within eighteen months to three years of the loss of control of house prices in late 1996. Prior to this loss of control, the housing market had been in rough balance, and prices had been moderate. By contrast, Housing for All was launched after six years of acute difficulties, during which housing announcements and initiatives have been devalued by overuse, and which was preceded by two decades in which the property market lurched from one extreme to another. As a result, the Irish housing system is routinely referred to as 'dysfunctional' and 'broken'.

So this time round the bar is set higher, and there is more focus on whether the measures in the package are durable, and offer the longer-term, systemic reforms needed. The authors of Housing for All seem well aware of this, and have included in it proposals for structural reform, including land value sharing, the land assembly role of the LDA, and support for home ownership through a shared equity system.

However, it does not address construction cyclicality directly enough, and seems over-reliant on state land banking and active land management by the LDA to do this. Without offering any definitive estimate of the share of overall activity the LDA and associated agencies will account for in the late 2020s, the majority of development, property investment and development land transactions will probably still be largely independent of the LDA. If so, there will be a continuing need to make that largely independent activity less cyclical.

While governments and commentators tend to be prisoners of the current phase, and to underestimate future divergences from it, the role of cyclicality in disrupting the housing system over the last quarter of a century can scarcely be denied. Convincing proposals on how to cope with it should increase the credibility of any wider package, and prospects for its success.

It would probably be possible to introduce measures to cope with construction cyclicality on the lines suggested in this book as a minor theme in a programme developed in response to housing availability and affordability problems in the upper part of the cycle, if that programme was a consolidated set of measures like Housing for All, rather than a succession of initiatives undertaken at intervals. To illustrate this, ways of adapting proposals in Housing for All have been discussed in Chapters 3 and 5.

While it is easier to fund actions in late recovery and early boom phases of the cycle, in other respects conditions are less favourable for the introduction of measures to reduce long-term cyclicality than at a reset. More developers and investors are likely to be more heavily committed to an intended course of action at that stage, and opportunities to influence their expectations and plans are likely to be fewer than at the start of the recovery. Gradual implementation of new incentives and disincentives may be necessary when there is strong growth already, so as not to artificially inflate the price of the limited amount of development of the desired type which is already available or committed, nor disrupt already committed development of a type which it has been decided should be scaled back. Some tension between this gradualist approach and the perceived urgency of overall housing programmes adopted at this stage in the cycle may result.

Durable policies to help us escape construction cyclicality may be more difficult to implement at intermediate points between the top and bottom of the cycle, as they would be at more risk of subsequent disruption by responses to the next housing crisis, or by a policy reset in the next trough.

INFRASTRUCTURE QUEUES

Openness to lower cost ways of meeting infrastructure needs is naturally greater in periods where the higher cost ones seem most likely to result in lengthy delays before they come on stream. However, it typically only affects a few high-profile proposals, which are discussed more at individual project level than on any systematic basis. Project design teams, the consultants they employ and, presumably, also the agencies and government departments which fund them, generally remain loyal to the high-cost options, and are prepared to wait until conditions for their implementation improve again.

Openness to lower-cost options is not necessarily confined to the lower part of the economic cycle. It may occur at other times, if the cumulative cost of planned projects seems unusually high, relative to likely resources, due to unexpected slowing of economic growth, or a steep increase in estimated construction costs.

The latter conditions applied at the time the revised 2021–30 NDP was published in October 2021. It became evident at that stage that the final cost of high-profile transport projects like Metrolink and the M20 might be around three times previous estimates (see Chapter 4B). The capacity to fund road schemes was also reduced, as they were collectively limited to one third of transport investment. Continued adherence to high-cost road improvement options could thus result in unusually lengthy funding queues.

However, the specialist agencies created by the state from the 1990s onwards control most infrastructure funding, and usually prefer higher-cost alternatives. Worthwhile cross-compartment funding, perhaps as outlined in Box 4.1, or top-down coordination led by a government department with a cross-compartment remit, as discussed in Chapter 6D, may be a precondition for change in the relevant incentives and behaviour.

EXPECTATIONS

The suggestions in this book face two 'chicken and egg' problems. The first is that the Irish experience is one of continually changing construction policies, with the unusually cyclical character of the sector being a prime cause. This promotes scepticism on the permanence of any set of reforms. Such scepticism can be self-fulfilling, because it reduces the ability to influence medium- to long-term expectations, and makes it more likely that some landowners, investors and developers will sit out reforms, and wait for them to be diluted or go away.

To cope with this, reforms need to demonstrate they can anticipate cyclically generated problems, early enough to allow for the lead times involved in interventions in the construction sector. Since the future cannot be foreseen accurately or reliably, I have argued that various semi-automatic ways of matching different market conditions with more timely and more appropriate responses are needed. These rely partly on damping down instinctively pro-cyclical public expenditure patterns, such as diversion of public funding away from social housing and local infrastructure in recessions, and partly on reshaping the expectations of landowners, investors and developers, through advance announcements on how the state will respond to different market situations.

The latter approach requires these groups to believe that there has been a permanent and durable policy shift, which will apply throughout the cycle. They may well not do this to start with, but the tax-related measures suggested are designed to be introduced on a step-by-step basis, intensifying in rising markets and being scaled back in falling ones, in accordance with principles which make it clear how governments will respond to changing economic circumstances well in advance. Each annual adjustment in accordance with these principles would reinforce the perceived commitment of governments, and the effect on market expectations.

SPONSORS

Reforms need sponsors, and a second chicken and egg problem arises in finding effective sponsors for long-term measures to address cyclicality. The instability created by a highly cyclical construction sector instead promotes a focus on short-term, reactive policies to cope with its more acute effects, and these are more likely to increase cyclicality than reduce it.

Construction firms and governments are, in any case, inclined to give priority to short-term issues, and not just because they are prompted to do so by the cycle. If construction firms cannot make a profit on current projects, or have follow-on ones lined up, ready to start as soon as the current ones are complete, they will not have any longer-term future to worry about. Governments are elected for five-year terms, and individual ministers may have less than this in a relevant department, as the cabinet is often reshuffled mid-term. They will be judged mostly by results which become apparent while they are still in office.

On the other hand, experience may perhaps make institutions more willing than individuals or individual firms to think long term. Political parties and government departments have suffered from the effects of the construction cycle in the recent past, with adverse effects ranging from a perceived failure to deliver through political and social backlashes to financial meltdown. They are naturally optimistic on prospects for the measures they are currently proposing or implementing, but must also be aware that outcomes in the Irish housing market in particular have been driven more by the cycle than by policy for the last quarter of a century, and that the chances of this continuing or recurring are high, leading to further damage to belief in the government's capacity to solve problems.

The CIF and other property sector lobby organisations have been effective in advancing the short-term interests of its members, but at the cost of a very bumpy medium-term ride. The SHD system, advocated by PII, has greatly boosted judicial reviews. Ultimately successful CIF opposition to effective measures to control cyclicality in the last cycle – other than supply-side ones with direct short-term benefits for its members – has permanently destabilised the housebuilding industry, with the effects still being felt now. This has not been helpful for builders who have built up a reputation for value and reliability over several decades, and who value stable conditions which allow them benefit from this. Some of the investment funds which have been set up in Ireland over the last decade see a long-term role for themselves here, but this will be complicated if they are tarred with the same brush as other, more obviously predatory funds with short-term objectives.

Cyclicality in the construction industry may be an important, long-term, endemic problem, but institutions do not currently perceive it in those terms, so it is not surprising it is not given the priority accorded to more immediate and pressing issues. If this perception changed, periodic cyclically prompted disasters would be seen more as extreme symptoms of this problem, and less as aberrations, arising from periods when the industry and government temporarily lost the run of themselves. They did, of course, and sometimes admit this after the event, but they were almost propelled into doing so by the logic of the cycle, the short-term opportunities it offers, and the difficulty of dissuading those in a position to benefit from those opportunities from taking full advantage of them. Growing awareness of this might perhaps lead to the emergence of sponsors in unexpected places.

Unfortunately, it is human nature to believe what we are doing now is enough of an improvement on what we did in the past to avoid the repetition of past crises. Reinhart and Rogoff gave their 2009 account of economic crashes the rather satirical title This time it will be different, their point being that conditions prior to crashes differ sufficiently to give rise to this belief, but not enough to prevent recurrence.

While the interval between crashes may be a quarter of a century or more, dysfunctional construction markets and processes can become the norm, and it is widely accepted they have in fact done so in Ireland, at least in relation to housing. This may well result in more committed attempts at systematic reform. If and when this happens, it will not be enough to propose, enact and implement whatever reforms to the construction process are deemed necessary at that time. It will need to be done on a basis where they stay implemented, which, amongst other things, means they will have to be able to cope with the cycle, and the assistance it will give to vested interests which oppose them.

ABBREVIATIONS

AFF   An Foras Forbartha
BSM   Brady Shipman Martin
CEC   Commission of the European Communities
CIF   Construction Industry Federation
DKM   Davy Kelleher McCarthy
DoEd   Department of Education and Science
DoE   Department of the Environment (plus varying additional responsibilities in title)
DoF   Department of Finance
DoH   Department of Housing, Planning and Local Government
DoH   Department of Housing, Local Government and Heritage
DoLG   Department of Local Government
DPER   Department of Public Expenditure and Reform
DoT   Department of Transport
ESRI   Economic and Social Research Institute
EU   European Union
HA   Housing Agency
IAE   Irish Academy of Engineering
IDA   Industrial Development Authority
IHF   Irish Hotels Federation
IPA   Institute of Public Administration
IPI   Irish Planning Institute
IW   Irish Water
MITR   Mortgage Interest Tax Relief
NESC   National Economic and Social Council
NIRSA National Institute for Regional and Spatial Analysis

NRA   National Roads Authority
NTA   National Transport Authority
OECD   Organisation for Economic Cooperation and Development
PBO   Parliamentary Budget Office
PRTB   Private Residential Tenancies Board
QEC   Quarterly Economic Commentary (ESRI)
SCSI   Society of Chartered Surveyors of Ireland
SERA   South East Regional Authority
SWRA   South West Regional Authority
TII   Transport Infrastructure Ireland
UCC   University College Cork
UCD   University College Dublin
UCL   University College London

BIBLIOGRAPHY

Advisory Expert Committee (1991) 'Local Government Reorganisation and Reform', Pl . 7918, Dublin: Stationary Office (Chairman T. Barrington).

AECOM (2014) *Fingal/North Dublin Transport Study: Stage 1 Appraisal Report*, Dublin: NTA.

AECOM (2015) *Fingal/North Dublin Transport Study: Stage 2 Appraisal Report*, Dublin: NTA.

All Party Oireachtas Committee on the Constitution (2004), 9th Progress Report 'Private Property', Dublin: Government of Ireland.

Andersen, L.S. (2017) 'Denmark: The Constitution of a Happy Nation' in Harrison, F. (ed.) *Debt, Death and Deadweight*, London: Land Research Trust, Ch. 4.

Bacon, P., McCabe, F., Murphy, A. (1998) 'An Economic Assessment of Recent House Price Developments', Dublin: Stationary Office.

Bacon, P., McCabe, F. (1999) 'The Housing Market: An Economic Review and Assessment', Dublin: Stationary Office.

Bacon, P. (2000) 'The Housing Market in Ireland', Dublin: Stationary Office.

Bacon, P. and Associates (2009) *Overcapacity in the Irish Hotel Industry and required Elements of a Recovery Programme*, Dublin: IHF

Ball, M. (1988) *Rebuilding Construction – Economic Change in the British Construction Industry*, London: Routledge.

Ball, M., Lizieri, C. and MacGregor, B.D. (1998) *The Economics of Commercial Property Markets*, London: Routledge.

Bannon, M.J., Eustace, J.G. and O'Neill, M. (1981) 'Urbanisation: Problems of Growth and Decay in Dublin', Dublin: NESC (Prl 9031).

Bannon, M.J. (ed.) (1989) *Planning: The Irish Experience 1920–88*, Dublin: Wolfhound.

Bannon, M.J, (2004) 'Irish Urbanisation: Trends, Actions and Policy Changes', Planning and Environment Working Paper 04/03, Department of Planning and Environmental Policy, UCD.

Bannon, M.J, (2005) 'Spatial Planning Frameworks and Housing' in Norris. M. and Redmond D. (eds) *Housing Contemporary Ireland – Policy, Society and Shelter*, Dublin: IPA.

Barret, S, and Fudge, C. (eds) (1981) *Policy and Action: Essays on the Implementation of Public Policy*, London: Methuen.

Barry, F. and Bradley, J., (May 1997) *FDI and Trade: the Irish Host Country Experience*, Dublin: Centre for Economic Research, Department of Economics, UCD.

Barry Transportation, SWECO and WSP (BSW) (2020a) 'N/M20 Cork to Limerick Road Improvement Scheme: Phase 1 – Multi Criteria Analysis', Feb. 2020.

Barry Transportation, SWECO and WSP (BSW) (2020b) 'N/M20 Cork to Limerick Road Improvement Scheme: Public Consultation – Information Brochure', Nov. 2020.

Barrington Committee (1991) – see Advisory Expert Committee (above).

Bentley, D. (2017) *The Land Question*, London: Civitas.

Biehl, D. (1986) *The Contribution of Infrastructure to Regional Development*, Luxembourg: CEC.

Blair, S. (1997) *Spatial Planning and the European Spatial Development Perspective*, Waterford: Waterford Corporation.

Boland, B. (Winter 1986) 'Planning Administration in Local Authorities', *Pleanáil*, Vol. 1, No. 6.

Boudeville, J.R. (1966) *Problems of Regional Economic Planning*, Edinburgh: Edinburgh University Press.

Brady, Shipman, Martin (1999) 'Strategic Guidelines for the Greater Dublin Area', Dublin: BSM.

Bradley, J., O'Donnell, N., Sheridan, N. and Whelan, K. (1995) *Regional Aid and Convergence*, Aldershot: Avebury.

Bramley, G., Bartlett, W. and Lambert, C. (1995) *Planning, the Market and Private Housebuilding*, London: UCL Press.

Breathnach, P. (1982) 'The Demise of Growth Centre Policy: The Case of the Republic of Ireland' in Hudson, R. and Lewis, J.R. (eds) *Regional Planning in Europe*, London: Pion.

Breathnach, P. (1985) 'Rural Industrialisation in the West of Ireland' in Healey, M.J. and Ilberry, B.W. (eds) *The Industrialisation of the Countryside*, Norwich: Geo Books.

Breathnach, P. (1995) 'Porter's Clustering Concept – implications for industrial and regional policy', Paper given at RSA Conference, Maynooth, 14–15 Sept. 1995.

Breathnach, P., van Egeraat, C. and Curran, D. (2015) 'Regional Economic Resilience in Ireland: The roles of industrial structure and foreign inward investment', *Regional Studies, Regional Science* 2:1 pp. 497–517.

Breathnach, P. (2017) 'The National Policy Framework: Key Governance Issues', Paper to Political Studies Association of Ireland Annual Conference, Dublin City University, 13–15 Oct. 2017.

Brindley, T., Rydin, Y, Stoker, G. (1989) *Remaking Planning – the Politics of Urban Change in the Thatcher Years,* London: Unwin Hyman.

Buchanan,C. (1968) *Regional Studies in Ireland*, Dublin: AFF.

Buttler, F. (1975) *Growth Pole Theory and Economic Development* (translated by J. Cuthbert-Brown), Westmead, Hants: Saxon House.

Callanan, M. and Keegan, J.F. (2003) *Local Government in Ireland – inside out*, Dublin: IPA.

Chisholm, M. (1990) *Regions in Recession and Resurgence*, London: Unwin Hyman.

Clancy, P., O'Malley, E., O'Connell, L. and van Egeraat, C. 'Culliton's Clusters: Still the way to Go?' in NESC *Sustaining Competitive Advantage*, Proceedings of NESC seminar, Nov. 1997, Dublin: NESC Research Series, Ch. 4.

Commission of the European Communities (1985) *The European Community and its Regions*, Luxembourg: CEC.

Commission of the European Communities (1986) 'Information note on procedures, content and implementation of an integrated approach to regional development', Luxembourg: CEC.

Commission of the European Communities (1994a) *Europe 2000+: Cooperation for European Territorial Development*, Luxembourg: CEC

Commission of the European Communities (1994b) *Study of Prospects in Atlantic Regions*, Luxembourg: CEC.

Committee on the Price of Building Land – Report (1974) Dublin: Stationary Office.

Construction (monthly periodical, 1974+) Dublin: CIF.

Construction Industry Federation (2021) 'Budget Submission 2022', Dublin: CIF.

Cork County Council (2015) 'Monard Development Contributions Scheme', Cork: Cork Co. Co.

Coughlan, M. and de Buitleir, D. (1996) *Local Government Finance in Ireland*, Dublin: IPA.

Cullingworth, J.B. (1960) *Housing Needs and Planning Policy*, London: Routledge and Kegan Paul.

Culliton (1992) – see Industrial Policy Review Group.

Darlow, C. (ed.) (1988) *Valuation and Development Appraisal* (2nd edition), London: Estates Gazette.

Daly, G. and Kitchin, R. (2012) 'Shrink Smarter? Planning for spatial selectivity in population growth in Ireland', *Administration*, Vol. 60, No. 3, pp. 159–86.

DKM (2014a) 'Rent Stability in the Private Rented Sector', Final Report, Dublin: HA/PRTB

DKM (2014b) 'Future of the Private Rented Sector', Final Report, Dublin: HA/PRTB.

Department of Education and Science (2008) 'The Provision of Schools and the Planning System', Dublin: Government of Ireland.

Department of the Environment (1997) 'Sustainable Development – A Strategy for Ireland', Dublin: Stationary Office.

Department of the Environment and Local Government (2002) 'The National Spatial Strategy, 2002–2020 – People, Places and Potential', Dublin: Stationary Office.

Department of the Environment, Heritage and Local Government (2005) 'Planning and Development Acts 2000–2002 Part V, section 96(3)(d)(ii) – Profit on the costs', Circular AHS 7/05, Dublin: Government of Ireland.

Department of the Environment, Heritage and Local Government (2006) 'Part V of the Planning and Development Acts – Implementation Issues', Circular 4/06, Dublin: Government of Ireland.

Department of the Environment, Heritage and Local Government, Press Release (Aug. 2008) 'Finneran Outlines Developing Areas Initiative'.

Department of the Environment, Heritage and Local Government (2010) 'Water Services Programme for 2010–12', Dublin: Government of Ireland.

Department of the Environment, Community and Local Government (June 2011) 'Housing Policy Statement'.

Department of the Environment, Community and Local Government (2015; revised DoH version March 2018) 'Sustainable Urban Housing: Design Standard for New Apartments', Dublin: Government of Ireland.

Department of the Environment, Heritage and Local Government (2013) 'Development Contributions Guidelines for Planning Authorities' Dublin: Government of Ireland.

Department of the Environment, Heritage and Local Government (May 2014) 'Construction 2020 – A Strategy for a Renewed Construction Sector', Dublin: Government of Ireland.

Department of Finance (1958) 'Economic Development', Pr.4808, Dublin: Stationary Office.

Department of Housing, Planning and Local Government (2016) 'Implementation of the Vacant Sites Levy as provided for in the Urban and Regeneration and Housing Act, 2015', Circular PL7/2016, Dublin: Government of Ireland.

Department of Housing, Planning and Local Government (2018) 'Project 2040 – National Planning Framework', Dublin: Government of Ireland.

Department of Housing, Local Government and Heritage (September 2021) 'Housing for All: A new housing plan for Ireland', Dublin: Government of Ireland.

Department of Housing, Local Government and Heritage (2021) General Scheme, Land Value Sharing and Urban Development Zones Bill, Dublin: Government of Ireland.

Department of Housing, Local Government and Heritage (June 2022), 'Residential Zoned Land Tax – Guidelines for Panning Authorities', Dublin: Government of Ireland.

Department of Housing, Local Government and Heritage (December 2022, released April 2023) Land Value Sharing and Urban Development Bill General Scheme, Explanatory Memorandum, Dublin: Government of Ireland.

Department of Housing, Local Government and Heritage (2023): 'Sustainable and

Compact Settlements' Draft Guidleines for Planning Authorities, Dublin: Government of Ireland

Department of Local Government (1971) 'Local Government Reorganisation' (White Paper), Dublin: Stationary Office.

Department of Public Expenditure and Reform (2019) 'Public Spending Code: Evaluating, Planning and Managing Public Investment', Dublin: Government of Ireland.

Department of Public Expenditure and Reform (2019) 'Prospects: Ireland's Pipeline of Major Infrastructure Projects', Project Ireland 2040, Dublin: Government of Ireland.

Department of Public Expenditure and Reform (2020) 'Project Ireland 2040: Annual Report 2019', Dublin: Government of Ireland.

Department of Transport (2016, updated 2020) 'Common Appraisal Framework for Transport Projects and Programmes', Dublin: Government of Ireland.

Dublin Chamber of Commerce (2018) 'Submission on Ireland 2040 – National Planning Framework'.

Dunleavy, P. (1981) *The Politics of Mass Housing in Britain*, Oxford: Clarendon.

Edwards, M. (1985) 'Planning and the Land Market: problems, prospects and strategy' in Ball, M., Bentivegna, V., Edwards, M. and Folin, M. (eds) *Land Rent, Housing and urban Planning – a European perspective*, London; Croom Helm, pp. 201–15.

English, J., Madigan, P. and Norman, P. (1976) *Slum Clearance: The Social and Administrative Context in England and Wales*, London: Croom Helm.

European Union (1997) 'European Spatial Development Perspective', 1st Official Draft, presented to ministers responsible for spatial planning at Nordwijk, The Netherlands, Luxembourg: Office for the Official Publications of the European Union.

European Union – see also Commission of the European Communities.

Eustace, J.G. (1982) 'Ireland: The Industrial Development Authority' in Yuill, D (ed.) *Regional Development Agencies in Europe*, Aldershot: Gower, pp. 235–96.

Evans, A.W. (2004a) *Economics, Real Estate and the Supply of Land*, Oxford: Blackwell.

Evans, A.W. (2004b) *Economics and Land Use Planning*, Oxford: Blackwell.

Faludi, A. and van der Valk, A. (1994) *Rule and Order: Dutch Planning Doctrine in the 20th Century*, Dordrecht: Kluwer.

Fitzgerald, J. (Spring 2005) 'The Irish Housing Stock: Growth in the number of vacant dwellings', ESRI Quarterly Economic Commentary.

Flinter, D. (1991) 'Overseas Industry in Ireland: Future Considerations' in Foley, A. and McAleese, D. (eds) *Overseas Industry in Ireland*, Dublin: Gill and Macmillan, pp. 191–8.

Flyvbjerg, B., Bruzelius, N. and Rothengater, W. (2003) *Megaprojects and Risk: An anatomy of ambition*, Cambridge: Cambridge University Press.

Gardner, D. (2012) *Future Babble: How to stop worrying and love the unpredictable*, London: Virgin Books.

George, S. (1991) *Politics and Policy in the European Community*, Oxford: Oxford University Press.

Glasson, J. (1974) *An Introduction to Regional Planning*, London: Hutchinson.

Gleeson, L (2003) 'Water Services' in Callanan, M. and Keegan, J.F. (eds) *Local Government in Ireland – inside out*, Dublin: IPA, pp. 209–20.

Goodbody Economic Consultants (2005) *Review of Area Based Tax Incentive Renewal Schemes*, Dublin: Department of Finance.

Goodchild, R. and Munton, R. (1985) *Development and the Landowner*, London: Allen and Unwin.

Harrop, J. (1996) *Structural Funding and Employment in the European Union*, Cheltenham: Edward Elgar.

Hart, J. (1985) 'The European Regional Development Fund and the Republic of Ireland' in Keating, M. and Jones, B. (eds) *Regions in the European Community*, Oxford: Clarendon Press, pp. 204–33.

Hearne, R. (2020) *Housing Shock: The Irish Housing Crisis and how to solve it*, Bristol: Policy Press.

Hearne, R. (2022) *Gaffs: why no-one can get a house... and what we can do about it*, Dublin: Harper Collins Ireland

Healey, P. and Nabarro, R. (eds) (1990) *Land and Property Development in a Changing Context*, Aldershot: Gower.

Hegarty, O., (2021) 'Housing and Sustainability') in Sirr (ed) *Housing in Ireland: Beyond the Markets*, Dublin: IPA, Ch. 6.

Hession, P. (2019) 'Update on the Affordable Purchase Scheme and the Serviced Sites Fund' (presentation), Dublin: Department of Housing, Planning and Local Government.

Higgins, B. and Savoie, D.J. (1988) *Regional Economic Development – Essays in honour of Francois Perroux*, Boston: Unwin Hyman.

Hillebrandt, P.M., Cannon, J. and Lansley, P. (1995) *The Construction Company in and out of Recession*, London: Palgrave Macmillan.

Hillebrandt, P.M. (1985 & 2000) *Economic Theory and the Construction Industry* (2nd & 3rd editions), Basingstoke: Macmillan.

Housing Agency (2014) 'Part V Review', Dublin: DoE

Howard, E. (1965) *Garden Cities of Tomorrow*, London: Faber and Faber.

Indecon (2005) 'Review of Property Based Tax Incentive Schemes', Dublin: DoF.

Indecon (2018) 'Report on the Taxation of Vacant Residential Property', Dublin: DoF.

Industrial Development Authority (1972) 'Jobs to the People: Regional Industrial Plans 1972–77' (summary), Dublin: IDA.

Industrial Development Authority (1978) 'IDA Industrial Plan 1977–80', Dublin: IDA.

Industrial Policy Review Group (1992) 'A Time for Change: Industrial Policy for the 1990s' (Culliton Report), Dublin: Stationary Office.

Ireland (1989) 'National Development Plan 1989–93' Dublin: Stationary Office.

Ireland (1993) 'National Development Plan 1994–99', Dublin: Stationary Office (Pn 0222).

Ireland (1999) 'National Development Plan 2000–06', Dublin: Stationary Office (Pn 7780).

Ireland, Government of (2016) 'Rebuilding Ireland – Action Plan for Housing and Homelessness', Dublin: Government of Ireland.

Ireland, Government of (2018) 'Project 2040: National Development Plan 2018–2027', Dublin: Government of Ireland.

Ireland, Government of (2021) 'National Development Plan 2021–2030', Dublin: Government of Ireland.

Irish Academy of Engineering (2011) 'The Cost Effective Delivery of Essential Infrastructure', Dublin: Forfas.

Irish Water (2019) 'Connection Charging Policy', Dublin: IW.

Irish Water (2019) 'Investment Plan 2020–2024', Dublin: IW.

Ive, G.J. and Gruneberg, S.L. (2000) *The Economics of the Modern Construction Sector*, Basingstoke: Macmillan.

Jacobs and Systra (2019) 'Cork Metropolitan Area Transport Strategy 2040', Dublin: NTA.

Jenkins (2020) *A Short History of London*, London: Penguin.

Jennings, R. and Grist, B. (1983) 'The Problem with Building Land', *Administration*, Vol. 31, No. 3, pp. 257–83.

Joint Oireachtas Committee on Building Land (1985) 'Report', Dublin: Stationary Office.

Joint Oireachtas Committee on State Sponsored Bodies (2 Oct. 1980) 'The National Building Agency Ltd.', Dublin: Stationary Office (Prl 9480).

Joyce, L., Humphreys, P.C. and Kelleher, A. (1988) *Decentralisation: The Civil Service Experience*, Dublin: IPA.

Kavanagh, C. (May 1996) 'Public Capital and Private Sector Productivity', Cork: UCC Department of Economics (Working Paper Series).

Kenny Report (1974) – see Committee on the Price of Building Land.

Kitchin, R., Hearne, R. and O'Callaghan, C. (Feb. 2015) 'Housing in Ireland: From crisis to crisis', Working Paper no. 77, Maynooth: NIRSA.

KPMG (1996) *Study on the Urban Renewal Schemes*, Dublin: Stationary Office.

KPMG (2023) Land Value Sharing – Update to General Scheme Released OK???

Kunzmann, K.R. and Wegener, M (1991) 'The Pattern of Urbanisation in Western Europe, 1960–1990', Report for DG XVI, CEC, Dortmund: Institut fur Raumplanung, Universitat Dortmund.

Lansley, P. (1991) 'Organisational Innovation and Development' in Male, S. and

Stocks, R. (eds) *Competitive Advantage in Construction*, Oxford: Butterworth Heinemann, pp. 128–38.

Lee, J.J. (1989) *Ireland 1912–1985*, Cambridge: Cambridge University Press.

Lennon, M., and Waldron., R., (2019) De-democratising the Irish Planning System, *European Planning Studies,* vol. 27, no. 8, pp. 1607–25.

Lewis, E. (2010) *Competing in an Uncertain World – Institutional Change in the Irish State*, Dublin: IPA.

Lewis, J.P. (1965) *Building Cycles and Britain's Growth*, London: Macmillan.

Lichfield, N. and Darin-Drabkin, R. (1980) *Land Policy in Planning*, London: Allen and Unwin.

McCartney (Winter 2008) 'An Empirical Analysis of Development Cycles in the Dublin Office Market 1976–2007', ESRI Quarterly Economic Commentary, pp. 68–92.

McCarthy (2003) 'Where have all the houses gone?', Dublin: Davy Stockbrokers Research Report.

McDonald, F. (1985) *The Destruction of Dublin*, Dublin: Gill and Macmillan.

McDonald, F. (1989) *Saving the City*, Dublin: Tomar Publishing.

McDonald, F. (2000) *The Construction of Dublin*, Kinsale: Gandon.

McDonald, F. and Nix, J. (2005) *Chaos at the Crossroads*, Kinsale: Gandon.

McDowell, M. (1982) 'A Generation of Public Expenditure Growth: Leviathan Unchained' in Litton, F. (ed.) *Unequal Achievement: The Irish Experience 1957–1982*, Dublin: IPA, pp. 183–200.

Mansergh, N.B.K (Apr. 1983) 'The Taxation of Development Land – A Proposal', *Administration*, Vol. 30, No. 4, pp. 114–28.

Mansergh, N.B.K (Apr. 1985) 'The Value of Cost Benefit Analysis of Road Projects', ESRI Quarterly Economic Commentary, pp. 36–47.

Mansergh, N.B.K (1998) 'Cork's Role as a Regional Core' in B. Brunt and K. Hourihan (eds) *Perspectives on Cork*, Maynooth: Geographical Society of Ireland, pp. 52–68.

Mansergh, N.B.K (2001) 'Spatial Planning and the Construction Policy Sector', unpublished PhD thesis, Cork: UCC.

Mansergh, N.B.K (2005) 'Planning and Development' in J. Crowley, R. Devoy, D. Linehan, P. O'Flanagan (eds) *An Atlas of Cork City*, Cork: Cork University Press, pp. 424–43.

Mansergh, N.B.K (Spring 2007) 'Social and Affordable Housing in Ireland: Transfers of Houses under Part V of the Planning Act', *Pleanáil*, No. 17, pp. 61–74.

Mitchel, P., (October 2022) 'Development Costs: Implications for Planning and Housing for All', IPI Autumn Conference (Malahide), Dublin: IPI

Morgenroth, E. (2012) 'Economics: The missing link in the National Spatial Strategy', *Administration*, Vol. 60, No. 3, pp. 41–60.

Morgenroth, E. (Jan. 2018) 'Prospects for Irish regions and Counties: Scenarios and Implications', ESRI Research Series 70.

Morgenroth, E. (27 Nov. 2019) 'Developing Ireland's Sustainable Transport System', Statement to Joint Oireachtas Committee on Climate Change.

Morley, C., Duffy, D. and McQuinn, K. (Winter 2015) 'A Review of Housing Supply Policies', ESRI Quarterly Economic Commentary, pp. 75–94.

Moylan, K. (2011) 'Irish Regional Policy: in search of coherence' Dublin: IPA

National Economic and Social Council (1975) 'Regional Policy in Ireland: A Review', Report no. 4, Dublin: NESC.

National Economic and Social Council (2004) 'Housing in Ireland: Performance and Policy', Report no. 112, Dublin: NESC.

National Economic and Social Council (2014) 'Ireland's Rental Sector: Pathways to Secure Occupancy and Affordable Supply', Report no. 141, Dublin: NESC.

National Economic and Social Council (2018) 'Urban Development Land, Housing and Infrastructure: Fixing Ireland's Broken System', Report no. 145, Dublin: NESC.

National Economic and Social Council (2019) 'Transport Orientated Development: Assessing the Opportunity for Ireland', Report no. 148, Dublin: NESC.

National Economic and Social Council (2020) 'Housing Policy: Actions to Deliver Change', Report no. 150, Dublin: NESC.

National Roads Authority (1998) 'National Road Needs Study' Dublin: NRA.

National Transport Authority (2016) 'Transport Strategy for the Greater Dublin Area 2016–2035', Dublin: NTA.

National Transport Authority (2018) 'Bus Connects', Core Bus Corridor Project Report, Dublin: NTA.

National Transport Authority (2018) 'Metrolink Emerging Preferred Route' Public Consultation Report, Dublin: NTA/TII NESC

National Transport Authority (2021) 'Greater Dublin Area Transport Strategy, 2022–2042', Dublin: NTA.

Nevin, E. (1990) *The Economics of Europe*, Basingstoke: Macmillan.

Norris, M (2016) *Property, Family and the Irish Welfare State*, London: Palgrave Macmillan.

Norris, M. and Hayden, A. (2018) 'The Future of Council Housing – an analysis of the financial sustainability of local authority provided public housing', The Community Foundation for Ireland/UCD.

Nowlan, Bill (2020) 'Turnkey approach is ideal for high volumes of houses at affordable prices', *Irish Times*, 20 August 2020.

Ó Broin, E. (2019) *Home – why public housing is the answer*, Newbridge: Merrion Press.

O'Callagnan, C., and Stokes, K., (2021) 'Housing and Vacancy' in Sirr. L., *Housing in Ireland: Beyond the Markets*, Dublin: IPA , Ch. 16.

O'Connell, D. (2005) 'Urban design and Residential Environment' in Norris, M. and Redmond, D. (eds) *Housing Contemporary Ireland – policy, society and shelter*, Dublin: IPA. Ch. 16.

O'Connell, H. (2021) 'Homes Plan misses target by thousands' *Sunday Independent*, 8 August 2021, p. 2.

O'Donnell, R. (1998) 'Post Porter: Exploring Policy for the Irish Context' in NESC Sustaining Competitive Advantage', Proceedings of NESC Seminar, Nov. 1997, Dublin: NESC Research Series.

O'Farrell, P.N. (July 1974) 'Regional Policy in Ireland – the Case for Concentration: A Reappraisal', *Economic and Social Review*, Vol. 5, No. 4, pp. 499–513.

O'Hegarty, R., Wall, S., Kinane, O., (October 2022) 'Whole Life Carbon in Construction and the Built Environment' (4th draft), Irish Green Building Council

O'Leary, E. (2007) 'Regional Policy and Agglomeration Economies in Ireland' in Forfas *Perspectives on Irish Productivity*, Ch. 15, Dublin: Forfas

Organisation for Economic Cooperation and Development (2011) 'Housing and the Economy: Policies for Renovation' in *Economic Policy Reforms: Going for Growth*, Paris: OECD, Ch. 4.

O'Sullivan, M.C. (1998) 'National Road Needs Study', Dublin: NRA.

Padoa Schioppa, T. (1987) *Efficiency, Equity and Stability*, Oxford: Oxford University Press.

Parliamentary Budget Office (2019) 'An Overview and Analysis of the Help to Buy Scheme', Dublin: PBO.

Parliamentary Budget Office (2022) 'An Overview of the Help to Buy Scheme from 2016–2021', Dublin: PBO.

Porter, M.E. (1990) *The Competitive Advantage of Nations*, London: Macmillan.

Quinn, K. (Summer 2021) 'With "G" greater than "R", should we be borrowing to increase Irish housing supply?', ESRI Quarterly Economic Commentary, pp. 51–63.

Redmond, D., Williams, B. and Punch, M. (2005) 'Planning and Sustainability: Metropolitan Planning, Housing and Land Policy' in Norris, M, and Redmond, D. (eds) *Housing Contemporary Ireland – Policy, society and shelter*, Dublin: IPA, Ch.15.

Reidy, J., and Breen, B., (December 2022) 'Planning Permission and Housing Supply' IGEES Unit, Dublin: Department of Public Expenditure and Reform.

Reynolds, M, 2021) 'Housing and the Dynamics of Land', in *Housing in Ireland: Beyond the Markets*, Dublin: IPA, Ch. 4.

Roche, D. (1982) *Local Government in Ireland*, Dublin: IPA.

Sabel, C. (1996) *Ireland: Local Partnerships and Social Innovation*, Paris: OECD.

Schofield, J.A. (1987) *Cost Benefit Analysis in Urban and Regional Planning*, London: Allen and Unwin.

Society of Chartered Surveyors Ireland (2016) 'The Real Cost of New House Delivery', Dublin: SCSI.

Society of Chartered Surveyors Ireland (2017) 'The Real Costs of New Apartment Delivery', Dublin: SCSI.

Society of Chartered Surveyors Ireland (2020) 'The Real Cost of New Housing Delivery' , Dublin: SCSI.

Society of Chartered Surveyors Ireland (2021) 'The Real Costs of New Apartment Delivery', Dublin: SCSI.

Sectoral Consultative Committee (1984) *The Construction Industry*, Dublin: AFF.

Sirr, L. (2019) *Housing in Ireland – The A-Z Guide*, Dublin: Orpen Press.

Sirr, L, (ed.) (2021) *Housing in Ireland: Beyond the Markets*, Dublin: IPA.

Sirr, L, (October 2022) 'Housing for All: What are we building?', IPI Autumn Conference (Malahide), Dublin: IPI

Shannon Development (1996) 'Regional Policy', Dublin: Forfas.

Sieverts, T. (2003) *Cities without cities: An interpretation of the Zwischenstadt*, London: Spon Press.

South-East Regional Authority (1996) 'Regional Report, 1996–2000', Waterford: SERA.

South-West Regional Authority (1996) 'Regional Action Plan, 1996–2001', Ballincollig: SWRA.

Strategic Review Committee (1997) 'Ireland: Building our Future Together – Strategic Review of the Construction Industry', Dublin: Stationary Office.

Telesis Consultancy (1982) 'A Review of Industrial Policy', Pl 409, Dublin: NESC.

van Duijn, J.J. (1984) 'Fluctuations in Innovations over Time' in Freeman, C. (ed.) *Long Waves in the World Economy*, London: Frances Pinter, Chapter 3, pp. 19–30.

van Egeraat, C., Breathnach, P. and Curran, D. (2012) 'Gateways, Hubs and Regional Specialisation in the National Spatial Strategy', *Administration*, Vol. 60, No. 3, pp. 91–113.

Waldron, R., (2019) 'Financialisation, Urban Governance anf the Planning Sytem: Utilising "Development Viability" as a Policy Narrative for the Liberalisation of Ireland's Post-Crash Planning System' *International Journal of Urban and Regional Research*, pp. 685–704.

Walsh, B. (July/Aug. 1977) 'The Construction Industry at the Cross Roads', *Construction*, p. 23.

Walsh, F. (1976) 'The Growth Centre Concept in Irish Regional Policy', *Maynooth Review*, Vol. 2, No.1, pp. 22–41.Journal number??

Williams, R.H. (1996) *European Spatial Policy and Planning*, London: Paul Chapman.

NOTES

Chapter 1

1   Figure 1.3(a) shows the proportion of total employment in the construction sector in West Germany until 1990, and in Germany as a whole from 1991 onwards.

2   Lead times are more of a problem in the larger urban areas, because these are the areas in which demand usually recovers first after a recession, and where, as a consequence, there is little or no time in which to remedy infrastructure deficiencies before increased demand leads to rapidly rising prices.

3   Average house prices nationally were around £55,000 (€70,000) in 1992 (c. £62,000/€79,000 in Dublin). The CSO House Construction Cost Index showed that material and labour costs approximately doubled between 1992 and 2016.

4   Housing output averaged 23,400 per annum between 1990 and 1995, and the population of the state was 39% higher in 2016–22 than in 1991–96. While housing output was almost 30,000 in 2022, it was only 21,240 in 2019, immediately before the pandemic, and averaged 12,700 p. a. in the 2014–19 period.

5   A recent collection of essays (Housing in Ireland – Beyond the Markets) explicitly focuses on these qualitative aspects, which are seen as having been 'pushed further down the list of priorities' by the quantitative requirements of governments and investors (Sirr, 2021, p.xiv). This involves real risks. Unattractive new housing units may be accepted when there are acute shortages, but may have a short life and wasteful end, if in the medium term they turn out to be unpopular with users, difficult to manage and maintain, or too tightly designed to be readily adapted to changing needs and expectations.

6   Strictly speaking, there are several pipelines. In addition to the main one, involving development of farmland on the edge of urban areas, there are subsidiary ones, involving recycling and redevelopment of previously developed urban land, and rural devel-

opment. The main flows involved are summarised diagrammatically at the beginning of Chapter 3 (Figure 3.1).

Chapter 2

1   McCartney (2008) describes this model, and applies it to the Dublin office market.

2   Lennon and Waldron's (2019, p. 1618) account of the origins of the Strategic Housing Development (SHD) system suggests alignment, at least in that particular case. They describe how a PII representative proposed on Marian Finucane's radio programme that planning applications for 100 or more housing units should bypass local authorities and go direct to An Bord Pleanála. The then Minister for Housing, hearing this, rang PII to arrange a series of meetings, at which PII put forward their recommendations 'and they took it lock, stock and barrel, and stuck it into the new housing bill' in 2016. Removal of the right to appeal planning decisions led to a large increase in judicial reviews, so the SHD system was phased out in 2021–22 and replaced by a restored two stage process, with such applications once again being made to local authorities.

3   The 1.6% growth line bisects actual output in the downward part of the cycle approximately halfway between peaks and low points (i.e. between 1979 and 1988, and 2007 and 2012). This can be regarded as a possible definition of sustainable average growth, if it is considered that the peaks were unsustainable, and the subsequent troughs involved over-correction, to roughly equal degrees.

Chapter 3

1   The ratio is approximate, and intended to convey orders of magnitude. Development land costs to developers include stamp duty and legal costs, which may be c. 5% of the amount paid to the previous owner.

2   Such ratios are not peculiar to Ireland, or to the recent past. Goodchild and Munton (1985, p. 48) cite development values of 50–80 times agricultural ones in outer London in the 1970s and 20–25 times agricultural values for a provincial city like Leicester in 1980. The ratio in Ireland seems to have been lower than that then, as Jennings and Grist (1984, p. 279) cite prices of £3–4,000 per undeveloped site in the late 1970s – 10–15 times agricultural value.

3   Sales are often in two stages, with the developer taking an option initially, and completing the purchase later (e.g. if and when land is zoned or planning permission granted).

4   Data on land values in the Review and Outlook series are expressed in terms of land costs (to developers), which include transaction costs, fees etc as well as the price paid to the seller. However, land price accounts for the great majority of land cost. The 2020 SCSI Cost of Housing Delivery Report estimated (p. 14) that stamp duty and fees would be 5% of the purchase price of land for an average semi in Dublin.

5   The increase in land value which occurs when land becomes available for development is often referred to as 'betterment' in government reports in the UK and Ire-

land. Estate agents sometimes use the term 'upgrading'. In recent government documents such as Housing for All (2021), the term 'uplift' is used instead.

6 While leases could also be used to control the timing of development (e.g. through clauses by which land was clawed back by the local authority if not developed within a specified time), the Kenny report does not specifically refer to this (p. 41). It was also not worried (p. 44) by potential delays due to local authority acquisition and disposal of land prior to development, citing the large volume of social housing they had provided since 1922, and their ability to cope with extensive additional responsibilities under the 1963 Planning Act.

7 For instance, the Community Land Act also involved the designation of areas likely to be needed for development in the next ten years, and its stage 2 provisions required all designated land to pass through public ownership.

8 In the remainder of this book, references to the Kenny report should be taken as referring to the recommendations of the majority on the Kenny Committee.

9 Department of the Environment, Construction Industry Review and Outlook series.

10 See Bacon (1999, pp. 58–62) for discussion of innovative options which could address the affordability problem.

11 Or its value when last sold or inherited, prior to publication of the Bill in August 1999, whichever was the greater.

12 The Planning and Development (Amendment) Act, 2002.

13 Circular AHS 2/05 (8 September 2005).

14 Contractor's profit is the profit a contractor makes on a contract to, say, build a housing scheme, and developer's profit is the additional profit made by a developer who employed a contractor to carry out the actual construction work. Developer's profit is necessary. If the selling price of houses was only sufficient to recover the cost of building them (with contractor's profit) plus the development value of the land, the developer could realise the same return with far less risk and delay by simply reselling the land at full development value and (if he was a builder as well as a developer) taking on contract work.

15 E.g. *Cork County Council v Shackleton and Murphy Construction, Glenkerrin Homes v Dun Laoghaire Rathdown County Council* (both 2007).

16 Circular AHS 4/06 (27 November 2006).

17 The Review (p. iv) estimated that provision of social housing under Part V had saved the state €614 million in the 2002–11 period, relative to the cost of providing the same houses.

18 Including VAT and 15% profit.

19 In the SCSI calculations, VAT and profit are shown as a percentage of overall cost, and so increase the effect of changes in land cost. A reduction of €50,000 in land costs thus reduces the overall cost by c. €65,000.

20 The use of national maxima may have complicated the task of fixing appropriate percentages. Outside the larger cities, there was no need for Part V affordable housing in 2015. The Act could, however, have retained provision for it, with the Minister hav-

ing power to lower the upper 20% limit on Part V transfers, in parts of the country and at times where full Part V transfers were not needed.

21 Despite widely accepted claims to the contrary, this mechanism was inoperative in the 2002–7 period, as housing output was not reduced, but grew rapidly. Development gains were so large then that house-building remained highly attractive, despite Part V and the increase in development contributions also provided for in the 2000 Act.

22 A Joint Oireachtas Committee is one composed of members of both the Dáil and the Senate.

23 This was at a late stage in the cycle, when a downturn had already taken hold, but the three general elections held in 1981–2 may have prevented it being established earlier.

24 This is reflected in the structure of the Joint Committee's report. The first five chapters deal with allocation, supply and distributional issues. Ch. 1 is entitled 'Ensuring the Best Use of Land'. Ch. 2 is largely a warning against making policy proposals for those related areas which affect land, without regard for their effects on land allocation/use. Ch. 3 deals with demand and supply of land, Ch. 4 with prices and costs, and Ch. 5 with the size and distribution of gains. The sequence is then repeated: Ch. 6 deals with the operation of the land market (supply), Ch. 7 with the local authority framework (allocation and procedural matters), and Ch. 8 with 'The Question of Equity'.

25 While the Committee also considered prohibiting non-building interests from holding development land, or discouraging them from doing so, by applying higher tax rates where land had been sold on without development occurring, it opted for wider and more aggressive use of compulsory purchase.

26 It may have felt that the greater use of compulsory purchase it recommended would solve this problem. Also, in the depressed housing market of the 1980s, many builders were happy to sell completed houses to local authorities, and the barriers to local authority property acquisition were lower than usual.

27 The Supreme Court decided (13 May 1983) in the Short case that an applicant for planning permission had a right to connect to a public sewer under the 1878 Public Health Act, and that the planning authority could not argue the capacity of the sewer was reserved to serve other development, and escape compensation on the grounds that the application was premature having regard to sewerage capacity other than that so earmarked (judgement quoted in P. O'Sullivan and K. Shepherd, *A Sourcebook on Planning Law in Ireland*, Abingdon, Professional Books 1984, pp. 432–3).

28 Where refusals remained compensatable, the 1990 Act reduced the amount, from what the applicant would have gained if granted permission to the actual reduction in value consequent on refusal. Sch. 1 of this Act provided (s.3(2)(b)) that in deciding the pre-decision value of the land, regard shall be had to the likelihood or unlikelihood of permission. If permission is unlikely, the value will be low, as buyers would want a large discount on the development value. Thus, only a small amount of compensation can be claimed for predictable refusals. Schedule 3 (s.11) excluded claims

which contravene the zoning. These provisions were carried over into the 2000 Act.

29 Sch 1, s.2(b)(i) and Sch. 3, s.1(b) of the 1990 Act.

30 See Chapter 4.

31 This provided for the construction of 10,000 additional affordable houses on publicly owned land.

32 State Authorities (Public Private Partnership Arrangements) Act, 2002.

33 John Coleman (interim CEO of the LDA), quoted by Olivia Kelly in 'Land Development Agency should stop spending and focus on State sites', *The Irish Times*, 5 February 2019, p. 6.

34 Opening Statement of John Coleman to Joint Committee on Housing, Planning and Local Government, 1710/18.

35 This works out at slightly over €8,000 per house, presumably implying that the operation was expected to be largely self-funding, with initial capital outlays being largely recovered and recycled once land was developed.

36 Advance acquisition of land under Part V – suggested in Box 3.3 above – is, to some extent, vulnerable to the same objection, but would be a more standardised process, whose legal and constitutional status would be more likely to be resolved by a Supreme Court decision on the relevant Bill or on a test case.

37 Unlike the 2021 General Outline of the proposed Land Value Sharing and Urban Development Zone bill, the December 2022 version makes no reference to land credits or land equalisation payments, but the explanatory memorandum attached to the latter to explain the changes in it does not refer to their omission. It is possible that it was decided to leave them on a non-statutory basis.

38 The term used in Housing for All.

39 As noted in Box 3.4, network infrastructure which serves a number of adjacent development sites does not necessarily give rise to a valid claim under s.34.4(m). Developers of sites in the lowest part of a neighbourhood or at the main entrance to it may have a valid claim payment for the extra cost of upsizing their sewers and roads to serve sites further up or into it. Such upsizing costs are likely to be minor, relative to those the local authority would incur if it built the road or laid the sewer itself. Also, developments higher up or further into the neighbourhood should not be in a position to make such claims, as any works they carry out on their own sites in excess of their immediate needs will be balanced by the works they benefit from, on other sites lower down or closer to the main entrance. S.34.4(m) is concerned with the balance between their immediate needs (which may be met partly by works carried out by others on adjoining sites) and what they have actually provided themselves. If this principle is not followed, collective over-compensation of the developers involved is likely.

40 This was misleading. As noted earlier, the Kenny majority proposals relied on compulsory acquisition rather than a tax on voluntary sales to capture gains. Ironically, in 2010, the state could have acquired large amounts of development land through the National Asset Management Agency (NAMA), much of it at or close to existing use

values, but was in no position to use this to start implementing Kenny, being under extreme pressure to reduce its debts.

41 The criteria include the availability of surface water drainage and public lighting, which are often matters only resolved during the processing of planning applications, and the need for the land or part of it for physical or social infrastructure. This presumably includes future needs, which may be ill-defined and subject to considerable uncertainty at present.

42 Local authorities would be expected to make submissions on these appeals, and there is also provision for seeking further information from Irish Water and the National Roads Authority.

43 The Planning and Development (Amendment) Act inserted a new clause to this effect into s.5.1(a) of the 2015 Act.

44 There is a general, widely discussed case for a more comprehensive system of site value taxation (SVT). It would not be politically practicable to apply this to agricultural land without development potential, so the majority of land would be exempt. Also, incentives to switch to high margin activities like dairy farming are arguably strong enough already. In areas which are already built up, there would be a similar risk of squeezing out diversity by making lower margin activities uneconomic. If applied to housing, it would face the same difficulty in updating values as Residential Property Tax (RPT), in a more acute form, as site/development land values are even more volatile than house prices. The advantage of limiting SVT to development land and vacant property is that the principle is already largely accepted in that area, so a carefully designed reform based on it might remain in place in the medium term.

45 General Scheme, Land Value Sharing and Urban Development Zones Bill 2021, pp. 21–2.

46 Land already zoned residential, or zoned commercial or industrial, was excluded from the first version of the outline legislation so as not to adversely affect the viability of development. It was included in the second version, as it was felt distinguishing between newly zoned and other zoned land could lead to distortions, issues of fairness, and potential for litigation (Land Value Sharing and Urban Development Bill General Scheme, Explanatory Memorandum, Dec. 2022, p. 10. The date on the document preceded its actual publication).

47 If this assumption was correct, housing land prices should already be lower than they otherwise would be, so as to take full account of Part V obligations.

48 The draft legislation adds a number of new items which can be funded by LVS, in addition to the list of items fundable under existing local authority Development Contributions Schemes. These include flood defences, sites for hospitals, facilities for the elderly, and programmes and facilities relating to training.

49 Other ways in which such funding could be used to improve local infrastructure provision and make it less cyclical are discussed in Chapter 4.

50 The relatively modest percentage annual levy rates used notionally in Table 3.4 are similar to the Danish land value tax rates of 0.6–2.4% cited by Barker (2003, para

7.23), and 0.6%–3.4% (with the maximum rate reduced there to 3% in 2017), cited by Andersen (2017). A general tax on the value of land has been in place in Denmark since the 1920s, and in view of its longevity is presumably effective in influencing expectations as well as current behaviour. Values are frequently updated in Denmark, so liability rises in line with development value, which 'generally results in land becoming available where most needed' (Morley, 2015, p. 76).

51   This effect is not allowed for in Figure 3.4, because of the difficulty of estimating how much lower land prices would have been under the assumptions used.

Chapter 4

1   The main exceptions are individual rural houses, farms etc relying on their own wells and septic tanks.

2   Discussed in Chapter 3 (section 2) above.

3   Sewerage and water supply were described collectively as sanitary services up to the 1990s, and as water services thereafter. Both terms are used in this chapter, depending on the period under discussion.

4   Developers would be obliged to provide these where the boundary of their development ran along an existing road as a condition of planning permission, but in developing suburbs this typically resulted in discontinuous footpaths.

5   Department of the Environment press release 'Finneran outlines proposals for Developing Areas Initiative'.

6   LIHAF – Call for Proposals, Department of Housing, Planning, Community and Local Government, Circular PL 10/2016, 26/8/16.

7   Presumably this related to cases where the local authority would normally have charged a special contribution, to cover investment made necessary by the particular developments involved. Infrastructure straddling a number of adjacent sites was also eligible under LIHAF.

8   The Serviced Site Fund was incorporated into or rechristened as the Affordable Housing Fund by Housing for All (2021, p. 38) – a shift of emphasis from input to output.

9   This is the scheme involving a 170 km pipe taking water from the River Shannon to Dublin and the surrounding counties.

10   However, Budget 2022 front loaded the increase, raising the capital allocation to Irish Water for 2022 to €1.6 billion, which might allow total investment in servicing new development to be around one third of the increase the CIF considered necessary.

11   House prices figures from the Annual Housing Statistics Bulletin Series.

12   Chapter 6 questions this view.

13   Strategic planning for metropolitan areas was previously carried out patchily, and mostly on an informal basis, as local authority boundaries rarely coincided with the journey to work areas used to define metropolitan areas.

14   A draft Metropolitan Area Transport Strategy for Cork was published in 2019. The

shift from integrated land use transportation studies such as the 1978 Cork LUTS plan and the 2001 Cork Area Strategic Plan reflected the segmentation of central government infrastructure functions, and the growing dominance of the agencies responsible for them.

15 Plans typically assume conditions will be more favourable than at the time of preparation, and do not allow for the lower part of the economic cycle.

16 Essentially, this would involve the local authority acting in the role of a developer under Irish Water's Connection Charging Policy (April 2019). This provides for (p. 24) 'self lay' – situations in which a developer is allowed to carry out works on its behalf, and becomes liable for reduced connection charges to reflect this. The local authority could similarly carry out works by agreement, and the amount by which connection charges would have been reduced if this had been done by the developer could be passed back to the local authority. The alternative of transferring responsibility for network water services infrastructure is discussed in Box 4.2 below.

17 Local Government (Planning and Development Act, 1963, s.26.2(g)–(h).

18 Department of the Environment Planning Statistics series; DKM Construction Industry Review and Outlook series.

19 Section 48.2–3.

20 Department of the Environment Planning Statistics series; DKM Construction Industry Review and Outlook series.

21 The most recent instance of this tendency was the announcement that contributions and water connection charges on housing developments would be waived for a year, from April 2023 (Department of Housing Circular PL 04/2023). While the circular provides for reimbursement of local authorities for income lost during that year, it reflects a broader view that housing developers should only be expected to make the most minimal payment for the infrastructure which makes their developments possible through the (existing) contributions system. The SCSI estimated (2020, pp. 11–14) that local authority contributions accounted for 2.4% of the total cost of a new house in the Dublin area (including profit), and Irish Water charges for a further 1.1%.

22 Obviously, this has to be 'early enough' to allow for planning and procurement processes, as well as actual construction. While these processes may sometimes be over-elaborate, they may also contain an element of concealed queuing, in the sense that speeding them up would not necessarily bring the completion date forwards, as funds for construction would not be available any earlier. Preliminary processes which take longer than strictly necessary can help demonstrate agency commitment to a project, and that progress towards its realisation is being made.

23 The study estimated (p. 52) the cost of reduced characteristics dual carriageway at £3.1m per km, and motorways at £4.5m. Multiplying the difference by the mileage, and dividing it by the cost per km of dual carriageway, $((4.5-3.1)*478)/3.1 = 216$ km (more if 2 + 1 roads were used). Many congested towns could have been bypassed.

24 NRA et al. 'N24 Western Corridor Improvement: Pallasgreen to Bansha – Preferred

Route' (leaflet, April 2001).

25   Tipperary County Council 'N24 Cahir to Limerick Junction: Public Consultation –
      Constraints Study', Board 1 (online display at n24cahirlimerick.ie, January 2021).

26   South Tipperary County Development Plan 2009–15, p. 76.

27   Tipperary County Council 'N24 Cahir to Limerick Junction: Public Consultation –
      Constraints Study', Board 1.

28   In theory, the short link connecting the existing and proposed N24s east of Bansha,
      and the section NW from there to the far side of Tipperary town, could be built as a 14
      km first phase. However, this is clearly not the intention, as these sections are not aligned
      in a way which would facilitate this. The desirability of prioritising the section bypassing
      Tipperary town itself is listed as the first item in a list of points raised by the public in
      participation exercises in the Option Selection Report (February 2023, p.83), but it
      makes no further reference to this possibility. Procedurally, the Report selects
      (pp.1544–7) preferred options for the NW, central and SE sections of the route separ-
      ately, with no reference to the desirability of facilitating an initial bypass for the town
      itself first in its discussion of any of them. Effectively, the issue was subdivided out of
      existence.

29   The 2019 Cork Metropolitan Area Transportation Study (CMATS) envisaged two
      new northern ring routes, one to cater for traffic within the Cork sub-regions, and
      the other to cater for national traffic. In the absence of Scenario D, one might be suf-
      ficient.

30   The Irish Times (4 October 2021), reporting comments by the Minister for Transport.

31   The main section of the proposed motorway/dual carriageway route which coincides
      with the existing N20 is the part between Blarney and Mourneabbey, just south of
      Mallow. This road was already improved c. 1990, with a substantial portion of it laid
      out as a 2+1 road. It runs alongside the main Cork–Mallow–Dublin rail line. Raising
      speeds on this part of the route may divert passengers from Cork–Mallow commuter
      rail services, which have been improved, and it is planned to improve further.

32   Existing 2+1 sections of the N20 and N24 are conversions of existing roads, with
      right turns through gaps in the central reservation and frontage access still
      allowed. These would be avoided on a purpose-built version. Aggressive overtak-
      ing at points where two lanes merge into one can be a problem on 2+1 roads, but
      could be controlled by suitably located speed cameras or other enforcement
      measures.

33   Due to greater segregation of local traffic on the existing N20 corridor, which would
      probably outweigh the safety benefits of segregation for local traffic between Mit-
      chelstown and Limerick.

34   A variety of cost estimates for Metrolink have been produced, using different meth-
      odologies, with results expressed in terms of the percentage probability that a spec-
      ified cost will not be exceeded. Estimates of this at 50% probability range from
      €9.5–10.68 billion. This rises to €12.25–14.2 bn for 80% probability, €12.61 –
      18.06 bn for 90%, and €12.92 – 23.39 bn for 95% (Major Projects Advisory Group,

Review Note on Metrolink Preliminary Business Case, 2022, p. 13).

35 This optimisation has subsequently been reversed, and Metrolink now has a design capacity back up at 20,000 per hour, and the surface section north of DCU has been put back underground.

36 Many would also prefer it for symbolic reasons. The absence of a metro in Dublin is widely seen as a symptom of underdevelopment, inappropriate in a wealthy country, but those who hold this view tend not to address cyclicality and coverage issues directly. For instance, Fintan O'Toole commented (*Irish Times*, 16/7/22) that 'Plans - like those re-announced yet again last week for the Dublin Metro – are made, shelved, remade, shelved again. It is as if our rulers have never really had faith in their own boasts. They have been unable fully to believe that Ireland is on a trajectory of long-term growth in which the workforce has doubled in size and the population is finally recovering from the disasters of the 19th century'. However, Ireland has not been wealthy for very long, its growth has been rapid but not consistent, and periods in which the state had sufficient resources to undertake megaprojects have alternated with ones in which it did not. The latter included the years in which the public finances were gradually rebuilt during recoveries, as well the downturns and troughs which preceded them.

37 The *stated* overall capital cost of the Strategy (p. 235) up to 2042 is 'of the order of €25 billion in current prices' (i.e. an average of €1.25 billion per annum). This overall estimate was presumably drawn up before the estimated cost of Metrolink rose from €3 billion to €9.5 billion, as Metrolink would otherwise absorb all capital funding for transport in Dublin for around eight years. Construction cost inflation has presumably affected other components of the Strategy as well, so the *implied* cost of fully implementing the GDTS projects is much higher than its stated cost.

38 An EIAR must include 'an outline of the main alternatives studied by the developer and an indication of the main reasons for his or her choice, taking into account the effects on the environment' (Planning and Development Regulations, 2001, as amended, Schedule 6).

39 Irish public agencies are often reluctant to publish project cost estimates in case this distorts the subsequent tendering process and raises prices. Describing any cost estimate as 'middle of range' might help convey the message that the agency would be seeking a final tender at its lower end. If they insist on redacting cost estimates from publicly available versions of their documents, comparison would still be possible if the cost of the coverage-friendly option was expressed as a percentage of the preferred one.

40 Aidan Corkery in the *Sunday Business Post*, 8 November 2020, p. 16, quoting Minister for Public Expenditure and Reform Michael McGrath.

41 Table 4.1 in the 2021–30 NDP splits public capital expenditure into exchequer and non-exchequer funded, and proposes the first of these will be around 5% of GNI per annum. If non-exchequer investment is added back in, this brings average public investment back up to 6%. The 2018–27 NDP noted (p. 18) that the EU average was 3%.

Chapter 5

1 While planning policies also influence the volume and mix of development, they have more effect on where particular types of development are located than on overall output in an area. While they also contain objectives on the volume of particular types of development, the predominantly negative character of planning powers makes it easier for them to limit – or abstain from limiting – the amounts provided than to actually increase the number of private sector development projects put forward.

2 *Construction*, January/February 1975, p. 7; October 1975, p. 8; February 1976, p. 6; June 1976, p. 4.

3 *Construction*, December 1974, p. 5; July/August 1975, p. 4; February 1976, p. 6; December/January 1981/2, pp. 5–7; December/January 1985, pp. 2–3).

4 Department of the Environment, Annual Report, 1978, p. 19.

5 Department of the Environment, Annual Report, 1979, p. 26.

6 This was agreed as part of a 'National Understanding'.

7 *Construction*, May 1983, p. 9.

8 *Construction*, July/August 1983, p. 5.

9 *Construction*, November 1984, p. 6.

10 The Housing Agency website: Housebuilding Historical Data (at http://www.housingagency.ie/data-hub/house-building-historical-data).

11 As noted in Chapter 2, state-funded social infrastructure tends to peak late in the cycle, probably due to the higher level of overall public expenditure possible in a boom, the more obvious inadequacy of existing infrastructure then, and increasing impatience with such inadequacies the longer they continue. The peaks of 1975 and 1984 both occurred after the relevant booms had ended, which may be explained partly by lead times, and partly by the relevant ministers being from the Labour Party, and more committed to public housing.

12 It was felt that targets for slum clearance in the UK needed to be raised, in view of the number of obsolete dwellings. Political parties competed in terms of who could promise the largest number of new dwellings. In 1964, the incoming Labour government promised to increase overall housing output to 500,000 units a year (Cullingworth, 1960, p. 53; English et al., 1976, pp. 24–31; Dunleavy, 1981, p. 118).

13 Even in the early 1980s, when the need for greater social mix in peripheral housing estates was well understood, development of the local authority owned 600-acre Mahon peninsula in Cork was destabilised by government pressure to increase public housing there beyond the planned 40% public/60% private ratio, with the result that it proved impossible to attract private developers there for over a decade.

14 Cost rental housing works on the principle that rents reflect historical cost of provision, rather than current market rents. Tenants are mixed income, rather than the more exclusively low income groups found in conventional social housing.

15 Rehabilitation of housing was also promoted by a generous but short-lived House Improvement grant (1985–7).

16 *The Irish Times*, 4 December 1996, p. 14.

17 The report recommended removing the requirement to operate the hotel for seven years, on the basis that this would not be an additional cost to the Exchequer, as the allowances would be claimed anyway.

18 The CSO Capital Goods Index showed a 6% increase in building and construction costs (i.e. labour and materials) between 1996 (when the CIF started lobbying to prevent demand-side measures) and 1998 (when the first Bacon report was published). Average house prices rose by 44% in the same period. Some of this price rise would have benefited landowners, as development land costs rose by 92%. However, net house prices exclusive of land costs rose by 35% (DoE Review of 2000, Outlook for 2001, p. 112). The excess of growth in net house prices (+35%) over construction costs (+6%) offered scope for large increases in profits over a short period.

19 Providing terrace housing with reasonable open space and parking becomes more challenging at densities above 14 per acre/35 per ha. Some quite successful public housing schemes were built in the 1930s and '40s at 16–18 per acre/40–45 per ha but are in inner areas with little open space, many destinations within walking distance, good public transport and older populations, which keeps car ownership low enough to avoid serious parking problems. More recently, ingenious site-specific design has sometimes combined higher densities with own front door access, but typically at a substantial extra cost. One option is to reduce the standard 22m back-to-back distance, while avoiding overlooking through layout, and orientation or height of upper floor windows.

20 This was due to the inclusion of Part V. In other respects, the Bill contained many of the changes to speed up the operation of the planning system and the supply of development land which the CIF had been pressing for.

21 This applied to new private sector housing, and was not merely a side effect of the increase in social housing. Terrace housing was 21% of new private estate housing in 1983, and 19% in 1984, but only 8% in 1976 (An Foras Forbartha, *Construction Industry Statistics 1986*, p. 34).

22 The extent to which the formula in Box 5.2 encouraged this type of apartment would depend on where the lower end of the eligible floorspace range was set.

23 On the basis of the benchmark simulation, as amended by the Policy Induced Supply Response (Bacon, 1998, pp. 75, 82).

24 Bacon (2000, p. 10) had actually recommended graduated stamp duty rates for non-owner occupiers, ranging from 3.75% for transactions under £100,000, to 9% for ones over £500,000. The government substituted a flat rate 9% (*Construction*, September 2000, p. 23).

25 Reports by John McManus, *Irish Times*, April 16, 2001, p. 16.

26 Carefully defined exemptions would be needed for houses which had been residences of the owners, and agricultural buildings

27 *Construction*, December 2008/January 2009, p. 5; September 2010, pp. 12–13; December/January 2010, p. 8; April/May 2011, p. 17.

28 *Construction*, June/July 2011, p. 12.

29 *Construction*, December 2009/Jan 2010, p. 18; June/July 2009, p. 38.

30 *Construction*, October/November 2009, p. 9.

31 This is a good example of the type of drastic measure which can seem unavoidable in dealing with market trends with a lot of momentum behind them, referred to in Box 5.4. The seven-year requirement had to be modified subsequently, because holding land back from the housing market became undesirable as housing demand recovered. This illustrates the advantages of tax measures which are modified on a preannounced basis as market conditions change: they do not need to make possibly erroneous assumptions about future conditions, or to offer incentives which turn out to be unnecessarily generous.

32 The National Asset Management Agency (NAMA) was set up in December 2009 to recover some of the bad loans transferred from the banks to the state as a result of the 2008 bank guarantee.

33 The Ireland Strategic Investment Fund (ISIF) was established in 2014 with funds transferred from the National Pension Reserve Fund.

34 *Construction 2020*, pp. 12–13.

35 *Construction 2020*, pp. 8–10; DKM, 2016, pp. 33, 37. Even in 2019, the director general of the CIF felt parents were discouraging their children from entering the industry due to memories of the 2008 crash (*Irish Times*, 11 Sept. 2019, p. 4), though he saw such fears as misplaced, as 'such a shock could never happen again as there was a concerted move away from the boom-bust cycle'.

36 Dual aspect units have windows facing in more than one direction. The requirement for them was reduced to 33% in urban locations.

37 'Rebuilding Ireland', 2015, p. 64.

38 These take 'precedence over any conflicting policies and objectives of development plans' under s.28.1(c) of the Planning Acts.

39 Bedsits in the traditional sense had been banned by the Housing (Standards for Rented Houses) Regulations 2008, with the prohibition coming into effect in 2009 (for units being let for the first time) and in 2013 (for existing units). While this measure was prompted by valid, long-standing concerns, its timing (in December 2008) may have been influenced by a desire to shore up the housing market, find occupants for recently constructed buy-to-let units, and help the owners of these units maintain payments on bank mortgages. Once the market recovered, rents in newly constructed studios were likely to be much higher than for traditional bedsits in converted nineteenth century houses.

40 Quoted by Gene Kerrigan in the *Sunday Business Post*, 30 June 2018.

41 Most commentators saw the scheme as likely to increase prices. E.g. John Fitzgerald saw (*Irish Times*, 15 October 2021) continuation of Help to Buy in 2022 as unwise, as it would add to the inflationary pressures in the housing market arising from sav-

ings accumulated in the pandemic. However, the PBO reports considered that the Help to Buy scheme had had little effect on house prices (PBO, 2019, pp. 7–9, 2022, pp. 1, 10).

42 There are considerable discrepancies between different estimates of housing completions, depending on the method used. CSO figures are used here, on the assumption that the targets they are being compared with were calculated on the same basis.

43 As noted in Chapter 1, this was the incoming Fine Gael–Labour coalition's comment on the policies of its predecessors.

44 Reducing the discretion of local authorities and An Bord Pleanála through centrally determined mandatory requirements on the SPPR model may also make objectors feel those bodies will not be allowed to give appropriate weight to local and site-specific concerns, making recourse to the courts more likely.

45 This term has largely displaced the older one of 'Housing Associations'

46 Reynolds (2021, pp. 66–70) shows how this gap can be reduced, if undeveloped parts of the site in a phased development are used as collateral for loans to help finance parts under construction.

47 Long-term leasing of social housing from investment funds is on 25-year leases, with the housing reverting to the fund at the end of the lease. The basis for this seems to be that Eurostat would treat total costs over the 25 years as an addition to the national debt at the time of contract, as it would be a contract to purchase, whereas annual rent for each particular year counts as state expenditure for that year if there is no provision for transfer of ownership. The aim seems to be to avoid frontloading. Killian Woods quotes a letter to the Minister from the financier Dermot Desmond describing the practice as 'insane' (*Sunday Business Post*, 10 October 2021, Business News supplement, p. 3). Leasing sometimes led to state supported purchasers being in competition with each other. Declan Dunne, Chief Executive of Respond, was quoted as saying that investment fund purchases of homes for leasing to local authorities were driving up the cost of Respond's acquisitions by about €50,000 – from an average of c.€297,000 to almost €350,000 (Killian Woods, *Sunday Business Post*, 18 July 2021, p. 6). Long term leasing is scheduled to end in 2025.

Chapter 6

1 *Construction*, March 1989, p. 4; April 1989, p. 4.

2 These statements are reproduced in NESC (1975), pp. 77–86.

3 Galway City was the only city to be included in the Industrial Designated Areas.

4 IDA (1972, pp. 23–31), NESC (1975, p. 48).

5 The IDA Regional Industrial Plans cover the period 1973/77 and assign job targets in manufacturing industry to each region in that period ... The Government endorse the approach adopted by the IDA which is consistent with longer term regional strategy outlined above' (from government press statement 'Review of Regional Policy', 4 May 1972, reproduced in NESC, 1975, pp. 85–6).

6   E.g.: 'The Government considers that the dispersal of industrial activity throughout the country, where this is economically feasible, yields important social advantages, and, in the administration of the industrial grants scheme, the location of industries in other (ie non primary) centres will be encouraged' (from government press statement, 31 August, 1965). The IDA will continue, as heretofore, to support the preference of some industrialists for locations outside the main population centres. The provision of serviced sites locally, and where the prospects warrant it, the provision of advance factories will be further incentives for such industrialists' (from government press statement, 19 May 1969). Both are reproduced in NESC (1975), pp. 78, 81.

7   The Telesis consultancy was commissioned by NESC to make recommendations on Irish industrial policy 'appropriate to the creation of an internationally competitive industrial base which will support increased employment and higher living standards' (Telesis, 1982, preface).

8   The Irish Foreign Minister, Dr Garret Fitzgerald, threatened to veto the holding of the Paris summit unless sufficient progress was made on the regional fund (*The Irish Times*, 11 December, 1974, p. 5).

9   On the principle that the industry diverted would export, boost demand and have positive multiplier effects, offsetting falling demand from declining industries in such regions (Chisholm, 1990, pp. 65–75).

10 A 1985 Commission report commented on the ironies involved in a traditional regional policy focusing on heavy industry in southern Italy. Building, say, a steel plant there would involve importing all the raw materials, and exporting most of the steel produced. Meanwhile, the extensive citrus fruit production of the region was being exported unprocessed to northern European fruit juice and marmalade factories. Encouraging use of local resources also implied promoting the new, small innovatory businesses which were most likely to do this (CEC, 1985, p. 42).

11 Bradley et al. (1995, Ch. 5) provide a historical account of economic growth theories, and, in many of these, specific supply-side variables were seen as playing a critical role in explaining variations in economic performance between regions.

12 This last view seems to have influenced the way the Structural Funds were actually applied in Objective 1 regions most. Padoa Schioppa (1987, pp. 96–7), writing from a Commission viewpoint, saw the structural funds as supporting the major categories of investment 'needed to endow the regions with a strong productive potential', including human physical and human capital, and complemented by support for national investment aid. His report (1987, App. E) estimates the structural funding required to produce a given percentage increase in the GNP of less favoured regions, given an assumed marginal efficiency of investment.

13 Under s.43.1 of the Local Government Act, 1991.

14 An appendix in the 1994–9 NDP described the sub-regional review committee for the Dublin region as aiming to 'provide and maintain the number and types of sustainable jobs needed by the people of Dublin through creating an environment in which industry, services and tourism can flourish ...'. Infrastructure was (understand-

ably) seen as a means of attracting jobs, not as a way of keeping pace with an unmanageable influx.

15 Arguably, national government action will always be required for this type of problem. However, some effective tools were available to local authorities and the IDA. The former could have used their power to impose conditions to planning permissions on 'the purposes for and the manner in which structures may be used or occupied', to prevent too high a percentage of new housing being bought by investors. The IDA could have sought to redirect industrial projects away from Dublin at an earlier stage, and on a larger scale. A proactive response to such problems at regional level was not impossible, but the authority and resources to coordinate it were largely absent.

16 The initial impetus came from the Netherlands, whose national planning agency produced a study of spatial development options for NW Europe in 1991. This promoted a European spatial policy, and used the two scenarios approach, later followed by trans-national studies, such as the Atlantic Arc (Williams, 1996, p. 107). National identification with the ESDP varied. Blair (1997, pp. 32, 39–40) noted differing national attitudes to the ESDP, including a 'Germanic' preference for strong, uniform principles, a Mediterranean tendency to want to differentiate between types of spatial area, and the relatively inactive role of the Irish and British.

17 For unexplained reasons, Cork lost the technology centre status shown in the trend scenario, and was shown as a medium-sized town and regional hub with a tourist access function in the active one (CEC, 1994b, p. 211).

18 Breathnach (2017, p. 2) suggests that this was not adequately explained to politicians and the public. However, the perception that Irish cities were in competition with more rural areas for public investment may have been deeply rooted enough to be impervious to explanations.

19 The definition of regions has been subject to constant change by successive governments. In the 1970s and 1980s, Dublin, Kildare Meath and Wicklow constituted the Eastern region, while in the 1990s, Dublin became a separate region, and the three surrounding counties became the Mid-East region. In the NSS, these were reunited for descriptive purposes as the GDA. Currently, both are included in the Eastern and Midland Regional Assembly area, which also includes the outer counties of Leinster, other than Kilkenny, Carlow and Wexford.

20 Mallow, Ennis and Tuam.

21 Cavan, Monaghan, and the paired hubs of Ballina/Castlebar and Tralee/Killarney.

22 The closure of Dell in 2009 had a major effect on employment in Limerick.

23 In practice, urbanisation economies rely mainly on greater opportunities for specialisation and interaction between local businesses, as urban size grows. However, government back offices are linked primarily to their head office, direct interaction with local businesses is low, and they affect the local economy mainly via local spending of employees on local services. In gateways and hubs, decentralised staff would be a small addition to the population, but would make more difference in smaller towns trying to maintain a range of local services.

24 Overall, 3,559 jobs were decentralised between 1987 and 1998. Of these, 40% went to the four provincial cities, 24% to secondary growth centres proposed in the Buchanan report, and the remaining 36% to other towns. The aims were 'to foster economic growth in certain parts of the country by bringing more jobs into the area' and 'to relieve congestion in Dublin' (Katie O'Donovan, *The Irish Times*, 9 June 1998, p. 13).

25 Both the NSS and the NPF seem to have been over-optimistic on the distances over which combined agglomeration effects are likely. Morgenroth (2018, p. 79) cites studies estimating that the agglomeration benefits extend to 40–80 km. The distance between Cork and Limerick, and between Limerick and Galway, is slightly over 100 km in both cases.

26 See section B of this chapter.

27 These in combination constituted the East region in the 1970s and 1980s.

28 The NPF saw the other two regions growing by 480,000–560,000 in that period – i.e. by more or less the same amount as the EMRA area.

29 The status of the statement on p. 21, that 'In setting out a context for future growth, this Framework does not seek to cap or limit the growth of places' may be relevant. It seems to be specific to its context (a discussion of smaller towns not specifically referred to in the NPF), but might be argued to be of more general application.

30 Less encouragingly, it seems MASPs may be land use strategies, with parallel transport plans being prepared separately. Cork, for instance, was recently the subject of a Cork Metropolitan Area Transport Strategy (CMATS, 2019). While CMATS has some merit as a plan, in terms of method it represents regression towards compartmentalised metropolitan planning, as Cork pioneered integrated planning strategies in Ireland through the 1978 Cork Land Use Transportation Study (LUTS) and the 2001 Cork Area Strategic Plan (CASP).

31 Sufficient state agency involvement was achieved by setting up area-based partnerships as limited companies, so local state agency representatives would be responsible under company law to the partnerships, rather than the bodies that nominated them, allowing them to promote an integrated approach without having to defend it 'against the well informed, but perhaps self-interested objections of the concerned departments' (*Ibid.*).

32 More recently, the success of the current North East Inner City project in Dublin has been attributed to the involvement of the Minister for Finance and the Secretary General of the Department of the Taoiseach (Pat Leahy 'Dublin inner city project punches above its weight', *Irish Times*, 26 December 2020, p. 11.

33 In evidence to the Joint Oireachtas Committee on Climate Change on 27 November 2019.

34 Transport and property markets obviously vary a lot by urban size, and policies differentiated enough to take account of this are no longer national ones, and may be complicated to administer and open to the criticism that different parts of the country are being treated unequally. If treated uniformly, this does not necessarily always result in

policies which best match Dublin's needs being adopted. In a section headed 'National housing policies for local problems', Norris and Hayden criticised (2018, p. 95) application of relatively uniform social housing funding arrangements to radically different rural and urban housing areas as damaging to the latter.

Chapter 7

1   See Boxes 3.5–3.7, 5.2–5.5.
2   See Box 4.1.
3   See Box 5.1.
4   See Boxes 3.2 and 3.3.

INDEX

Public bodies and other organisations are listed under the names in use in the period under discussion on the pages referred to. In some cases, these names are different from the current names of those organisations.

active land management, 37, 61–6, 70, 276; by
    local authorities, 55–6, 67–9
Adamstown SDZ, 150
AECOM (consultants), 145–8
agricultural land values, 35–36, 37, 46–7, 51,
    89, 296n2
affordable housing, 46, 53, 63, 77, 115, 160,
    197, 203, 213; in Housing for All, 208–9;
    provided via Part V, 47, 49–51, 190;
Affordable Housing Act (2021), 51, 53
Affordable Housing Fund, Serviced Site Fund
    renamed as, 301n8
Affordable Housing Initiative (2003), 61
Affordable Housing Scheme (1999), 61, 209
Affordable Purchase Scheme (local authority),
    208
allocative function of the property market, 57,
    59–60
Andalucia, 246
Annual Housing Statistics Bulletin series, 183
Anois (urban design consultants), 99
apartment guidelines,195, 203
apartments, 48, 51–2, 99, 158, 191, 194,
    203–6, 242–5; block sales of, 26, 196; cost
    of, 51–2, 184, 194–6, 208–10;high rise,
    166, 205, 210; labour mobility and, 197;
    low rise, 51–2
Approved Housing Bodies (AHBs), 193, 206–7,
    308n45

Area Plans, Integrated (IAPs), 172
asset values, 58, 71, 89, 103, 165, 177, 185,

191, 201
Athlone, 222, 249, 253
Atlantic Arc scenarios (ESDP), 246
Atlantic corridor, 253, 310n16
Austria, 4, 6

Bacon, Peter, 118
Bacon report on hotel industry (2009), 174
Bacon reports on house prices, 77, 86, 99, 176–8,
    187, 208, 275; *1st report (1998)*,73, 74,
    112–3, 176–8; *2nd report (1999)*, 73–4,
    158, 178–82, 297n10; *3rd report (2000)*,
    77, 185–6, 200, 306n24
Bacon measures, lobbying on, 186–7
balanced regional development/growth, 15, 121,
    247, 251, 253, 262–70
Ball, Michael, 29

Ballymun, 145
banks, 25, 26, 27, 159, 174, 191, 307n32
Bannon, Michael, 58, 224, 251, 266
Bansha, 135–7

Berlin, 214, 247
Belgium, 4, 6
betterment, 39–40, 45, 68, 75–6, 90, 94,
    296–7n5, *see also* uplift
Biehl, D., 234–6
Blair government (UK), 268
Blair, Stephen, 310n16
Boland, B.J., 56
boom phases of the cycle, 14, 16–17, 24,

52–3, 91–3, 95; passing back (of taxes to landowner), 91–3

Part V, 17, 33, 47–54, 60, 90, 104–6, 180, 190, 211, 273, 275, 297n17; suggested transfer of land in advance of planning application, 53

participation rate, 239

pauses in the cycle, 30–31, 88; (1980–81), 163; (1991–3), 175; (2000–2), 1, 77, 186

Perroux, Francois, 220

pharmaceutical industry, 228

planning process, 46, 69, 204; fast–track versions of, 195; pressures on, 59–61; specific planning policy requirements (SPPRs) for, 195, 203; speeding up of, 194

Planning and Development Act (2000), 55, 121, 129

Planning and Development (Amendment) Act (2002), 48

Planning and Development Bill (1999), 47, 77; (2023), 127, 204

planning controls, effect on house prices, 101–3

planning permissions, 8, 11, 34, 50, 55, 58, 69, 73, 83, 94, 103, 211; conditions attached to, 47, 53, 91, 110; non–compensatable reasons for refusal of, 59; outline, 73, 178; unimplemented, 71, 194, 205, 209–10

Planning Regulator, 266

plasterers, 192

policy histories, 13–14

polycentric regional development, 245, 247

Port Access Tunnel (Dublin), 146

Portugal, 4–6

potentiality factors (in regional development), 235–6, 239–40, 249, 254

private rented housing sector, 158, 170, 190, 192–3, 196–201, 208–9; lower income households in, 199–200, 202; ownership of, 198–9; regulation of, 201; rents in, 192–3, 195, 198–210, 205; standards for, 198, 210, 307n39; rebalancing of incentives for, 200–1; role of, 197; security of tenure in, 198;

private non–residential construction, 19–23, 25–6, 29; commercial, 18, 21–22, 40, 55–6, 75, 80, 126–7, 130, 172, 182, 191, 196; industrial, 18, 22, 40, 55–56, 77, 80, 221; office, 21, 71, 172, 264, 268; retail, 22, 136

Private Rented Sector, Strategy for, 201

procurement, 24, 68, 212

pro–cyclical: incentives, 174, 274; ;public

expenditure, 23, 156, 279; provision of new social housing, 158, 167–70

profit margins, 8, 243

Project Tosaigh, 208–12

property bubbles, 7–8, 177

property-based welfare, 165

property markets, 1, 12, 46, 100, 159, 186, 214, 276; and CGT rates, 72, 75; and Dublin, 16, 215–7; and timing of infrastructure, 118–20; expertise in, 63, 244; suburban 171

propulsive firms (in growth poles), 220–1

Public Capital Programmes (PCPs), 108, 133, 161, 164

public expenditure, 15, 72, 132, 156, 162

public finances, 9, 72, 132, 156, 162

Public Expenditure and Reform, Department of (DPER), 119; public spending code of, 153

public housing, 48, 165–7, 213; *see also* local authority housing, social housing

public–private partnerships, 61, 70, 194

public sector investment, *see* PCP

public transport, 23, 108, 110, 149, 178, 262

Queuing of infrastructure projects, 14, 107, 131–2, 145, 149, 157, 272, 277–8, 302n22

Randstad, 246

ratchet principle (on infrastructure investment), 131, 156

reactive policy measures 1, 11–12, 99, 245, 275–6, 279

Rebuilding Ireland, 158, 193–5, 197–8, 201–3, 205–6, 208–9

Real Estate Investment Trusts (REITs), 191, 199–200, 207

recentralisation of new development, 171, 260

recessions, 9, 16, 31, 54, 107, 120, 123, 129–30, 167, 170, 216, 245, 260, 279; of mid-1970s, 161–3; of 1980s, 47, 72, 110, 145, 173, 272; after 2008, 205

recovery phases of the cycle, 9–11, 16, 28, 30–1, 44, 57, 76, 85–8, 95, 97, 105–7, 120, 128, 160, 182, 188, 260, 264, 267, 273–4, 277; in late 1970s, 161–3; 1989–90, 172, 175; in mid–1990s, 2, 173; after 2014, 180, 191–2, 197, 203, 206, 241, 243, 252

reforms, packages of, 16, 17; permanence of, 45, 272, 278–9, 281; public support for, 16, 38, 101, 276; to planning system (2015+),